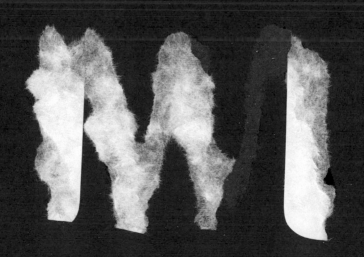

Safeguarding
Canada
1763–1871

Safeguarding Canada

Canada J. MACKAY HITSMAN

1763-1871

UNIVERSITY OF TORONTO PRESS

1867 1967

Published on the occasion of the Centennial of Canadian
Confederation and subsidized by the Centennial Commission

Ouvrage publié à l'occasion du Centenaire de la Confédération
Canadienne, grâce à une subvention de la Commission du Centenaire

FOR KAYE

PREFACE

This study of British plans to defend Canada during the years 1763–1871, and the extent to which they were implemented, is based primarily on manuscript sources now easily accessible to students of military history. Undoubtedly additional information will be discovered from time to time in private collections of documents but, since the subject is one which today would be classified TOP SECRET, the pickings are likely to be thin. Little attention has been directed to what was going on "at the other side of the hill," an apt phrase coined by the Duke of Wellington, because of a personal conviction that the answer was very little in the way of plans to attack Canada. Next to nothing in this volume relates to tactics, which Cyril Falls has very simply defined as "the art of conducting a battle or section of a battle." Rather this book is a study of strategy, a word which, in this case, may simply be substituted for "plans" in the opening sentence above.

A word about titles is in order. The last officer of the British Army to hold the appointment of Commander-in-Chief in North America was Sir Guy Carleton in 1783. The first Governor General was Lord Durham in 1838. In between, Sir George Prevost and other soldier-governors held lesser appointments as Commander of the Forces and Governor-in-Chief. The first appointment of Secretary of State for the Colonies was made in 1854, following the outbreak of the Crimean War when it was decided that the Secretary of State for War and the Colonies, the Duke of Newcastle, would have enough to do as Secretary of State for War. Yet Canadian historians, obsessed by the importance of the struggle to achieve responsible government and conveniently forgetting that there were potential enemies without, refer to Lord Glenelg and Lord Grey as merely Colonial Secretaries. Their illogical step was to accept, or make, such fatuous statements as the following, which appears in the

Cambridge History of the British Empire, VI, *Canada and Newfoundland* (1930, 259):

At the centre was the Lieutenant-Governor, ruling in spite of legal technicalities, at his little capital, York, as a despot limited only by inexperience and the British Parliament. Such was the position, inevitable in 1815, when colonial posts were not attractive to Englishmen of the first rank, and when the additional pay which soldiers drew made it natural to appoint officers of Wellington's army.

Some explanation of military and naval ranks is also indicated. Officers normally acquired promotion within cavalry and infantry regiments by purchase, whereas artillery and engineer officers were promoted on merit and seniority within their own corps. Captains, majors, and lieutenant-colonels could have a higher army or brevet rank because of distinguished service or employment on staff. Whether a colonel "owned" a regiment or merely had brevet rank, promotion was to major-general. During most of these years, the lesser brigadier-general was only a local rank. This and other local ranks were given to offset an officer's lack of seniority for a particular service. For example, annual *Army Lists* show Guy Carleton as colonel of the 47th Regiment of Foot (April 2, 1772), major-general in the Army (May 25, 1772), and general in North America (January 1, 1776). Field-Marshal was a more senior appointment given for life by the sovereign, as was the corresponding Admiral of the Fleet.

Naval ranks used in this book are those given in *The Commissioned Sea Officers of the Royal Navy, 1660–1815* (Greenwich, 1954) and the annual *Navy Lists* which begin with 1816. Prior to 1864, flag officers were Admirals, Vice-Admirals, and Rear-Admirals of the Red, White, and Blue squadrons into which the fleet was still theoretically divided. Promotion was by seniority from Rear-Admiral of the Blue to Admiral of the Red. As Professor Michael Lewis has noted, in *England's Sea Officers* (London, 1939): "Nelson, who was only forty-seven when he died, had merely got as far as Vice-Admiral of the White." Commodore was an appointment given to the senior captain in command of a small squadron. Captains commanded ships of the line and the larger frigates (or fifth raters). Commanders and lieutenants commanding lesser war vessels were merely called "captain."

My original purpose in undertaking this study was to produce a doctoral dissertation for the University of Ottawa. The subject was suggested by Dr. Arthur R. Vanasse, then Chairman of its History Department. A thesis was completed under his direction and accepted by the University of Ottawa in October, 1964. Extensive revision and expansion of the manuscript to its present form was accelerated by financial assistance from the Canadian Centennial Commission, making early publication possible. Publication was also assisted by a grant from the Social Science Research Council using funds provided by the Canada Council, and by a subsidy from the Publications Fund of the University of Toronto Press.

My research was facilitated by residence in Ottawa. Members of the staff of the Public Archives of Canada did everything possible to help with my varied problems. Mr. T. E. Layng, Chief of the Map Division, took some pains to ensure that I should gain some knowledge of the work done in Canada by the British officers who compiled Ordnance Maps and Admiralty Charts. Miss Barbara Wilson of the Manuscript Division revised and simplified the Bibliographic Note which follows. Librarians of the National Library, the Parliamentary Library, and the Department of National Defence made available a wide variety of printed material. The state of my health precluded extended travel, but Admiral of the Fleet The Earl Mountbatten of Burma very kindly directed that I might be furnished with xerox copies of relevant letters from among Lord Palmerston's Papers in the Broadlands Archives; the Director of the William L. Clements Library of the University of Michigan, Mr. Howard Peckham, supplied me with photostat copies of letters from the Gage and Germain Papers; the Librarian of the Royal Military College of Canada, Mr. John W. Spurr, lent me a copy of the letters written by Captain Robert Barrie, R.N., to his relatives in England. Other primary material not available on microfilm in Ottawa was obtained from the British Museum and the Public Record Office in London, and from the National Archives in Washington. Members of these staffs, and of the historical staffs of both the Department of the Army and the Department of the Navy in Washington, were kind enough to supply answers to specific questions.

Quotations from unpublished Crown-copyright material in the Public Record Office have been made by permission of the Controller of H.M. Stationery Office. Quotations from Lord Palmerston's Papers have been made by permission of the Broadlands Archives. Similar permission to quote from collections of private papers was given by the William L. Clements Library of the University of Michigan, the British Museum, and the Royal Military College of Canada.

Illustrations were obtained from the Department of National Defence, the Public Archives of Canada, the Canadian Travel Bureau, the McCord Museum, and the Confederation Life Collection in Toronto. The maps are the work of my long-time friend, Major C. C. J. Bond, who was good enough to make detailed comments about the manuscript as he read.

Major W. A. McDill, Mrs. W. O. Sorby, and Mr. Thor Thorgrimsson were kind enough to read and comment upon the revised manuscript as it progressed, chapter by chapter. Professor R. A. Preston provided detailed comments and criticism. Dr. George F. G. Stanley of the Royal Military College of Canada also read the manuscript. Two readers, whose identity could not be divulged to me by the University of Toronto Press, supplied a number of most interesting comments. My son Tony indexed the book, which is dedicated to my wife. Kitty-Cat insisted on helping. Once again I found the advice given me about the manuscript by the Editorial Department of the University of Toronto Press most stimulating. Responsibility for what now appears in print, however, is mine alone.

Ottawa, Canada   J. M. H.

BIBLIOGRAPHIC NOTE

A few words of explanation are necessary respecting the unpublished manuscript material cited in the detailed references; collections of printed documents, newspapers and secondary works are, however, adequately described when first cited.

Papers of the Colonial Office, War Office, and the Admiralty are now in the custody of the Public Record Office, London, England. Microfilm copies of most of the papers relating to Canada are in the Public Archives of Canada, Ottawa. Official correspondence between colonial governors and the Colonial Office is arranged by colony: C.O.42 for Canada, C.O.60 and C.O.398 for British Columbia, C.O.188 for New Brunswick, C.O.217 for Nova Scotia, and C.O.226 for Prince Edward Island. Series C.O.43, entitled "Entry Books, Canada," includes what would now be considered TOP SECRET instructions to governors of Canada. Despatches and correspondence relating to Canada, not included in C.O.42 or C.O.43, are in C.O.537. The most useful of the War Office Papers are in-letters (W.O.1) and monthly strength returns (W.O.17). Despatches and letters from naval commanders-in-chief in North American waters are in Adm.1.

In addition to official British records, the Public Record Office has some private papers, including those of Edward Cardwell (P.R.O. 30/48) and Sir William Eyre (P.R.O.30/46). The Public Archives of Canada has microfilmed documents relating to Canada from the Cardwell and Eyre papers.

The principal French source is C^{11A}, entitled Correspondance Générale, Canada. The series is part of the Archives des Colonies and is in the custody of the Archives Nationales in Paris. The Public Archives of Canada has a microfilm copy.

The Public Archives of Canada has transcripts of the bulky Haldimand

Papers, which are known as the "B" Series. The originals are in the British Museum.

The most important manuscript material in the Public Archives of Canada for this study is in the surviving records accumulated by the British Army in Canada. Included are volumes relating to the Provincial Marine and the Royal Navy. These records are generally known as the "C" Series and form part of the Public Archives' Record Group 8. Also in this group are the Admiralty Pacific Station records and copies of the reports on Canadian defence made by Major-General Sir James Carmichael-Smyth, Lieutenant-Colonel E. W. Durnford, Lieutenant-Colonel W. F. D. Jervois, Colonel Gother Mann, Lieutenant-General Sir John Michel, and the Defence Commission of 1862. Manuscript Group 24 includes the private papers of Sir Isaac Brock, George Brown, Lord Durham, Sir George Prevost, and Lake Service Letters Received, 1815–1817 (F 25). The papers of Sir John A. Macdonald are in Manuscript Group 26. Canadian militia records are in Record Group 9. Record Group 7 comprises the records of the Governor General's Office; the most relevant series in this group are G. 1, G. 3, G. 5, G. 10, G. 12, G. 20, and G. 21. "New Brunswick Letter Book, Volume 1" (Record Group 7, G8B, Volume 62) contains copies of the Lieutenant-Governor's outgoing correspondence for 1861–64. State Books, containing the minutes of meetings held by the Executive Council of Canada, are in Record Group 1.

The William L. Clements' Library of the University of Michigan at Ann Arbor holds the papers of Lieutenant-General the Hon. Thomas Gage and Lord George Germain. Lord Palmerston's Papers are in the Broadlands Archives, Romney, Kent, England. John Bright's Papers are in the British Museum (Add. Mss 43392). The library of the Royal Military College of Canada at Kingston has some letters written by Captain Robert Barrie, R.N.

The National Archives in Washington has the Records of the Office of the Secretary of War (RG 107) and the Naval Records Collection of the Office of Naval Records and Library (RG 45).

CONTENTS

$$\left(\begin{array}{c} \text{Safeguarding} \\ \text{Canada} \\ \text{1763–1871} \end{array} \right)$$

(1)

THE BRITISH CONQUEST

As early as 1664 conquest of the Dutch colony of Niew Amsterdam had given the subjects of King Charles II of England control over the whole Atlantic coast from Virginia to the region known both as Nova Scotia and Acadia. There sovereignty was disputed with the King of France, Louis XIV, whose subjects, the Acadians, had established several small settlements. The Acadians were separated from the 2,500 French colonists of New France in the lower St. Lawrence valley by miles of wooded wilderness, crossed only by occasional couriers following streams which flowed on either side of the most northerly range of the Appalachian Mountains.

New France had become a royal colony a year earlier and had been placed under the administration of the *ministère de la Marine*. French army regulars, or *troupes de terre*, controlled by the *ministère de la Guerre*, were soon posted temporarily to New France to put an end to the menace posed by the Iroquois Confederacy of the Five Nations. When this task had been accomplished, the *troupes de terre* were withdrawn and garrison duty was left to small independent companies recruited by the *ministère de la Marine* for permanent service in New France. Subsequently these companies became known as *troupes de la Marine*. Over the years an increasing number of officers for these *troupes de la Marine* were found from among the sons of Canadian seigneurs, but the men continued to be recruited in France from members of the urban lower classes. In addition, there was the *milice*, or militia, which included practically all the physically fit male settlers between the ages of sixteen and sixty, organized locally into companies and drilled once a month. Discharged members of the *troupes de la Marine* and other veterans who settled in New France provided the militia with a trained nucleus. The marksmanship of the militiamen could be an important factor when there was actual fighting, but their principal duty seems to have been service as military pioneers, supporting the regulars by transporting supplies by *bateau*, canoe, or sleigh and by building roads and fortifications. For this arduous, compulsory service (*corvée*) they received no pay. Anything resembling a *levée en masse* was normally possible only between the planting and harvesting of crops. At other times each captain of militia selected from his company the number of men required for each particular service.[1]

French explorers and fur traders steadily pushed into the heart of the heavily wooded continent via the St. Lawrence River and the Great Lakes. Portaging their canoes around rapids and waterfalls and carrying them short distances overland, they came to tributaries of the Mississippi River leading to the Gulf of Mexico, which La Salle reached in 1682. France thus claimed prior discovery and attempted to extend her sovereignty over the entire Ohio and Mississippi valleys.

This French claim was disputed by the English-speaking American colonists, who had been handicapped by the Appalachian Mountains in their efforts to expand westward. Mountain barriers restricted easy settlement to the coastal plain and forced the venturesome to travel westward on foot with supplies on pack-horses or on their own backs. The mountains were broken by only two narrow corridors—both in the colony, or province, of New York—running north and west, respectively, from Albany, the farthest point to which ocean-going sailing ships could ascend the Hudson River. Travellers to the north could portage from the upper Hudson first to Lake George and then to Lake Champlain, which empties into the Richelieu River; the Richelieu joins the St. Lawrence River at the seigniory of Sorel, about forty-five miles below Montreal. West from Albany was a canoe and portage route along the Mohawk River, Wood Creek, Lake Oneida, and the Oswego River to the eastern shore of Lake Ontario. This territory, however, was guarded by the Iroquois who wanted to profit from the fur trade by serving as middlemen between all white men and the tribes of the interior, who refused to recognize either English or French sovereignty over themselves or their hunting grounds, and who did not welcome strangers in their midst.

Iroquois attacks on New France were renewed during the 1680s, and the Governor, Marquis de Denonville, could not combat them without help from France. The few hundred *troupes de la Marine* sent from France in reinforcement drafts made the garrison posts strong enough to beat off any Indian attack and enabled Denonville to mount a puni-

---

[1]Gustave Lanctôt, "Les Troupes de la Nouvelle-France," *Canadian Historical Association, Annual Report*, 1926.

tive expedition against the Senecas. He then suggested retaliating against the Americans who were supplying the Indians with muskets and ammunition. This policy was approved after an Anglo-French war broke out in Europe in 1689, and the Governor was authorized to lead an expedition along the Lake Champlain–Lake George–Hudson River route to Albany. After capturing Albany he was to continue downriver to the port of New York, which was to be attacked simultaneously by French warships. If successful, this strategy would have separated New England from the rest of the American colonies and would have permitted French forces to overrun both segments at their leisure. French resources were, however, insufficient for the new Governor, the elderly Comte de Frontenac, to make such an attempt.[2] The best Frontenac could do during the winter of 1690 was to send strong raiding parties against the most exposed settlements of New York and New England. Tactically, these hit-and-run raids were excellent examples of *la petite guerre*, but they resulted in the massacre of defenceless women and children at Schenectady, Salmon Falls, and Casco Bay and aroused the people of New York and of New England to demand that the French colony be conquered.

The only British regulars in continental North America were ineffectual garrison companies in New York. The Royal Navy was busy in Europe contesting control of the English Channel with Louis XIV who was trying to restore James II to the English throne. The "disunited" American colonists, as they were later described, had to act on their own. The courses open both to the makeshift coalition of the colonists that ensued and to its enemy in New France were governed by the principles that the great American naval historian, Rear-Admiral A. T. Mahan, would later summarize:

The strength of Canada against attack by land lay in its remoteness, in the wilderness to be traversed before it was reached, and in the strength of the line of the St. Lawrence, with the fortified posts of Montreal and Quebec on its northern bank. The wilderness, it is true, interposed its passive resistance to attacks from Canada as well as to attacks upon it; but when it had been traversed, there were to the southward no such strong natural positions confronting the assailant. Attacks from the south fell upon the front, or at best upon the flank, of the line of the St. Lawrence. Attacks from Canada took New York and its dependencies in the rear.[3]

---

[2]Gustave Lanctôt, *A History of Canada,* II: *From the Royal Regime to the Treaty of Utrecht, 1663–1713* (Toronto, 1964), 113–14; W. J. Eccles, *Canada under Louis XIV, 1663–1701,* Canadian Centenary Series (Toronto, 1964), 161–4.
[3]A. T. Mahan, *The Major Operations of the Navies in the War of American Independence* (London, 1913), 7–8.

The principal American effort in 1690 was directed at Quebec, which was attacked by a provisional fleet and an army of volunteers commanded by colonial-born Sir William Phips who had already and easily captured Port Royal on the Bay of Fundy. Since the militia service required of physically fit males between the ages of sixteen and sixty was normally restricted to the defence of a colony, volunteers were enlisted into special provincial regiments for the campaign. Phips successfully navigated the lower reaches of the St. Lawrence River, but after Frontenac refused to surrender Quebec on demand the New Englanders proved incapable of conducting a successful siege. A subsidiary, overland expedition aimed at Montreal proceeded up the Hudson River but got no farther than the head of Lake Champlain. Port Royal was returned to France in 1697 by the Treaty of Ryswick; nothing was gained by the American venture.

In 1701 the long and bitter quarrel between the French and the Indians of the Five Nations was peacefully settled, with important consequences for New France. When the War of the Spanish Succession broke out in Europe in 1702, which again put France and England at military odds, only individual Iroquois tribes rallied to the support of the American colonists. The group of Mohawks who had been induced by Jesuit missionaries to move to Caughnawaga, near Montreal, joined the Abenakis and other Indian allies of the French in hit-and-run raids on American settlements.[4]

In 1710, with the War continuing, Port Royal was again easily captured by an expedition from New England. However, the two-pronged attack aimed at Quebec and Montreal in the following year was a complete fiasco. A considerable portion of the British fleet and army was shipwrecked in the lower St. Lawrence River, and once again the American overland expedition halted at Lake Champlain. Elsewhere, the War was more favourable to British arms, and Queen Anne was able to retain possession of the ill-defined Acadia by the treaty signed at Utrecht in 1713. France also recognized Queen Anne's sovereignty over Hudson Bay and Newfoundland.

Port Royal had served as a base for the French privateers that preyed on New England fishing vessels. But, as Annapolis Royal, under British rule, it was of little use, and its tiny garrison of regulars maintained an ineffectual rule over those Acadians who chose to remain on their farms. A more serious matter for France was the loss of a foothold in Newfoundland, for that island dominated the Gulf of St. Lawrence and the sailing route to Quebec.

[4]G. F. G. Stanley, "The Significance of the Six Nations Participation in the War of 1812," *Ontario History*, LV (December, 1963), 215–16.

French activities were transferred to Isle Royale (later Cape Breton), where the fortress of Louisbourg was built in an effort to regain command of the Gulf of St. Lawrence. However, without a fleet in its harbour, Louisbourg would prove to be only as strong as the limited range of its fortress guns, and, on June 15, 1745, after a six-week siege, it surrendered to a nondescript force of New Englanders supported by a squadron of the Royal Navy from the West Indian Station.[5] The challenge reappeared when Louisbourg was returned to France by the Treaty of Aix-la-Chapelle in 1748, and the British Government decided to establish their own town and naval base on the Atlantic shore of the Nova Scotian peninsula. In 1749 Halifax was begun. A militia was mustered in December of that year, but a regular militia system, modelled on that of New England, was not introduced until 1753. A "sea militia," maintained by the Governor at the expense of the Board of Trade in London, was also copied from the American colonies.[6]

The French and American colonists came into open conflict in the Ohio valley in 1754, because of French efforts to prevent American settlement and trade from spreading westward beyond the Appalachian Mountains. The governments in both Paris and London tried to keep the fighting localized by sending only limited military help to North America in 1755. Four battalions of *troupes de terre* were sent to Quebec with Baron Dieskau, a protégé of the great Maréchal de Saxe, to reinforce the forty-two companies of *troupes de la Marine* in New France; two further battalions were added to the garrison of Louisbourg.[7] Two under-strength regiments of British Army regulars, which were normally kept in Ireland and which were of poor quality, were completed by enlistments from the Virginia and Maryland militia following their arrival; two regular regiments (Shirley's and Pepperell's) were raised in New England; the seven independent companies scattered along the American frontier and the three regular regiments garrisoning Nova Scotia were brought up to strength locally.[8] The legislatures of the American colonies were asked to help finance the two operations envisaged by the newly arrived Commander-in-Chief, Major-General Edward Braddock: his own principal expedition against Fort Duquesne in the Ohio country, and an attack by Lieutenant-Colonel Robert Monckton on Fort Beauséjour, on the Isthmus of Chignecto, part of the ill-defined boundary between British Nova

[5]Gerald S. Graham, *Empire of the North Atlantic: The Maritime Struggle for North America* (Toronto, 1950), 120.
[6]W. A. B. Douglas, "The Sea Militia of Nova Scotia, 1749–1755: A Comment on Naval Policy," *Canadian Historical Review*, XLVII (March, 1966).
[7]Maurice Sautai, *Montcalm au combat de Carillon, 8 Juillet 1758* (Paris, 1909), 14, 21.
[8]Stanley Pargellis, *Lord Loudon in North America* (New Haven, 1933), 29–33.

Scotia and continuing French Acadia. The colonial legislatures, however, were more interested in retaining control of the money they had voted and the provincial regiments they had raised separately than in co-operating one with the other or with the British Government. Yet Governor William Shirley of Massachusetts did manage to persuade the northern colonies to put their own army in the field under the command of William Johnson, Superintendent of Indian Affairs for what were now the Six Nations, for an attack on the French fort at Crown Point on Lake Champlain. Shirley then tried unsuccessfully to mount an expedition of his own against Fort Niagara with the same object as Braddock: to cut the enemy line of communication between New France and Louisiana.[9]

North American tradition has attached far too much importance to the ambush and defeat of Braddock's army near Fort Duquesne on June 9, 1755, by a much smaller French force of *troupes de la Marine*, militia, and Indians employing the tactics of *la petite guerre*, and has glossed over the fact that the local levies on neither side could be depended on as fighting troops. Had Braddock's force been organized, as suggested in manuals such as Humphrey Bland's *Treatise of Military Discipline* (1753), when marching in country where an ambush was possible, and had the advanced guard charged forward boldly instead of falling back on the still advancing main party, there would have been no milling mass of confused redcoats for the French and Indians to shoot down at their leisure from behind cover. Among the fatalities was Braddock himself. The American provincials made no contribution to the final outcome by emulating the tactics of their opponents. In short, the British failure here was primarily one of leadership, a neglect of the fundamentals of the then current European art of war.[10]

Conditions were reversed later that summer when Baron Dieskau launched a frontal attack against Johnson's American provincials who were camped at the head of Lake George. To Dieskau's surprise and undoing his Indian allies immediately vanished, and the Canadian militiamen contented themselves with firing from behind trees: only the 230 *troupes de terre* charged in a proper manner and, lacking support, they were repulsed by withering cannon and musket fire from the entrenched Americans. Johnson used this defensive victory and the capture of a wounded Dieskau as a convenient excuse for not continuing against Crown Point. Instead he built Fort William Henry where he was. The

[9]*Ibid.*, 35–6, 41.
[10]Stanley Pargellis, "Braddock's Defeat," *American Historical Review*, XLI (January, 1936).

French halted their retreat at Ticonderoga on Lake Champlain and began the construction of Fort Carillon.[11]

Only the British expedition against Fort Beauséjour succeeded. Once the fort had been isolated, standard siege procedures, including the employment of large mortars, ensured British success. Thereupon the French abandoned their other fort on the Isthmus and their post on the St. John River.[12] Fort Beauséjour was renamed Fort Cumberland.

In 1756 a general conflict erupted in Europe, which would continue, as the Seven Years' War, until 1763. Great Britain left Frederick the Great, of Prussia, and lesser allies to ward off the military might of France, Austria, and Russia, and to safeguard George II's beloved Hanover, supported only by British gold and a small expeditionary force. She directed her own effort against French possessions overseas.

Major-General Lord Loudon was sent to North America as Commander-in-Chief, accompanied by a sizable reinforcement of British regulars, but few attempts to fight were made, and nothing was gained during 1756 and 1757. A much publicized plan to raise four battalions from among German and other European-born settlers brought only 1,800 recruits, and the rest of the manpower for this 60th (or Royal American) Regiment of Foot had to be found from direct enlistments in Europe and drafts from regiments stationed in Ireland.[13] American enlistments in the British Army declined to a trickle, and 11,000 regulars had to be sent from Britain during 1757.[14] Many of the poorly disciplined American provincial troops, recruited anew for each summer's campaigning season, came from long-settled communities. They had never seen Indians in war paint, were ill-trained, and knew nothing of forest fighting. They were no match for either *troupes de terre* or *troupes de la Marine* in the open and were better employed transporting supplies by canoe or *bateau* and building fortifications. On the other hand, the backwoodsmen serving in ranger companies were so invaluable that Loudon was glad to maintain them from his military chest. His appreciation of August 20, 1756, describes his intention:

When I arrived, I found there was a disposition in the Soldiers, to go out with Indians and *Rangers*, and that some of them were then out; I shall encourage it all I can, and if the parties that are now out, have success and escape, we shall

---

[11]Guy Frégault, *La Guerre de la conquête* (Montreal, 1955), 148–52.
[12]Stanley Pargellis, ed., *Military Affairs in North America, 1748–1765: Selected Documents from the Cumberland Papers in Windsor Castle* (New York, 1936), xv–xvi.
[13]Pargellis, *Lord Loudon in North America*, 111–12.
[14]*Ibid.*, 107–10.

soon get a knowledge of this Country, and be able to March with much more safety than at present; for I am convinced, that till we have every thing necessary, for carrying on the War here, within ourselves, Independent of Aid from this country, we shall go on very slowly.[15]

The result was the addition of a light infantry company to each regular battalion in North America and the recruitment locally of an 80th Regiment of Foot (Light Armed).

France, on the other hand, planned to mount major campaigns in continental Europe and India. Only two battalions of *troupes de terre* were sent to Quebec in each of 1756 and 1757, providing a maximum establishment of 3,988 rank and file in Canada; the establishment of the 42 companies of *troupes de la Marine* was increased to 2,600 men, but actual or effective strengths were normally considerably less.[16] Moreover, Dieskau's successor as commander of the *troupes de terre*, Marquis de Montcalm, was continually frustrated by the actions of the Governor General, Marquis de Vaudreuil, who had served in the *troupes de la Marine* as a young man and who believed that *la petite guerre* was still the best course to follow.[17] Montcalm knew better and later wrote:

La constitution de la guerre dans cette colonie a changé totalement. Jadis les Canadiens croyoient la faire, c'étoient des courses ressemblant à des parties de chasse, aujourd'huy entreprises suivies, jadis les Sauvages en faisoient le fond, aujourd'huy l'accessoire. Il faut donc d'autres vues, d'autres maximes. Je le dis mais les anciens préjuges subsistent.[18]

Montcalm had to concentrate on holding what he had. Canadian militia transported his regulars to Oswego in 1756 and to Fort William Henry in 1757, and helped with the successful siege of these American outposts. Capture of Oswego, before the small vessels under construction for the Royal Navy were completed, ensured continued French control of Lake Ontario, and the destruction of Fort William Henry delayed the inevitable British attempt to advance along Lake George and Lake Champlain towards Montreal. Montcalm was stalling for time in the hope that French victories in Europe or India might bring about a peace conference before Canada was lost.

Lord Loudon had made no offensive move against New France. Thus, he was now replaced as Commander-in-Chief in North America by Major-General James Abercrombie.

[15]Pargellis, *Military Affairs in North America*, 223.
[16]Sautai, *Moncalm au combat de Carillon*, 14, 21; Lanctôt, "Les Troupes de la Nouvelle-France," 44.
[17]Frégault, *La Guerre de la conquête*, 95.
[18]C[11A], Montcalm to Le Normand, April 12, 1759.

During the first week of July, 1758, Canadian militiamen felled trees to make log breastworks and abatis to form outer defences for Fort Ticonderoga. Then they added the fire of their muskets to that of the *troupes de terre* and *troupes de la Marine* to repulse Abercrombie's much larger assaulting force of British regulars and American provincials. Montcalm complained in his journal, however, that too few militiamen had been present, blaming their absence on the financial inducements offered by both the Montreal fur traders and the commissariat department for the freighting of stores.[19]

Less than three weeks after Montcalm's defensive victory at Ticonderoga, which put an end for another year to any British attempt to move down the Lake Champlain route to Montreal, the French fortress of distant Louisbourg surrendered to the expedition headed by a recently promoted Admiral of the Blue, the Hon. Edward Boscawen, and Major-General Jeffrey Amherst, of the 15th Regiment of Foot, a young colonel who had been specially promoted to hold this rank in North America. Although a total of fourteen French ships had managed to elude the British blockading squadrons in European waters that spring and get to Louisbourg before the attackers, the presence of Boscawen's fleet thereafter prevented any possibility of further succour. The successful British landing west of Louisburg itself meant that it would be only a matter of time until orthodox siege operations in the European manner forced the French to surrender. The decision at Louisbourg, when it came, was the turning point of the war in North America.

During the second half of August, 1758, Lieutenant-Colonel John Bradstreet advanced along the water route from Albany to Oswego with a small part of the Anglo-American army which had been defeated earlier at Ticonderoga. Bradstreet's men crossed the eastern end of Lake Ontario in *bateaux* and took the French garrison of Fort Frontenac by surprise, while its sizable naval force sat in the harbour. Fort Frontenac and the surrendered vessels were destroyed, and Bradstreet returned the way he had come, throwing away an opportunity to exert naval control of Lake Ontario and hasten the surrender of Fort Niagara. However, Fort Frontenac had been the French supply depot for the entire west and its destruction made the fall of Fort Duquesne inevitable. With Brigadier-General John Forbes's mixed force of regulars and provincials only a single day's march away, Fort Duquesne was blown up by its own garrison on November 24.

[19]L'Abbé H.-R. Casgrain, ed., *Journal du Marquis de Montcalm durant ses campagnes en Canada de 1756 à 1759* (Québec, 1895), 421-2.

This favourable turn in British fortunes, which continued until 1762, must be attributed to the dynamic personality, energy, and foresight of William Pitt who had been appointed Secretary of State, Southern Department, on June 27, 1757. As such he was leader of the Government in the House of Commons and director of the over-all war effort, even though the Duke of Newcastle was titular Prime Minister. Pitt was a civilian, however, and obviously depended much more on professional advisers than most historians have suggested. Advice on naval matters was available to Pitt and the Cabinet generally from the First Lord of the Admiralty, the professionally competent Admiral Lord Anson. But there was no single corresponding authority in control of military matters. Even though the continued existence of the British Army had to be sanctioned annually by Parliament, the royal prerogative still extended to its government, command, and disposition, and George II was interested enough in military matters to try to control them personally. Normally a Master General of the Ordnance headed the Royal Artillery and the Corps of Engineers, as well as the Board of Ordnance which was responsible for the construction and maintenance of fortifications and for the provision of the guns, small arms, ammunition, and other munitions for both the Army and Navy, but the elderly and stubborn King delayed filling this political-military appointment, which carried with it membership in the Cabinet, until June 1759. At the instance of Newcastle and Pitt, the King then appointed Field-Marshal Lord Ligonier, who had been carrying on most of the duties as Lieutenant-General of the Ordnance and had also been attending Cabinet meetings in an advisory role.

Pitt, who valued this distinguished soldier's advice, had managed as early as the autumn of 1757 to get him appointed Commander-in-Chief in England. In that appointment Ligonier was directly responsible for the administration and employment of all the cavalry and infantry regiments of the British Army serving anywhere, and for the entire conduct of home defence in the event of a French attempt at invasion. As Pitt's adviser on military strategy Ligonier drafted the instructions that the Secretary of State sent to the Commanders-in-Chief serving overseas, based on the more detailed planning done by his staff at the Horse Guards in London. A Secretary at War, with access to the King, was independently and primarily responsible to Parliament for the money authorized and spent on the British Army.[20] (Although a member of Parliament, the Secretary at War was not a member of the Cabinet and should not be confused with the later appointment of Secretary of State for War.)

[20]Rex Whitworth, *Field Marshal Lord Ligonier: A Story of the British Army* (Oxford, 1958), 214 ff.

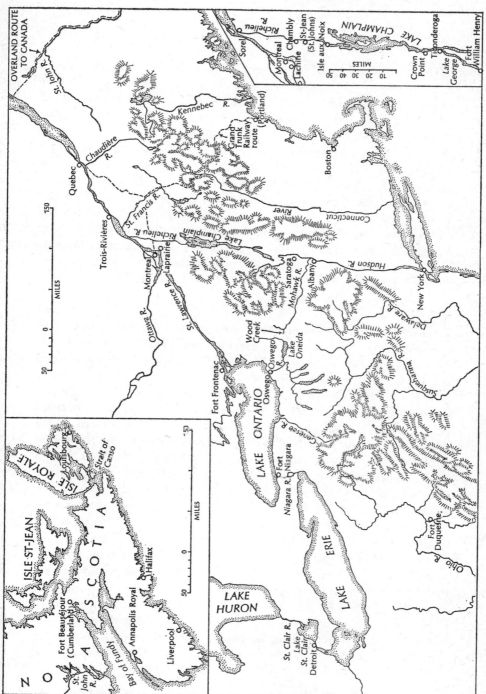

Invasion routes.

The strategy adopted by Pitt for 1759 envisaged a naval blockade of French ports so effective that no reinforcements or stores could reach New France. Major-General Amherst, now Commander-in-Chief in North America replacing Abercrombie, was to move along the Lake Champlain route against Montreal with 4,000 regulars and about the same number of provincials. Major-General James Wolfe was to attack Quebec with a separate army carried up the St. Lawrence River by a fleet under the command of a Vice-Admiral of the Blue, Charles Saunders. Ligonier reasoned that the French would divide their inferior numbers of *troupes de terre* and *troupes de la Marine* between Quebec and the Montreal frontier and he considered this action would make it impossible for them to defend either properly. Brigadier-General John Prideaux was to reoccupy Oswego with a smaller force and then continue on to Fort Niagara and force its surrender. Detailed planning was, however, left to the commanders on the spot.[21]

News of the approaching British expedition against Quebec reached Montcalm at Montreal about the middle of May, 1759. Montcalm had received only 400 reinforcements for his eight battalions of *troupes de terre*, about forty gunners, and a few specialists. He thus took a calculated risk and left only three battalions of *troupes de terre* and eight companies of *troupes de la Marine*, with some militia and four armed sailing vessels, to defend the Lake Champlain approach to Montreal. Ticonderoga could be abandoned as soon as it was seriously threatened by Amherst, but a stand was to be made at Isle aux Noix. The balance of the *troupes de terre* and *troupes de la Marine*, about 1,500 sailors of the ships then in the St. Lawrence River, and nearly 12,000 militia and Indians, were concentrated in and around Quebec. However, Quebec was not a proper fortress: its walls were neither well conceived nor well built; they lacked counterguards to protect them from the direct fire of a besieger's cannon; there were no proper ditches (with counterscarp and glacis) to slow down assaulting troops; and enemy batteries could be erected on high ground that overlooked the walls. As the launching of an assault seemed most likely to be carried out on the low ground east of the city, Montcalm disposed the bulk of his regulars and the militia there, behind field works. Only a small force was stationed above the city to interfere with any possible British attempt to land farther up the St. Lawrence River.[22]

On June 27 Wolfe's troops began landing on Isle d'Orléans from ships

21*Ibid.*, 278.
22C. P. Stacey, *Quebec, 1759: The Siege and the Battle* (Toronto, 1959) is the best account in English.

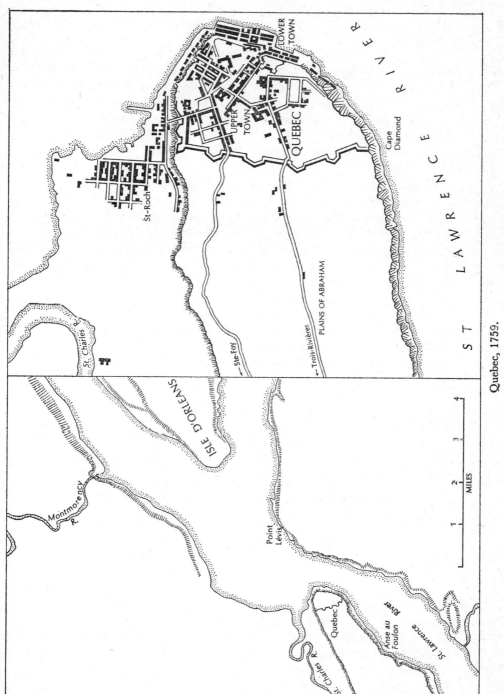

Quebec, 1759.

of Vice-Admiral Saunders' fleet. Except for six companies of rangers the 8,500 troops were all regulars; 300 provincials arrived later to serve as pioneers. Yet, apart from damaging the town by bombardment from the guns mounted on the high ground at Lévis, Wolfe was no more successful than Sir William Phips had been in 1690, until he finally gambled and landed with 4,400 troops at the Anse au Foulon before dawn on September 13.

When Montcalm learned that British troops had climbed the heights and were marshalling on the Plains of Abraham—high ground that commanded sections of the city walls—he decided to advance to the attack at once with 4,500 men who were immediately available and of whom about half were militia. For this he would be criticized in the future. Guy Frégault suggests that Montcalm was in a hurry to defeat the British before the Marquis de Vaudreuil could arrive with more troops to share the credit. Colonel C. P. Stacey contends that Montcalm, although he should have waited for Vaudreuil, had to attack Wolfe's field force, which was astride French communications with Montreal and could prevent food from entering the town. However, a distinguished British soldier, Major-General Sir James Carmichael-Smyth, R.E., writing in 1825 for the benefit of the Duke of Wellington, maintained that

. . . it would have been more advantageous to have profited of the near neighbourhood of the works of Quebec, and compelled General Wolfe to attack him behind them. The defences of Quebec were not so strong as respectable field-works. They were not, however, to be taken by assault, defended by such good troops as were under Montcalm's orders; nor had the English general such a superiority of regular regiments as to have justified his making the attempt. To have established batteries, and to have broke ground, would have been an operation requiring considerable time and labour. The season was slipping away rapidly, and the French had everything to gain from delay. It is also to be observed Montcalm had a corps of about 2,000 men in the rear of the British army . . . being employed to prevent any disembarkation at the mouth of the Jacques Cartier River, or at Pointe-aux-Trembles. This detachment would have harassed the British Army, and impeded their communications had they been obliged to remain before Quebec and to commence regular operations.[23]

As it was, devastating volleys of British musketry broke the French advance across the Plains of Abraham. In a matter of minutes a mortally wounded Montcalm and his men were headed for shelter in the city. The French field force soon abandoned its position and retreated up the St.

[23]Sir James Carmichael, ed., *Précis of the Wars in Canada, from 1775 to the Treaty of Ghent in 1814: With Political and Military Reflections.* By the late Maj.-Gen. Sir James Carmichael-Smyth (London, 1862), 81; cf. Stacey, *Quebec, 1759: The Siege and the Battle*, 154 and Frégault, *La Guerre de la conquête*, 348.

Lawrence River by a circuitous route, leaving the victorious British on the battlefield where their own commander lay dead. By September 18 the Chevalier de Lévis had rallied the French forces and had started back to relieve the garrison holding Quebec, but the commander in the city had already agreed to surrender and did so. Lévis thereupon retreated up the St. Lawrence and went into winter quarters, and the British fleet soon sailed for home, leaving a sizable garrison with Brigadier-General the Hon. James Murray to hold Quebec.

Meanwhile Amherst had achieved very little. The French had abandoned Ticonderoga on his approach and had blown up the fort at Crown Point when he continued his advance. When Amherst reached there on August 4, he learned that the French had surrendered Fort Niagara. Amherst, a cautious soldier, refused to advance further down Lake Champlain until he had acquired a navy strong enough to prevent the four tiny war vessels possessed by the French from destroying his troop-laden *bateaux*. By the time all was ready it was September 11. When the British flotilla advanced down the lake two of the four French war vesssels were sunk by their crews, a third ran aground, and the fourth retreated down the Richelieu River to Isle aux Noix. Amherst now held undisputed command of Lake Champlain. Nevertheless he decided not to venture further until the spring of 1760. News that the British had captured Quebec convinced him that all French forces would now be concentrating in front of him in the Montreal area.[24]

Activity in the European theatre added to Britain's advantage in the war, the Royal Navy having two major victories to its credit in 1759. On August 18 Admiral Boscawen destroyed in Lagos Bay the Toulon squadron which was trying to join the Brest squadron as a preliminary to a French invasion of England. On November 20 another Admiral of the Blue, Sir Edward Hawke, completely shattered the Brest squadron in Quiberon Bay. As a result little French aid was likely to reach Canada during the coming year.

In mid-April, 1760, the French force at Montreal moved down the St. Lawrence River against Quebec. It included more regulars than the physically fit men among Murray's garrison. Murray may have thought, when he led his troops outside the city on April 28, that superior British musketry fire would again bring victory. If so, he was mistaken. The British troops were defeated at Ste-Foye and retreated into the city. The

---

[24]J. Clarence Webster, ed., *The Journal of Jeffrey Amherst: Recording the Military Career of General Amherst in America from 1758 to 1763* (Toronto, 1931).

French commenced a close siege of Quebec. Only the arrival of a British warship from Halifax on May 9, followed by two more on May 15, forced the French to raise the siege and retreat towards Montreal. Since the Royal Navy was able to prevent any aid from arriving from France, it was only a matter of time before the French in Canada would have to surrender to British forces converging on Montreal: Brigadier-General Murray from Quebec with 2,450 regulars, Brigadier-General William Haviland from Crown Point with 3,300 regulars and provincials, and Major-General Amherst with 10,000 regulars and provincials from Albany, via Oswego and the upper St. Lawrence River. However, these separate expeditions moved carefully and ponderously, and it was early September before they neared Montreal. As there were less than 3,900 *troupes de terre* and *troupes de la Marine* remaining, and large numbers of the Canadian militia were deserting daily to their homes, the Marquis de Vaudreuil agreed to Articles of Capitulation on September 8, 1760.

Although historians have been careful to emphasize the part played by the Royal Navy in the conquest of Canada, they have ignored certain other factors, such as those indicated in the extremely pertinent military comments made by Sir James Carmichael-Smyth:

As General Amherst's operations were successful, hasty observers have taken it for granted they were judicious, and they have, in later days, even been attempted to be imitated. They will not, however, stand the test of investigation, and the movement by Oswego, Lake Ontario, and the St. Lawrence may be pronounced to have been imprudent and unnecessary.

The distance from Albany to Oswego is one hundred and sixty miles; from Oswego, across Lake Ontario to the commencement of the St. Lawrence, there are sixty miles of water conveyance, and from the commencement of the St. Lawrence to Montreal a hundred and seventy-four additional miles of a very rapid and dangerous river, making a total distance of three hundred and ninety-four miles for the conveyance of the troops, as well as the provisions, ammunition, and stores they required.[25]

Carmichael-Smyth emphasized the difficulty of descending the rapids of the St. Lawrence River, the ease with which a small party of French and Indians could have interrupted this movement, the fact that Amherst had to bring all his supplies from distant Oswego, and the possibility that complete disaster could have resulted had "the French opposed with spirit the advance of this corps."[26] On the other hand, Amherst's troops could easily have advanced down Lake Champlain and the Richelieu River, the route followed by Haviland's smaller force, and could then have joined

[25]Carmichael, *Précis of the Wars in Canada*, 84.
[26]*Ibid.*, 85.

Murray's regulars advancing up the St. Lawrence River. The French no longer had a base on Lake Ontario and their hold on the upper St. Lawrence River was limited to La Galette in the Thousand Islands, where they had built two brigs following the destruction of Fort Frontenac, and a small fort on Isle Royale just below Oswegatchie (Ogdensburg). The capture of these small bases could well have been left to a brigade of American provincials and Indians led by someone like Bradstreet.

Amherst soon removed his headquarters as Commander-in-Chief in North America to New York City. Since there no longer was employment in North America for 22,000 British regulars, he was ordered to mount expeditions against the French West Indian islands of St. Lucia and Dominica during late 1761 and to plan a larger operation against Martinique. He was also ordered to undertake operations in the south and west of continental North America in order to extend British territory to the Gulf of Mexico and the Mississippi River.[27]

The British troops remaining in Canada became an army of occupation. Murray's report of June 6, 1762, on the state of Quebec and its inhabitants, included a condemnation of the existing fortifications which could never be "rendered strong."[28] What was needed was a citadel on the rising ground of Cape Diamond, which commanded the town and the whole area, and which "may be defended 4 months at least by a small garrison, awe the Inhabitants, whose fidelity in case of attack we cannot for some years rely on, and secure our Magazines." Appended to the report were several fortress plans drawn by Captain Samuel Holland, one of the foreign Protestant engineer officers specially commissioned into the 60th (or Royal American) Regiment of Foot. Holland also participated in the detailed survey of the settled portions of the St. Lawrence valley, between the islands of Montreal to the west and Orléans to the east, and the compilation of the detailed maps ordered by Governor Murray. The *Gazeteer*, compiled during the years 1761–63, included a short description of each parish and the number of its male inhabitants capable of bearing arms. Lieutenant John Montressor of the corps of engineers, who was in charge of this project, also produced detailed maps of an overland route between Quebec and Fort Halifax at the mouth of the Kennebec River in Maine. This route followed the Chaudière and Kennebec rivers for the most part.

The British military governors of Quebec, Trois-Rivières, and Montreal

[27]Whitworth, *Field Marshal Lord Ligonier*, 338, 344.
[28]Haldimand Papers B/7, Report of General Murray on the state of Quebec, April 6, 1762.

conscientiously followed the principle that the laws of a conquered territory remain in effect until expressly altered by a new sovereign. The
Treaty of Paris, signed on February 10, 1763, recognized the British
conquest of all French territory in North America except the tiny fishing
colony of Saint-Pierre-et-Miquelon. The Treaty permitted those wishing
to retain French nationality a further eighteen months in which to return
to France with their possessions. The Canadians could not therefore be
considered British subjects until August 10, 1764. How loyal they would
be to their new sovereign was another matter, but hardly a pressing one.
There also was little urgency about planning Canada's future defence
because the Union Jack now waved over most of the known continent
of North America, and Britain's recent enemies in Europe were too busy
licking their wounds to cause trouble in the foreseeable future.

(2)

AMERICAN REVOLUTIONARY YEARS

The Seven Years' War had proved very costly to British taxpayers, but a great deal of the action had taken place overseas. The Government decided that the American colonists should be taxed to help maintain the considerable garrison of sixteen regiments of regular troops left in North America. A good part of it, indeed, was almost immediately required to suppress the uprising of former Indian allies of the French, led by Pontiac, chief of the Ottawas. Successive attempts to tax the American colonists, however, met with impassioned cries of "no taxation without representation," accompanied by widespread passive disobedience and some rioting.

Because the scene of Pontiac's Conspiracy was far distant from long-settled communities, most Americans conveniently ignored the British Army's role in its suppression. Several colonies had, however, furnished contingents. The Commander-in-Chief in North America, now Major-General the Hon. Thomas Gage, suggested that Canada contribute a battalion of three hundred men. He reasoned that "nothing can so effectually serve, to convince the savages how vain and erroneous, their expectations have been of French Supplies, and that the arms of Great Britain, have received additional strength by the Conquest of Canada, than their seeing a Body of Canadians in Arms, and ready to act hostilely against them, in conjunction with British Troops."[1] Although the Military Governor of Montreal, Colonel Thomas Burton, thought that it was "too Early in the day, for raising Canadians to act Hostilely against the Savages,"[2] both Colonel Frederic Haldimand at Trois-Rivières and Major-General the Hon. James Murray at Quebec disagreed. Murray, who was soon to become the first Civil Governor of the whole new

[1]C.O. 42/25, Gage to Haldimand, Feb. 12, 1764.
[2]C.O. 42/25, Burton to Murray, March 2, 1764.

province, thought that the *habitants* should be encouraged to undertake a service for which, incidentally, they would be relatively well paid. Murray's commission as Captain-General and Governor-in-Chief, dated November 14, 1763, gave him "full power & Authority to Levy, Arm, Muster, Command, and Employ all persons whatsoever, residing within our said province, and as occasion shall serve them to march, Embark or Transport from one place to another for the resisting and withstanding of all enemies, pirates, & Rebels, both at land and sea; and to Transport such Forces to any of our Plantations in America, if necessity shall require for Defence of the same against the invasion or attempts of any of our enemies."[3] But he was loath to embody militiamen at the risk of impeding the natural process of turning the French-speaking Canadians into loyal subjects of George III, which they would be expected to become after August 10, 1764. His letter of March 5, 1764, to Gage emphasized the desirability of using persuasion rather than the traditional policy of compulsion:

These poor people have hardly yet had time to breathe; after a long uninterrupted Series of Misfortunes, they have flattered themselves, that under our Government, they would be exempted, at least from the *intolerable* weight of Military Service under which they formerly groaned, hence an additional Necessity of making the service you require of them at present a Voluntary one, when put upon that footing, it will not be in the power of French Emissaries, Priests or other disaffected persons, to turn the measure to their purposes, and thereby persuade many to leave the province who otherwise would not have thought of it. . . .[4]

After some initial difficulty recruiting the quota assigned to Montreal, the required three hundred volunteers were obtained, and command of the battalion was entrusted to a former officer of the *troupes de la Marine*. Service as military pioneers and transportation troops with Colonel John Bradstreet's column during the campaigning season of 1764 was physically arduous, and the battalion did not return to Montreal until the last week in November. Colonel Haldimand subsequently reported from Trois-Rivières that "ces bonnes gens, qui n'avaient jamais reçu un traitement pareil, sont très contents et souhaitent qu'on aye besoin de leurs Services l'année prochaine."[5]

A few armed schooners had been providing lake transportation for

[3]Adam Shortt and Arthur G. Doughty, eds., *Documents relating to the Constitutional History of Canada 1759–1791* (Ottawa, 1918), I, 177.
[4]C.O. 42/25, Murray to Gage, March 5, 1764.
[5]Haldimand Papers B/2–2, Haldimand to Gage, Dec. 25, 1764.

military stores and troops since shortly after the Conquest. This service was soon transferred from Admiralty control to that by the Quartermaster General's Department of the British Army in North America and gradually became known as the Provincial Marine. Montreal merchants and others interested in the fur trade, which was centred about the British military posts in the interior, found it convenient to have their trade goods and the furs bartered from the Indians shipped in vessels belonging to the Provincial Marine. Initially it was also cheaper to pay the designated freight rates than to operate private vessels. The government schooners had to visit Army posts with supplies and reinforcements anyway, and the fur trade helped defray the cost of their operation.

Major-General Gage seems to have been so busy rebuilding the frontier forts destroyed by the Indians who had supported Pontiac that he did not give much thought to the crumbling state of the forts at Crown Point, Ticonderoga, and the foot of Lake George until late in 1766. He then sought an opinion from Colonel Guy Carleton as to whether they should be rebuilt. Carleton had been Quartermaster General of Wolfe's army in 1759. He was now Lieutenant-Governor of the province of Quebec while Murray was on leave of absence in Britain. On February 15, 1767, Carleton replied to Gage's letter in the affirmative. He further suggested the establishment of a munitions depot near New York City and the construction of a citadel at Quebec City where nothing had yet been done to repair the inadequate fortifications damaged during the sieges of 1759 and 1760.[6] Carleton outlined a plan that could have been employed to counter either a French threat in the St. Lawrence River or a rebellion by disgruntled American colonists. According to his reasoning, a chain of fortified bases between Quebec and New York—at Crown Point, Ticonderoga, the foot of Lake George, and upriver from New York— would "facilitate the Transport of ten or fifteen thousand Men in the beginning of a War, from the one to the other, as the circumstances may require."[7] As his letter to Gage continued:

This Communication so established, will give Security to the King's Magazines, till then precarious, and doubtful who may avail themselves of them; will separate the Northern from the Southern Colonies, will afford an easy and advantageous opportunity of transporting his Forces into any part of this Continent, and may prevent the greatest of all Inconveniences, Delay and Loss of Time in the beginning of a War.

---

[6]C.O. 42/27, Carleton to Gage, Feb. 15, 1767.
[7]Ibid.

It is not clear whether Carleton was aware of earlier and abortive French plans to split the American colonies in two by attacking along the Lake Champlain–Lake George–Hudson River route towards New York City, or whether he reached the same conclusion about strategy by independent reasoning.

Gage may have been impressed by Carleton's ideas, but the Treasury Board in far off London was in no mood to approve new military expenditure in North America when the world was at peace and likely to continue so for some time.

Carleton persuaded an engineer officer who was visiting Quebec to prepare a plan for a citadel. This was submitted on November 25, 1767, to Lord Shelburne, the Secretary of State responsible for administering the colonies in North America. Carleton's accompanying despatch reiterated that nothing had been done to repair the damage caused to Quebec's fortifications and added that the flimsy walls at Montreal were falling into ruin. He estimated that the English-speaking merchants who had flocked into the new province might furnish 500 men experienced in bearing arms, "supposing them all willing,"[8] and thought that these men should be capable of putting Quebec into a defensible state after two months of hard work. Carleton's military establishment called for 1,600 British regulars, but his actual strength was considerably less, and he would have to call on the French-speaking Canadians in the event of an emergency. He stated that the French-speaking inhabitants "could send into the Field, about eighteen Thousand Men, well able to bear Arms; of which Number, above one half have already served, with as much Valor, with more zeal, and more military knowledge for America, than the regular Troops of France, that were joined with them." It seems that he had not understood the lessons that the recent Anglo-French struggle had to teach about the relative merits of regulars and militia.

The rest of Carleton's letter argued that immigrants would be attracted to the "more chearful Climates and more fruitful Soil" of the more southerly American colonies and that, "barring a Catastrophe shocking to think of, this Country must, to the end of Time, be peopled by the Canadian Race, who already have taken such firm Root, and got to so great a Height, that any new Stock transplanted will be totally hid, and imperceptible amongst them, except in the Towns of Quebec and Montreal."[9] He therefore urged greater efforts to make the Roman Catholic and French-speaking Canadians happy and contented subjects of a Pro-

[8]C.O. 42/28, Carleton to Shelburne, Nov. 25, 1767.
[9]*Ibid.*

testant and English-speaking monarch. Carleton assumed that if the leaders were won over the rank and file would follow. Had not this doctrine of *cujus regio, ejus religio* been successful in Europe since the early years of the Protestant Reformation?

Carleton was particularly afraid that should there be another war between Britain and France a number of Canadian seigneurs, especially former officers of the *troupes de la Marine* settled in the province, might be persuaded by agents from France to head a revolt. A possible long-term solution was advanced in his despatch of January 20, 1768: the organization of a few companies of Canadian Foot would provide employment as officers for a number of the Canadian gentry and would encourage them in the belief that their sons could look forward to careers in the service of a British king.[10] Legally, it is true, Roman Catholics were barred from holding commissions in the British Army by the Test Act of 1672, but this was regularly being overlooked in Great Britain throughout the eighteenth century. Considerable numbers of Roman Catholics served as regimental officers by occasionally conforming to practices of the Church of England.[11]

Although Carleton's suggestions were ignored, the British Government was not lacking in plans for North America. It was even then discussing what military steps should be taken to give the Indians a vast hunting ground, from which white settlement would be barred, in the hinterland separated from the province of Quebec by the Royal Proclamation of October 7, 1763. On April 15, 1768, Lord Hillsborough, the first to be Secretary of State for the American Colonies, wrote directing Gage to withdraw British regulars from many of the existing forts in this interior and to concentrate his establishment of sixteen regiments of foot as much as possible in Quebec, Nova Scotia, East Florida, and the middle colonies "to serve effectually upon any emergency whatsoever."[12] Hillsborough indicated that British garrisons should remain at Forts Ticonderoga, Niagara, Detroit, and Michilimackinac, none of which, however, were within Carleton's military jurisdiction.

Carleton officially became Governor of Canada on October 26, 1768. A despatch of November 20, 1768, addressed to Lord Hillsborough, expressed his fear of a war with France and a rebellion within the American colonies. He felt that if the French regained Quebec they could

---

[10]*Ibid.*, Jan. 20, 1768.

[11]Charles M. Clode, *The Military Forces of the Crown: Their Administration and Government* (London, 1869), I, 69; II, 384–5.

[12]John Richard Alden, *General Gage in America; Being Principally A History of His Role in the American Revolution* (Baton Rouge, 1948), 142–3.

actively assist the Americans to win independence from the British Empire.[13] Since nothing had been done about building a citadel for Quebec, Carleton resubmitted his 1767 plan on May 9, 1769. The argument now put to Lord Hillsborough somewhat twisted the facts to suit Carleton's purpose:

I have found it the general opinion of the Canadians, that if Admiral Durell had pushed up in May 1759, with only a small part of the Army [from Louisbourg], the Town might have been taken before the [French] Governor in Chief could have sent them any Assistance from Montreal, where and in the upper Country all the Troops were collected to Defend the Entrance by the Lakes; That after the Defeat of their Army upon the Plains of Abraham the 13th of September, altho' they had eight Battalions and forty Companies of regular Troops, with fifteen or sixteen thousand warlike Militia in the Field, after having had four months Time to strengthen the Town, they apprehended the same so indefensible that they surrendered immediately before one single Battery could be opened against it; and that if in the Succeeding year the remains of ten Brave [British] Battalions were enabled to hold out until the Arrival of our Fleet, it was in a great Degree due to Monsieur de Lévis' Army being in want of Artillery and Ammunition.[14]

In the summer of 1770 Carleton returned to England and remained there for nearly four years. During that time he helped the Government draft the Quebec Act, which he hoped would expedite the conversion of French-speaking Canadians into loyal subjects of George III. Unfortunately Carleton's judgment seems to have been influenced by his association with Canadian seigneurs who had told him what he wanted to believe, namely that New France had been a feudal society in which tenants had turned out under their overlords to repel any aggressor. In actual fact, of course, the struggle for survival in the Canadian wilderness had mitigated against the establishment of a true feudal society, and the laxity of recent British rule had further eroded seigniorial bonds. Time alone would show that the *habitants* would be alienated, rather than won over, by an act intended to turn every seigneur into a real "lord of the manor."

The Quebec Act was passed in 1774 by the same British Parliament that enacted four so-called "Coercive Acts" aimed particularly at Massachusetts, but American fears that the Act was directed at them actually seem to have been groundless. Yet Americans could not be blamed for resenting the recognition given Roman Catholicism, the revival of French civil law, and the denial of a legislative assembly to their compatriots who had flocked to Quebec for primarily commercial reasons. They were

[13]C.O. 42/28, Carleton to Hillsborough, Nov. 20, 1768.
[14]C.O. 42/29, Carleton to Hillsborough, May 9, 1769.

also alarmed by the extension once again to the Ohio and Mississippi rivers, of Quebec's western boundary, which thereby encompassed most of the Great Lakes' region; this appeared a reversion to the French attempt to exclude them from the interior of the continent.[15] The radical element in Boston particularly resented the appointment of Lieutenant-General the Hon. Thomas Gage as Governor of Massachusetts. The more troops Gage ordered into Boston, in his other continuing capacity as Commander-in-Chief, the worse grew the discontent and the possibility of open rebellion. Newfoundland lost its regular garrison to Boston, and both Halifax and New York were left with less than a single battalion of troops. Although four regiments arrived from Britain during August, and more were expected, this did little to soothe a worried Gage.[16] On September 4, 1774, he wrote to Major-General Carleton, who was on his way back to Quebec from Britain, requesting that the 10th and 52nd Regiments of Foot be shipped to Boston in the transports he was sending to Quebec.[17] Gage also asked whether a body of Canadians and Indians might be recruited for service against the dissident element in New England, should the existing sparks of unrest be fanned into the flames of armed rebellion.

This letter reached Quebec only a few hours after Carleton had arrived on September 18, in a very optimistic mood. Carleton had a young wife and two infants with him, and he was extremely confident that success would attend his implementation of the new Quebec Act. He has been criticized for agreeing to the transfer of the 10th and 52nd Regiments to Boston, since the continuing 7th (or Royal Fusiliers) and the 26th Regiments numbered less than 800 effectives between them. (It should be remembered that the upper posts, garrisoned by detachments of the 8th (or King's) Regiment, would not be within his jurisdiction until promulgation of the Quebec Act on May 1, 1775.) But the following extract from Gage's letter suggests that neither the Commander-in-Chief nor the Governor of Quebec considered that there would be any undue risk involved in this course of action:

. . . at the same time I submit to you whether you think anything is to be dreaded from the absence of these Corps, internally, in the Province of Quebec, during the Winter, for, as these Regiments will come down the River so late in the Year, and may be replaced early in the Spring, I imagine no Danger can be apprehended from without. If, therefore, you think the Fusiliers at Quebec, and the part of the 26th at Montreal, with small Detachments from them at Trois-Rivières, &

---

[15]A. L. Burt, *The Old Province of Quebec* (Toronto, 1933), 184–8.
[16]Alden, *General Gage in America*, 209–14.
[17]C.O. 42/33, Gage to Carleton, Sept. 4, 1774.

Chambly, can preserve Peace and good Order in the Province, I am to beg you will order the 10th & 52nd Regiments to embark without delay on board the Transports, for, you will think with me they will have no time to spare in coming from the River St. Lawrence.[18]

Carleton sent off the 10th and 52nd Regiments and replied to Gage's letter that he would experience no difficulty in forming a Canadian regiment, which might in time be augmented to two, three, or even more battalions.[19]

As the months passed, however, Carleton became somewhat disturbed. A secret letter to Gage of February 4, 1775, expressed the hope that a reinforcement of British regulars would be sent to Quebec as soon as the navigation season opened.[20] Protest meetings were being held by the English-speaking minorities at Quebec and Montreal for, when the Quebec Act became effective on May 1, 1775, these "old subjects" would lose all hope of gaining an elected assembly. They would also lose their traditional right of *habeas corpus*, the right to have jury trials for civil, though not criminal, cases, and the right to have their suits determined by English civil law. Revolutionary agents from the American colonies fostered a rumour, widely believed by the French-speaking *habitants*, that the hitherto neglected militia would be drafted into the British Army for service in turbulent New England.[21] Carleton's letter to Gage conceded that the *habitants* would not be "pleased at being suddenly, and without Preparation embodied into a Militia, and marched from their Families, Lands, and Habitations to remote Provinces, and all the Horrors of War, which they have already experienced."[22] On the other hand, Carleton wrote, the raising of Canadian battalions of regulars would do much to recall the *habitants* to the "ancient Habits of Obedience and Discipline" from which they had been released by the Conquest.

Gage's reply, March 16, 1775, advised Carleton that a fort should be built at Crown Point from the ruins of the French fortification destroyed by fire in 1759.[23] A few days earlier Gage had written the commander at Ticonderoga to be on his guard against a surprise attack by American rebels. The importance of the line of communication between Montreal and New York could not be overemphasized.[24]

On April 19 came the skirmishes at Lexington and Concord. Against

18*Ibid.*; see also extract of the same letter in the Germain Mss, 1774–76.
19C.O. 42/33, Carleton to Gage, Sept. 20, 1774.
20C.O. 42/34, Carleton to Gage, Feb. 4, 1775.
21Burt, *The Old Province of Quebec*, 203–4.
22C.O. 42/34, Carleton to Gage, Feb. 4, 1775.
23Gage Papers, Gage to Carleton, March 16, 1775.
24Alden, *General Gage in America*, 228.

this background Gage felt justified in writing Carleton to send the 7th Regiment of Foot with some companies of Canadians and Indians to Crown Point to create a diversion on his behalf.[25] This letter reached Quebec on May 19, but next morning the news arrived that American rebels had surprised St. Johns (St-Jean) on May 18 and had carried off its military stores and tiny garrison; Ticonderoga and Crown Point had been captured on May 10 and 12, respectively, and were being held by Ethan Allen's Green Mountain Boys and Benedict Arnold's contingent from Connecticut.[26]

These aggressive steps ran counter to the wishes of the Second Continental Congress, most of whose members were not yet in favour of seeking independence from Britain and desired only to take the minimum defensive precautions.[27] However, the American inhabitants of the settlements bordering Canada had unpleasant memories of French and Indian raiding parties and believed that offensive action was the best defence. They regarded Canada

. . . as a base for attacks, of a kind with which they were painfully familiar, but to be undergone now under disadvantages of numbers and power never before experienced. [Therefore] it was desirable to gain possession of the St. Lawrence and its posts before they were strengthened and garrisoned. At this outset of hostilities, the American insurgents, knowing clearly their own minds, possessed the advantage of the initiative over the British Government, which still hesitated to use against those whom it styled rebels the preventative measures it would have taken at once against a recognized enemy.[28]

Letters of Ethan Allen and Benedict Arnold, and the former's personal appearance before the Second Continental Congress at Philadelphia, seem to have had the effect the aggressive party desired. On June 27 Congress authorized Major-General Philip Schuyler, commanding its New York Department, to proceed to Ticonderoga and Crown Point. If he found "it practicable and that it will not be disagreeable to the Canadians," he was instructed that "he do immediately take possession of St. Johns, Montreal and other parts of the country."[29]

Meanwhile Carleton had hurried to Montreal to supervise defensive preparations. That he had been further jolted is evident from the despatch he wrote to the Secretary of State for the American Colonies, now Lord

[25]Gage Papers, Gage to Carleton, April 19, 1775.
[26]C.O. 42/34, Carleton to Dartmouth, June 7, 1775.
[27]Christopher Ward, *The War of the Revolution* (New York, 1952), I, 139.
[28]A. T. Mahan, *The Major Operations of the Navies in the War of American Independence* (London, 1913), 8.
[29]Ward, *The War of the Revolution*, I, 140.

Dartmouth, on June 7. Instead of being able to relieve the pressure on Gage's army at Boston by marching a force along the Lake Champlain–Lake George–Hudson River route, Carleton suddenly realized that he might have difficulty defending his own province of Quebec against American rebels. He quickly despatched this intelligence to Dartmouth:

The little Force we have in the Province was immediately set in motion, and ordered to assemble at or near St. John's; The Noblesse of this neighbourhood were called upon to collect their Inhabitants, in order to defend themselves, the Savages of those Parts likewise had the same orders; but tho' the gentlemen testified great zeal, neither their Entreaties or their Example could prevail upon the People, a few of the Gentry, consisting principally of the Youth, residing in this Place [Montreal], and its neighbourhood formed a small Corps of Volunteers under the command of Mr. Samuel Mackay a half-pay officer, and took post at St. John's; the Indians shewed as much Backwardness as the Canadian Peasantry.

The consternation in the Towns and Country was great and universal, every Individual seemed to feel our present impotent situation, for tho' in no Danger of internal Commotions, we are equally unprepared for Attack or Defence; not six hundred Rank & File fit for duty upon the whole Extent of this great River [St. Lawrence], not an armed Vessel, no place of Strength; the ancient Provincial Force enervated and broke to Pieces; all Subordination overset, and the minds of the People poisoned by the Hypocrisy and Lies practised with so much success in the other Provinces, and which their Emissaries and Friends here have spread abroad with great Art and Diligence; had it not been for those few Troops, three hundred Rebels might have procured all the Arms, Ammunition and Provisions, this Province can afford, and have kept Post at St. John's with great security.

We are at present fortifying a Post there and at Oswegatchie, tho' there are other avenues into the Province, I hope the above may be made sufficiently strong to resist any sudden Attack of this sort; a considerable Force here might not only secure ourselves, but assist General Gage in extinguishing the Flames of Rebellion in the other Provinces more speedily, I feel he has none to spare and it may be too late in the year to have them from Europe.[30]

Two days later Carleton issued a proclamation which put martial law into effect and directed the militia to assemble whenever called upon by their captains, who had been continued in their appointments by the British Governors.[31] Up to this point Carleton had refrained from issuing a Militia Ordinance and there was not now time to reorganize this dormant force properly.[32] The English-speaking minorities at Montreal and Quebec, however, seem to have gone ahead and formed militia companies.[33] Those at Quebec, where less than 60 rank and file of the 7th

[30]C.O. 42/34, Carleton to Dartmouth, June 7, 1775.
[31]*Quebec Gazette*, June 15, 1775.
[32]C.O. 42/34, Carleton to Dartmouth, June 7, 1775.
[33]*Quebec Gazette*, July 6 and 27, Sept. 14 and 21, 1775.

Regiment of Foot remained, were embodied to guard the magazine and military stores.

Montreal, which Carleton considered to be the most likely American objective, had only 96 British regulars in garrison, but nearly 500 effectives from the 7th and 26th Regiments now occupied the advanced forts at Chambly and St. Johns.[34] Yet all his efforts to improve the defences of St. Johns and the smaller post at Chambly were frustrated by the unwillingness of the *habitants* to work on them.[35] The remainder of the 7th and 26th Regiments was disposed in patrols on other possible enemy avenues of approach: 24 men were at the mouth of the Chaudière River, which flowed into the St. Lawrence near Quebec City; 32 men were at St. Francis, near the mouth of that river which emptied into Lake St. Peter; and 13 men were beside the Lachine Rapids. A small company of the 8th Regiment was now stationed farther up the St. Lawrence River at Oswegatchie.[36] Four of the rest of the companies of this unit garrisoned Niagara, three were at Detroit, and two were at Michilimackinac.[37]

"What adds to our Distress," Carleton wrote Lord Dartmouth on August 14, "is the feeble state of the Vessels upon the upper Lakes, which are all very ill manned, and in no ways prepared for War, yet they are much threatened, and the consequences would be fatal to the Upper Posts and Country, should they fall into the Enemies Hands."[38] Since there was scant possibility of American rebels obtaining vessels to dispute the Provincial Marine's control of the Great Lakes, the lack of shipwrights and naval ordnance there was not nearly as serious a matter as Carleton's letter implied. The situation on Lake Champlain, however, was entirely different: here the Americans had an armed sloop and schooner, and were busy mounting guns on two row-galleys and ten *bateaux*. Carleton had ordered the construction at St. Johns of two vessels, one of which was to carry sixteen guns, but artificers had to be brought from as far away as Halifax, and work progressed slowly.[39] Carleton managed to persuade Lieutenant William Hunter, R.N., commanding the brigantine H.M.S. *Gaspé* which had arrived at Quebec seeking provisions, to remain and help prepare the lake vessels for action, but her crew was not

---

[34]C.O. 42/34, Carleton to Dartmouth, June 26, 1775.
[35]*Ibid.*, Nov. 5, 1775.
[36]*Ibid.*, June 26, 1775.
[37]W.O. 17/1494, Distribution of His Majesty's Forces in North America, June 11, 1775.
[38]C.O. 42/34, Carleton to Dartmouth, Aug. 14, 1775.
[39]*Ibid.*, Nov. 5, 1775.

sufficient to man the vessels being built on Lake Champlain, to say nothing of the Great Lakes.[40]

A *mandement* issued by Bishop Briand and the activity of the parish clergy helped to check active disloyalty among the French-speaking Canadians, but in a number of parishes around Montreal and Trois-Rivières the *habitants* defied those militia officers who tried to give some semblance of order to their companies. The majority of the people in the province merely wanted to remain aloof from a quarrel that was none of their choosing. Carleton therefore concluded that it would be inadvisable to try to muster any considerable number of militia except as a last resort.[41] Unfortunately, this negative attitude had the effect of further discouraging the Indians from going to war on Carleton's behalf.[42] About 100 of the discharged Scottish veterans of the Seven Years' War who had settled in the province were recruited for the provincial corps of Royal Highland Emigrants being raised by Colonel Allan Maclean and were posted to St. Johns, but a larger number of recruits enlisted in the Mohawk valley could not be brought into Canada immediately because of the presence of American forces about Lake Champlain.

Meanwhile Gage in Boston and Dartmouth in London, blissfully ignorant of the true situation in Canada, were urging Carleton to take positive action. Gage's letter of June 15, 1775, hoped that "with the 7th and 26th Regiments, and such Canadians and Indians as you may have been able to collect, that it's possible you may have secured a Post on Lake Champlain, to be in a position to penetrate from thence into the New England Governments."[43] He was sending Brigadier-General Robert Prescott to serve under Carleton and a number of cannon by sea, but no carpenters or shipwrights could be spared from Boston. On July 1 Dartmouth wrote authorizing Carleton to raise a force of 3,000 Canadians.[44] By July 3 Gage was in receipt of despatches detailing Carleton's difficulties, but he wrote optimistically that "when the present flurry is a little over, you will be able to do a great deal" and that "you will soon receive a good reinforcement of Indians from the back Country, which will rouse the spirit of those amongst you, and likewise of the Canadian Peasantry."[45] Another letter from Dartmouth, of July 12, directed Carleton to raise 6,000 rather than 3,000 men, for all of whom arms

[40]Gage Papers, Carleton to Gage, Aug. 5, 1775; see also Adm. 1/485, Carleton to Hunter, Aug. 6, 1775.
[41]C.O. 42/34, Carleton to Dartmouth, Aug. 14, 1775.
[42]C.O. 42/34, Cramahé to Dartmouth, Sept 21, 1775.
[43]Gage Papers, Gage to Carleton, June 15, 1775.
[44]C.O. 42/34, Dartmouth to Carleton, July 1, 1775.
[45]Gage Papers, Gage to Carleton, July 3, 1775.

and equipment were being shipped from Britain,[46] and Gage's letter of August 12 expressed the hope that Carleton might still accomplish something.[47]

A week earlier, on August 5, Carleton had written bluntly to Gage from Quebec that "so far from being in a Condition to act offensively against the Rebels, this Province is in no small Danger of falling into their hands."[48] Carleton's latest intelligence was that the rebels were collecting a large force in the Lake Champlain region for an invasion of Canada and that they had enough good seamen for their craft to defeat the "ill manned" vessels of the Provincial Marine which were still under construction at St. Johns. "While they see so weak a Force to support them," Carleton continued, "it will be very difficult to bring the Canadians even to defend their Country against an Enemy, who has vowed to destroy it with Fire and Sword, if they stir, and have Friends and Emissaries enough through the Country to whisper this constantly in their Ears." Even if the Indians remained in good humour and joined "heartily" against the Rebels, "what is or can be expected from them farther, than cutting off a few unfortunate Families, whose Destruction will be but of little avail towards a Decision of the present Contest."

The American commander, Major-General Schuyler, had promised General George Washington that he would invade Canada. Washington was well aware of the organizational problems faced by the conscientious but ineffectual Schuyler and counted on his having "a feeble enemy to contend with, and a whole province on your side, two circumstances of great weight in the scale."[49] Washington's own contribution from the rebel army investing Boston was to be a small force that Colonel Benedict Arnold would lead up the Kennebec River to the height of land and down the Chaudière River on the other side to the St. Lawrence River almost opposite the town of Quebec—the route that had been surveyed and mapped by Lieutenant John Montressor during 1761. Washington believed that the Arnold expedition would persuade Carleton "either to break up and follow this party to Quebec," leaving Schuyler's own army unopposed, or else to "suffer that important place [Quebec] to fall into our own hands, an event which would have a decisive effect and influence on the public interest."[50]

[46]Haldimand Papers B/37, Dartmouth to Carleton. July 12, 1775.
[47]Gage Papers, Gage to Carleton, Aug. 12, 1775.
[48]Gage Papers, Carleton to Gage, Aug. 5, 1775.
[49]Douglas Southall Freeman, *George Washington: A Biography* (New York, 1951), III, 537.
[50]*Ibid.*, 532.

*

The rebel advance down Lake Champlain did not get under way until late August when Brigadier-General Richard Montgomery, who was temporarily in command of Schuyler's army, learned that the two British war vessels were nearing completion at St. Johns and would soon be able to challenge the American vessels for supremacy on Lake Champlain. Montgomery's occupation of Isle aux Noix on September 4 made it possible for his small flotilla to block the Richelieu River, but he had the greatest difficulty getting his officers and men to undertake a proper siege of St. Johns. Montgomery had been a captain in the 17th Regiment of Foot during Amherst's campaigns of 1759 and 1760, but, as suggested earlier, fighting had not been the principal contribution of American provincial troops to the victorious conclusion of the Seven Years' War in Canada. Only after part of Montgomery's force had managed to slip downriver past St. Johns at night and force the surrender of the much smaller Fort Chambly, and only after Carleton's relief expedition from Montreal had been turned back, did the British commander of the now badly battered St. Johns surrender on November 3. Among those taken prisoner were Lieutenant Hunter and fourteen other members of the crew of H.M.S. *Gaspé*.

By this time Carleton knew that the British Government had issued the Proclamation of Rebellion on August 23, 1775, and was negotiating with both Catherine the Great of Russia and the German states of Hesse-Cassel and Brunswick for the hiring of up to 20,000 mercenary troops.[51] British regulars must be husbanded. It was painfully obvious that the colonial rebellion would turn into a general European war unless the rebels were quickly squashed. In that case France and Spain, smarting for revenge against the victor of the Seven Years' War, might attempt an invasion of Great Britain and Ireland should these be denuded of British regular troops. Gage was recalled to London, ostensibly for consultation, and the North American command was split. Major-General Sir William Howe in beleaguered Boston became Commander-in-Chief for the Atlantic colonies stretching from Florida to Nova Scotia, and Carleton became Commander-in-Chief of the more isolated Quebec, which the British Government now realized it might lose.[52] As early as August 2 Dartmouth had written Carleton that "His Majesty hopes to have an Army of 20,000 men in North America next spring exclusive of the Canadians & Indians, and you may depend upon a Reinforcement of the Regular Troops in

[51]Haldimand Papers B/37, Pownall to Carleton, Sept. 8, 1775.
[52]Piers Mackesy, *The War for America, 1775–1783* (London, 1964), 40.

Canada."[53] On September 25 Dartmouth issued orders to stop five battalions of troops in Ireland from sailing for Boston: four would go to Quebec and one to Halifax. One of these battalions did get to Halifax. However, two of the regiments had already sailed for Boston, and the other two were delayed by storms until it was too late in the season to attempt navigation of the St. Lawrence River. The suggestion that these two battalions might land in Nova Scotia and march overland to Quebec was discounted by senior officers on the spot, and they were added to an expedition heading for the Carolinas. Sir William Howe suggested that a battalion of marines be sent from Boston to Quebec, but Vice-Admiral of the Red Samuel Graves would not agree.[54] Possibly it was just as well that Carleton did not know any of this.

Carleton was convinced that the inhabitants of Montreal would insist on surrendering as soon as Montgomery's Americans appeared,[55] so on November 11 he started down the St. Lawrence River towards Quebec with his few remaining troops. But because American shore batteries erected at Sorel now commanded the St. Lawrence River, his ships and troops were forced to surrender two days later. Carleton himself, however, had been rowed past the American guns in a small boat during the dead of night, and he arrived at Quebec City safely on November 20.

Meanwhile Colonel Benedict Arnold had reached the St. Lawrence nine days earlier with only about 600 of the 1,100 Americans who had started out forty-five days earlier from the Atlantic coast of Maine. Because Washington and Arnold had greatly underestimated both the difficulties to be encountered and the distance to be travelled, the half-starved and ill-clad survivors of the expedition were incapable of offensive action and soon withdrew to the village of Pointe-aux-Trembles, about twenty miles above Quebec City. On December 2 Brigadier-General Montgomery arrived from Montreal with 300 men, several small guns, and a supply of ammunition, provisions, and clothing. The Americans then took up positions before Quebec: Montgomery's men occupied the Plains of Abraham and Arnold's men the partially burned suburb of St-Roch. With the ground frozen and covered with snow, and without heavy guns, it was, however, impossible to conduct normal siege operations.

Carleton had purged Quebec of the disaffected and was hopeful that his motley garrison of about 1,200 could withstand the numerically

[53]C.O. 42/34, Dartmouth to Carleton, Aug. 2, 1775.
[54]Mackesy, *The War for America, 1775–1783*, 43–5.
[55]C.O. 42/34, Carleton to Dartmouth, Nov. 5, 1775.

smaller enemy force outside the city walls. The garrison was made up of about 300 French-speaking militia, 200 English-speaking militia, 200 Royal Highland Emigrants (mostly recruits), 400 seamen and marines from the ships and vessels in ports, about 80 carpenters and artificers belatedly sent from Halifax for service at St. Johns,[56] and a miscellaneous handful of regulars.[57] Carleton's situation was similar to that of Murray during the winter of 1759–60, but he had no intention of repeating Murray's mistake of venturing outside the walls of Quebec and risking battle. He went further and even refused to accept the American messages sent to him by flag of truce.

Because the supplies and munitions stored in Quebec could sustain the rebel cause elsewhere, both George Washington and Congress counted upon its early capture. Moreover, Montgomery knew that he had little hope of retaining Arnold's men after their term of enlistment expired at the end of the year. He therefore decided to launch a direct assault against both ends of the Lower Town, which was the most poorly fortified part of Quebec, on the first dark and stormy night. This proved to be the early morning hours of New Year's Eve, when a near blizzard was raging. The defenders were alert, however, and defeated both attacking columns. Montgomery was killed, Arnold was wounded, and more than 450 Americans were killed, wounded, or taken prisoner. About 100 time-expired men left for New England, but the rest of the survivors stayed with Arnold, braving the Canadian winter, short rations, and an epidemic of smallpox.[58]

News of the American failure before Quebec placed George Washington in a quandary. He could not spare rebel troops for the campaign in Canada from the army besieging Boston, but Quebec must be captured. Otherwise the British might use it as the base for a summer offensive in 1776 along the Lake Champlain–Lake George–Hudson River route towards New York City, which could be simultaneously attacked by a British fleet carrying the troops with which General Sir William Howe was defending Boston.[59] Washington had already advised Congress not to launch an attack against Nova Scotia because there were no American troops to spare for any expedition that could be cut off from its base by British warships.[60] He had also tried to discourage the spread of hostilities

[56]Gage Papers, Gage to Carleton, Sept. 29, 1775.
[57]C.O. 42/34, Hamilton to Dartmouth, Nov. 20, 1775.
[58]Ward, *The War of the Revolution*, I, 186–96.
[59]Freeman, *George Washington*, IV, 10.
[60]John C. Fitzpatrick, ed., *The Writings of George Washington from the Original Manuscript Sources 1745–1799* (Washington, 1931), IV, 292.

to St. John's Island (later renamed Prince Edward Island), whose tiny capital of Charlottetown had been plundered by New England privateers on November 17, 1775. He released its acting Governor, Phillips Callbeck, and another member of the Executive Council who had been taken prisoner and brought to Washington's headquarters outside Boston.[61] The council of war now convened by Washington agreed that the New England colonies should divert some of the regiments they had promised for the campaigning season of 1776 to the siege of Quebec.[62] On March 25, 1776, Congress reaffirmed that "the reduction of Quebec and the general security of the province of Canada are objects of great concern."[63]

On the following day a British fleet removed the last of Howe's regiments from Boston, which had earlier been cleared of its loyal inhabitants. The troops were taken to Halifax where Howe found a greatly relieved Governor Francis Legge of Nova Scotia. Legge had convened a special session of his Legislature as soon as he learned of the American invasion of Canada. Martial law was proclaimed and orders issued to call out one-fifth of the militia to be selected by ballot (or lot) wherever there were insufficient volunteers. However, the large New England element in the population did not want to become actively involved in the struggle, any more than did large numbers of the inhabitants in the American colonies. The citizens of Halifax were largely dependent for their livelihood on British military and naval expenditure locally, but the majority of the people in the small and scattered out-settlements was determined on a neutral course that would permit them to continue trading with New England.[64] Hence many militia companies refused to muster, and there were local disturbances, accentuated by the recurring rumour that the embodied militia would be transported to New England for service against their compatriots. As a result Governor Legge had been forced, as early as January 12, 1776, to issue a circular letter instructing militia officers to reassure their men that they would be required for local defence only in the event of actual invasion; a provincial regiment would be recruited "purely for the defence of the Province."[65]

Howe now rejected appeals for arms and stores for the company which the acting Governor of St. John's Island was hoping to recruit for its defence, and his letter of June 4 advised Callbeck that Vice-Admiral of

[61]Ibid., 152; see also C.O. 226/6, Stewart to Dartmouth, Dec. 8, 1775.
[62]Freeman, George Washington, IV, 11.
[63]Ibid., 84.
[64]John Bartlet Brebner, The Neutral Yankees of Nova Scotia: A Marginal Colony during the Revolutionary Years (New York, 1937), 299–300.
[65]C.O. 217/52, Legge to Dartmouth, Jan. 21, 1776 and enclosures.

the Blue Lord Shuldham was sending a sloop to protect Charlottetown
and would order a frigate from Quebec to watch the area. The balance of
Howe's letter was equally specific:

As this is judged the most advisable Expedient at present, and the Cannon at
Charlotte Town, without an Established post or some force, only providing a
Temptation to the Rebells to disturb the peace of the Island, the Admiral at my
request, has given directions for bringing them away, in consequence of this
Determination, the Company you intended to raise becomes an unnecessary
measure.[66]

Shortly thereafter Howe embarked his army once again and sailed from
Halifax for New York. On July 2, 1776, he landed his troops on Staten
Island.

Early in April Major-General John Burgoyne had been sent from
Great Britain to the relief of Quebec, with nine British regiments of foot,
four companies of Royal Artillery, and about 5,000 German mercen-
aries.[67] On March 28, 1776, a new Secretary of State for the American
Colonies, Lord George Sackville-Germain, wrote Carleton, now advanced
to the local rank of General in North America, suggesting the sort of
campaign that George Washington had been worried the British might
adopt:

If the Rebels should attempt to keep Possession of Montreal, or any other place in
Canada, on your side of the Lakes, the Army under your Command will be
sufficient to drive them from that part of the Province, and there is no doubt if
you succeed in the first operation but that you will endeavour to pass the Lakes
as early as possible, and in your future progress contribute to the success of the
army under General Howe.[68]

Germain, however, had no intention of dictating Carleton's operational
plans from distant London. "These operations," his letter continued,
"must be left to your judgment and discretion, as it would be highly im-
proper, at such a distance, to give any positive orders, especially as so much
confidence is placed in your knowledge and military experience." In
point of fact, however, Carleton's defence of Quebec was his only experience of independent command in war, and Germain had displayed
much more military ability in the Seven Years' War as commander of

[66]C.O. 226/6, Howe to Callbeck, June 4, 1776.
[67]C. T. Atkinson, "The British Forces in North America, 1774–1781: Their
Distribution and Strength," *Journal of the Society for Army Historical Research*,
XVI (1937), 9.
[68]C.O. 42/35, Sackville-Germain to Carleton, March 28, 1776.

the British contingent serving under Prince Ferdinand of Brunswick until the fateful Battle of Minden in 1759. Whatever actually did occur that day, political enemies had managed to have the then Lord George Sackville declared unfit to serve George II in any capacity. His friends, however, managed to rehabilitate him politically during the early years of George III's reign, and in 1770 he changed his name to Germain in order to inherit a fortune.[69] Now he was as much in charge of the rebellion in North America as William Pitt had been of the Seven Years' War, since Lord North was as nominal a Prime Minister as the Duke of Newcastle had been. Unfortunately Germain was, and would remain, on bad terms with the Earl of Sandwich, who was the First Lord of the Admiralty.[70]

Despite the fact that the Americans camped before Quebec City had received reinforcements and more were on the way, they hurriedly retreated when the first British warships appeared in May and the defenders finally sallied forth. The Americans halted at Sorel where they were considerably reinforced. They recrossed the St. Lawrence River and tried on June 8 to surprise the British advanced guard at Trois-Rivières. This attempt failed, and the British troops, who had been carried farther up river by troopship, might have prevented their further escape. It was argued by some critics of Carleton then, and by others later, that he deliberately let the rebels escape up Lake Champlain in the belief that these disillusioned Americans would return to their homes and persuade their fellows to resume a loyal conduct towards George III.[71] On the other hand, having learned his lesson the hard way in 1775, Carleton was likely to have proceeded cautiously because the means of communication were not good enough to guarantee a successful pincer movement. Sir John Fortescue, in his monumental *History of the British Army*, noted that the "western column was entrusted to General Burgoyne, but with strict orders not to fight without the support of the eastern column; and it was thought that except for this caution, Burgoyne might have reached Chambly before the retreating Americans and compelled the whole of them to surrender."[72]

As for the Canadians, Carleton subsequently reported to Germain his belief that "there is nothing to fear from them while we are in a state of

[69]Mackesy, *The War for America, 1775–1777*, 47.
[70]*Ibid.*, 54.
[71]A. L. Burt, *The United States, Great Britain and British North America: From the Revolution to the Establishment of Peace after the War of 1812* (Toronto, 1940), 10–11.
[72]J. W. Fortescue, *A History of the British Army* (London, 1911), III, 181.

prosperity, and nothing to hope for when in distress; I speak of the People at large; there are among them [those] who are guided by Sentiments of honour, but the multitude is influenced only by hopes of gain, or fear of punishments."[73] Many of the *habitants* had been willing to sell provisions to the invaders until payment began to be made in paper currency. During the occupation they had elected new officers for militia companies in the districts of Montreal and Trois-Rivières, but less than 450 had enlisted in the two Canadian regiments which had been authorized by the Continental Congress and which had now fled the country.[74]

By the time Carleton had constructed a naval flotilla to dispute the American command of Lake Champlain, the campaigning season was drawing to a close. On October 11 and 13, Carleton's little navy managed to destroy 11 of 16 nondescript American war vessels, but he decided not to continue against Ticonderoga and attempt to establish contact with Howe's army, which had captured New York City and was cautiously probing northward.[75] Had there been sufficient shipping available to transfer Howe's army from Boston to New York during the autumn of 1775, as the British Government had directed, it might have been possible in 1776 to seize the whole line of the Lake Champlain–Lake George–Hudson River and thus cut off New England from the middle colonies.[76]

Carleton had been given a knighthood for his successful defence of Quebec City, but his dilatory conduct of the succeeding campaign was one of the reasons advanced for not giving him a field command in 1777.[77] Carleton was to remain in Canada, while Lieutenant-General John Burgoyne was to advance up Lake Champlain with 4,000 British and 3,000 German troops, as many loyalists and Indians as could be assembled, and enough Canadian militia to handle transportation problems for the whole army. Albany was his destination. Lieutenant-Colonel Barry St. Leger was to lead a small diversionary force along the water route from the British fort at Oswego to Albany. Here Burgoyne would come under Howe's command, even though the latter had no intention of advancing up the Hudson River himself. Howe hoped to capture Philadelphia and thereby put an end to rebellion in the middle colonies while leaving only a defensive screen of troops on the lower Hudson to "facilitate in some degree the approach of the army in Canada."[78]

Howe's army entered Philadelphia on September 26, 1777, but his

[73]C.O. 42/35, Carleton to Sackville-Germain, Sept. 28, 1776.
[74]Fitzpatrick, *The Writings of George Washington*, IV, 117n; VI, 479.
[75]C.O. 42/35, Carleton to Sackville-Germain, Oct. 14, 1776.
[76]Mackesy, *The War for America, 1775–1783*, 56.
[77]C.O. 42/36, Sackville-Germain to Carleton, March 26, 1777.
[78] Mackesy, *The War for America, 1775–1778*, 111.

summer campaign did not put an end to the rebellion in the middle colonies. St. Leger did not manage to advance farther than Fort Stanwix at the head of Wood Creek and the Mohawk River. Burgoyne's army captured Ticonderoga, but his further advance was so slow that American opposition had time to gather and force his surrender at Saratoga on October 17. Most historians have blamed Germain for the over-all British failure in 1777, which was the turning point of the conflict since it encouraged France to become an outright ally of the rebellious American colonists. The belief that Burgoyne expected Howe to advance to meet him was only recently shattered by Piers Mackesy in *The War for America, 1775–1783*:

The plan for Canada was launched in the full understanding that though Howe's army would eventually co-operate with Burgoyne's on the Hudson, it could not support his advance to Albany in strength. Carleton's instructions were signed on 26 March, in time for Burgoyne to take them to Quebec; and a copy was sent to Howe which he acknowledged before his departure for Philadelphia. But a legend was launched by [Lord] Shelburne that through the idleness of Germain and the carelessness of his office, Howe was never informed of Burgoyne's intentions. Knox, however, left a note which explains the truth.[79]

The soundness of the strategy, however, was discounted by Carmichael-Smyth in the confidential study he prepared in 1825 for the Duke of Wellington:

The object . . . of placing a corps at Albany, to threaten the rear of the Massachusetts and Connecticut provinces, was to be accomplished by water from New York at one quarter the expense and trouble; confining the operations from Canada to the capture of Ticonderoga, and the destruction of the American boats and flotilla upon Lake Champlain.[80]

During the same campaigning season of 1777, British forces based on Halifax eradicated American influences from the small settlement along the St. John River, Fort Howe was built at its mouth, and the local Indians were persuaded to abandon their hitherto neutral position. However, continued activity by American privateers and the French declaration of war against Great Britain in 1778 resulted in second thoughts on the desirability of establishing garrisons at each of the more important ports of Nova Scotia and St. John's Island. Yet the small detachments of provincial or loyalist troops intermittently made available for such duty were generally too small to be of much use and merely

[79]*Ibid.*, 117.
[80]Sir James Carmichael, ed., *Précis of the Wars in Canada, from 1775 to the Treaty of Ghent in 1814, With Political and Military Reflections.* By the late Maj.-Gen. Sir James Carmichael-Smyth (London, 1862), 132.

provided an excuse for New England privateersmen to plunder and burn wherever and whenever they landed. Good examples are the successful American raids against St. Peter's on the Island and Liverpool in Nova Scotia.[81] The best answer to privateering and commerce raiding by naval vessels, the *guerre de course* at which the French excelled, was to put overwhelming British naval strength in North American waters. Not until the summer of 1780, however, were enough British frigates and smaller war vessels available to keep the coastal waters generally free of privateers, to harry them out of their place of refuge in the Strait of Canso, and to prevent them from interfering with traffic in the lower reaches of the St. Lawrence River.[82]

The arrival at Quebec on June 26, 1778, of General Frederick Haldimand, who replaced Sir Guy Carleton as Governor of that province, had practically coincided with the first offensive action by France on the high seas. For the next five years Haldimand was faced by the bogey of attack by both land and sea and by fear of revolt by the French-speaking inhabitants of his province. What he did not know was that mutual suspicion and jealousy would always prevent one or other of the French Government and American Congress from agreeing to an effective co-operative undertaking.[83] General Washington authorized preparations to be made for attacks on Canada,[84] but the American patrols which twice kidnapped members of the British garrison on Carleton Island, off the south shore of the St. Lawrence River just below where it flows out of Lake Ontario, were the only enemy that came close to a Canadian fort.[85]

During the summer of 1778 Lieutenant William Twiss, of the Corps of Engineers had supervised the construction of Fort Haldimand on what then became known as Carleton Island. It was to serve as a transshipment point in place of the poorly located post at Oswegatchie for supplies bound for Fort Niagara by armed schooner. Lieutenant John Schank, R.N., who had been in charge of earlier naval construction on Lake Champlain, considered that the harbour at Carleton Island was an ideal site for a shipyard. Schooners were subsequently constructed there for the Provincial Marine and the island served as a jumping off place for raids against American settlements in central New York.[86]

[81]C.O. 226/7, Callbeck to Sackville-Germain, Aug. 18, 1778; D. C. Harvey, ed., *The Diary of Simeon Perkins, 1780–1789* (Toronto, Champlain Society, 1958), xxvi, 41–2.
[82]Haldimand Papers B/202, Haldimand to O'Hara, July 27, 1782.
[83]Freeman, *George Washington*, V, 85, 418.
[84]*Ibid.*, 189n.
[85]Major C. C. J. Bond, "The British Base at Carleton Island," *Ontario History*, LII (March, 1960).
[86]*Ibid.*

British operations, directed by Haldimand from Canada, were merely raids by comparatively small forces of regulars, provincials, and Indians. By this time the greater number of Indians, particularly those of the Six Nations, were assisting the British. Haldimand's despatches continually refer to the inadequacy of the military forces under his command because the British Government had transferred the scene of major operations far to the south in the hope of gaining active support from loyalists there.[87] Loss of New England was accepted, but it was hoped to secure adequate compensation by capturing the rest of the French islands in the West Indies.[88]

Worried by rumours of a pending attack, Haldimand wanted substantial garrisons for Quebec, the Montreal area, and the upper posts which had to be retained and improved as an encouragement to the fur traders and Indians. He also wanted a considerable field force for employment in a counter-attack against any invading army. Mere insufficiency of numbers, however, was not Haldimand's only reason for complaint. There were too few British regulars—only 166 officers and about 3,400 other ranks[89]—and too many of the 3,900 Germans seem to have been poor quality troops left behind from Burgoyne's expedition. According to Haldimand, these last were "lazy and inactive, unwilling to work, which here constitutes the greatest part of a Soldier's duty."[90] Moreover, so many Germans attempted to desert to join their countrymen settled in Pennsylvania that they could not be left for long at any frontier fort. Haldimand considered that the (provincial) King's Royal Regiment of New York, raised by Sir John Johnson from loyalists who fled the Mohawk valley, was a "useful Corps with the Ax," but "not altogether to be depended on with the Firelock."[91] Dread of another winter invasion made Haldimand a victim of the common delusion that all Americans were "trained to the woods from their infancy, know well how to shelter themselves from the cold, and are excellent Marks Men."[92]

Haldimand's original excuse for not embodying a corps of French-speaking Canadians, as his Instructions had directed, was that he would wait until the late autumn (in 1778) when the "most robust and active of the men" should have returned home from fur-trading activities in the western country or from the fisheries of the lower St. Lawrence River.[93]

[87]Mackesy, *The War for America, 1775–1783*, 159.
[88]*Ibid.*, 183.
[89]Atkinson, "The British Forces in North America," 15–16.
[90]C.O. 42/39, Haldimand to Sackville-Germain, Sept. 13, 1779.
[91]C.O. 42/39, Haldimand to Clinton, May 26, 1779.
[92]C.O. 42/38, Haldimand's "Sketch of the Military State of the Province of Quebec," July 25, 1778.
[93]C.O. 42/38, Haldimand to Sackville-Germain, Oct. 15, 1778.

Like the Marquis de Montcalm some twenty years earlier, Haldimand was faced with the fact that numbers of young *habitants* preferred any kind of employment to that of transporting military stores as militiamen. Even though the Militia Ordinance finally issued in 1777 had specified that men were to be paid for such *corvées,* no one could be certain that individual militia officers would not keep the money for themselves and thus unnecessarily alienate the more gullible *habitants.* Haldimand had, according to the balance of the letter addressed to Germain on October 15, 1778,

. . . received some assistance from the Country by Corvées, without which the Transport of Provisions between Montreal and Carleton Island would be impracticable; but in the present disposition of the People, I have judged it highly requisite to observe the utmost caution, not to make demands that from exciting Murmurs that might lead them to a declaration of Sentiments, which the French Alliance with the Rebels has undoubtedly raised in numbers of those who in regard of the Rebellion were unquestionably attached to Government and renewed in the others the Symptoms, of which change in the Canadians is everywhere manifest, and the more dangerous, as multitudes of them are but too sensible of our inability, with the troops we have in an open Country, to control them if any circumstances should invite their resolutions as their inclinations are but too much already.[94]

Realizing that he had insufficient resources to begin construction of a "formidable Citadel" at Quebec City, as his Instructions also had directed, Haldimand decided merely to make sufficient additions to the existing defences to foil any possible American attack during the current Revolutionary War.[95] Early in 1779 Lieutenant Twiss began the construction of an extensive outworks on the left flank of the old French walls so as to enclose the highest ground of Cape Diamond. The defences of St. Johns and Isle aux Noix were also strengthened; work was continued at Carleton Island; Fort Niagara was improved; and a new fort was built at Detroit. Haldimand explained in a despatch of October 24, 1779, that because of all this activity he was not able to construct a fortress at Sorel, but barracks for 1,200 troops had been set up there, and he planned to build it up as a base for counter-offensive operations against an enemy advance along either the St. Francis or Richelieu rivers or an enemy attempt to move across country from St. Johns to Laprairie for an attack on Montreal.[96]

[94]*Ibid.*
[95]Haldimand Papers B/54, Haldimand to Townshend, June 18, 1779.
[96]C.O. 42/39, Haldimand to Sackville-Germain, Oct. 24, 1779.

Germain approved the increase in the Provincial Marine's strength on Lakes Ontario, Erie, and Huron. He was convinced that the continued fidelity of the Canadians and Indians depended on retention of the upper, or western, posts, but his letter of March 17, 1780, emphasized that the lower posts were not to be denuded of troops to achieve this.[97] Presumably Germain had obtained this opinion from General Lord Amherst, who had been given the appointment of Commander-in-Chief in London and a seat in the Cabinet on March 19, 1778. Haldimand, who had a better grasp of the geography of the poorly mapped Old Northwest, was not seriously worried about the continued safety of the British forts there. Furthermore, although he realized the advantage to be gained by winning back the allegiance of Vermont, which would then become a partial buffer against any American attempt to invade Canada, he was not convinced that Ethan Allen and his brothers were sincere in the negotiations which had been started. As events turned out, he was correct in his belief that they were merely trying to intimidate the Continental Congress into agreeing that Vermont should be independent of both New York and New Hampshire.[98]

Haldimand's despatch of October 25, 1780, indicated that the inhabitants of his province were subconsciously aware that British retention of Quebec City was the key to the successful defence of Canada:

. . . the general Disposition & Behaviour of the Inhabitants, make it beyond a Doubt to a nice observer that we have little to expect from their assistance in Military Operations, & that they have learned to consider the arrival of the Fleet as an Event that will certainly happen and that it is equally sure their Efforts to reconquer the Province will be successful.[99]

After learning that a final peace treaty had been signed at Paris on September 3, 1783, Haldimand wrote to the Secretary of State of the Home Department, which would be responsible for the continuing British colonies in North America, to say that this "Province can only be preserved by bringing back the Canadians to a Regular Subordination, and by rendering them useful as a well Disciplined Militia."[100] Haldimand, of course, was not responsible for the safe preservation of Nova Scotia and St. John's Island, whose Governors were lulled into a feeling of security by the fact that the Royal Navy possessed a decided superiority in the North Atlantic.

[97]Haldimand Papers B/50, Sackville-Germain to Haldimand, March 17, 1780.
[98]See Haldimand despatches on C.O. 42/41–42.
[99]C.O. 42/40, Haldimand to Sackville-Germain, Oct. 25, 1780.
[100]Haldimand Papers B/56, Haldimand to North, Oct. 24, 1783.

(3)

UNEASY DECADE

Late in 1782 Great Britain had recognized the fact of American independence in an effort to split the colonists' alliance with France and Spain and to regain their goodwill and trade. Parliament and the British people were tired of a war which had been definitely lost, with Lord Cornwallis' surrender at Yorktown as early as October 19, 1781, and wanted peace on almost any terms. In consequence, the British peace commissioners agreed to a preliminary Anglo-American treaty that was not in the best interests of those possessions which King George III retained in North America. The population of these possessions—Newfoundland, St. John's Island, Nova Scotia, Quebec, and a vast but little known hinterland—was small, but in all except Newfoundland and the hinterland there was now a substantial influx of loyalists from the former American colonies.

The treaty set up a boundary for the shrunken British North America. Although British troops were in physical possession of Maine as far west as the Penobscot River, making nonsense of the American demand for the international boundary to follow the St. John River, the British plenipotentiaries supinely agreed to the poorly defined and much-disputed St. Croix River as a compromise. From the source of the St. Croix River the boundary was to follow the height of land as far as the 45th parallel of latitude and continue thereon to the St. Lawrence River. British troops were also in possession of the south shore of the Great Lakes, but it was agreed that the international boundary should follow the crooked line of the St. Lawrence waterway through the Great Lakes as far as the northwest corner of the Lake of the Woods.

The British commissioners secured an agreement from the American plenipotentiaries stating that Congress would "earnestly recommend" to the several states the restoration of confiscated property and civil rights to loyal subjects who had not borne arms; those who had fought in provincial regiments would be allowed to return temporarily to their former homes while they endeavoured to recover their property.[1] However, the British negotiators completely neglected the interests of their Indian allies, whose hunting grounds were in what it was agreed would become American soil.[2]

Before the final peace settlement of 1783, one of the British commissioners suggested an Anglo-American alliance for mutual defence of North American territory, to include an understanding that the Royal Navy would protect the United States if the Americans would support and strengthen it with naval stores and seamen. This idea foundered because of the certainty of the other commissioners that the British Government was not prepared to ratify a separate commercial treaty based on the principle of reciprocal freedom of trade and navigation by each party in all the dominions of the other.[3] A proposal by John Adams, which would have prohibited the fortification of the inland boundary and forbidden the introduction of armed vessels on the Great Lakes by either side, was also shelved.[4]

For the moment, the Royal Navy dominated the North Atlantic, and the United States possessed no naval force whatsoever. This fact suggested that the provinces of Nova Scotia and St. John's Island would remain safe from American attack. An attempt to ensure protection in the future for the overland route to Quebec was made by settling disbanded loyalist corps in the St. John valley. This portion of Nova Scotia north of the Bay of Fundy became the separate province of New Brunswick in 1784. In the same year Cape Breton was thrown open for settlement and given a separate government from Nova Scotia.

A Militia Act was passed by the Legislative Assembly in New Brunswick in 1787, and it closely resembled existing legislation in Nova Scotia and St. John's Island. It required compulsory military service from physically fit males aged sixteen to fifty, except for Crown officials, clergymen, ferrymen, millers, and others whose occupations were essential at all times, and conscientious objectors. In the event of an alarm, invasion, insurrection, or rebellion, every captain was to mobilize his company and be prepared to march to any part of the province. This Act obligated every militiaman

---

[1] Article V of the Treaty of Paris of 1783.

[2] A. L. Burt, *The United States, Great Britain and British North America* (Toronto, 1940), 85.

[3] Samuel Flagg Bemis, *The Diplomacy of the American Revolution* (New York, 1935), 249–250.

[4] *Ibid.*, 251.

to possess a musket, bayonet, cartridge box, nine cartridges, and nine bullets,[5] but most veterans had been forced to sell the army muskets they retained on discharge in order to buy additional provisions and farm implements to those provided by the authorities for homesteading.[6]

Since miles of wilderness separated New Brunswick from any existing American settlement, the Commander of the Forces in "Nova Scotia and its Dependencies" considered that half a battalion of regulars in garrison at the mouth of the St. John River would be sufficient immediate protection for both the maritime settlements and the overland route to Quebec. The rest of this battalion was stationed across the Bay of Fundy at Annapolis Royal. Similarly weak regiments of foot, having an establishment of only 408 rank and file and a much smaller actual strength, were at each of Fort Cumberland and Shelburne. Three regiments were in garrison at Halifax, less the two companies detached to Charlottetown. Total strength, including artillerymen, was about 2,400 all ranks.[7]

In the province of Quebec, Governor Haldimand had about 150 officers and 2,500 other ranks. These were organized as four companies of Royal Artillery and seven regiments of foot.[8] During the spring and early summer of 1784 Haldimand arranged to provide farms for the loyalists collected in refugee camps or still serving in provincial corps at the upper posts. He managed, however, to keep settlers out of the area near the Vermont frontier, later known as the Eastern Townships, on the plea that the subsequent expansion of French-speaking settlement there would create a racial and religious barrier to possible American penetration.[9] The largest loyalist settlement was along the north shore of the St. Lawrence River, extending west from the seigniory of Longueuil to the Bay of Quinte. Settlers were assigned land according to the corps in which they had served, except that Protestants and Roman Catholics were placed separately. Numbers of disbanded regulars and some former German troops were located in the most westerly township. Most of Butler's Rangers settled along the west bank of the Niagara River, whence they had set out on their raids against central New York. Only a handful of loyalists remained in the vicinity of Detroit, which was a predominantly French-speaking settlement for some years to come. These loyalist settlements were augmented by an inflow of families left behind earlier in the

[5]27 Geo. III, c. 1.
[6]C.O. 188/5, Carleton to Dundas, March 29, 1793.
[7]C.O. 217/35, Campbell to Sydney, June 14, 1784.
[8]W.O. 17/1579, Monthly Strength Return of British Troops serving in Canada, Jan. 1, 1785.
[9]Haldimand Papers B/56, Haldimand to North, Nov. 27, 1783; B/50, Sydney to Haldimand, April 8, 1784.

rebellious colonies; others now being persecuted as loyalists hastened to cross into British territory.

The American Congress had disbanded its Continental Army, retaining only one battery of artillery in service to care for ordnance stores, and had left the problem of defence to the militias of the individual states.[10] There would soon, however, be second thoughts about American disarmament. British garrisons had remained, allegedly temporarily, at several inland forts located in the territory ceded to the United States. They were there to cover the liquidation of fur-trading interests, but the need to hoodwink their Indian allies about the fate of the territory soon became a far more vital reason for remaining.[11]

Governor Haldimand quickly realized that the United States, the new owner, was in no mood to placate what most Americans considered to be bloodthirsty savages, particularly when land-hungry families were streaming westward. Furthermore, Joseph Brant and several chiefs soon suspected the truth—that the Indians had been ignored by the treaty-makers —and were impressed neither by a liberal distribution of presents nor by the harangues of Sir John Johnson, the Superintendent General of Indian Affairs. Haldimand therefore decided that the best way of avoiding an Indian conflict was to hold onto the forts indefinitely. The most important of these so-called "western posts" were Oswegatchie, Oswego, Niagara, Presque Isle, Sandusky, Detroit, and Michilimackinac. His view was subsequently accepted by Lord Sydney who had become Secretary of State for the Home Department when a new British Government was formed under the leadership of Pitt the Younger in December, 1783. The official excuse for reneging on the terms of the Treaty of Paris was that the British were retaliating against the Americans because loyalists were finding themselves unable to secure the restoration of their property and civil rights in individual states which refused to honour the commitments made in the Treaty.

The situation was still fluid when Carleton, now Lord Dorchester, returned to Quebec on October 23, 1786. He now held a commission as Captain-General and Governor-in-Chief over the whole of British North America, but the appointment of Commander-in-Chief in North America, which he had held while still Sir Guy Carleton from February 22, 1782, until November 25, 1783, was never again filled. Lord Dorchester's subsequent request for guidance on a policy to be followed for the western posts

[10]Maj.-Gen. Emory Upton, *The Military Policy of the United States* (Washington, 1904), 68.

[11]Thesis developed in Burt, *The United States, Great Britain and British North America*, 82–102.

crossed a despatch from Lord Sydney advising that it would not be proper to refuse the Indians "such supplies of ammunition as might enable them to defend themselves."[12] Dorchester was, however, instructed to supply them "in a manner the least likely to alarm the Americans" or to incite the Indians "to any hostile proceedings."

As early as June 3, 1784, Congress, in optimistic anticipation of the evacuation of the western posts by British troops, decided to ask four of the states of the very loose and weak Confederation to furnish militia quotas for a force of 700 enlisted men, properly officered, to take over garrison duty for a twelve-month period. During 1785 this force was converted into a regular regiment of infantry, the men engaging to serve for three years. Two companies of artillery were added to this embryo United States Army in 1786, and a second infantry regiment was authorized in 1787. Yet the framers of the American Constitution of 1789 compromised on the question of defence by leaving the militia under the control of the individual states, except when the President, as Commander-in-Chief, should call it into the "actual service of the United States."[13] The Militia Act finally passed by Congress in 1792 provided that all able-bodied, white males between the ages of eighteen and forty-five be enrolled as militia.[14] Clauses relating to actual training, which had doomed earlier bills to defeat, were omitted, and the state militias continued to be little more than organizations on paper.[15]

Meanwhile Lord Dorchester was trying to make the best possible use of his military resources. These, he argued in a despatch of November 8, 1787, were very limited:

Two thousand Troops extended Eleven Hundred Miles on a frontier (where several months of the year the communication is impracticable) in large forts falling into ruins, can neither cover the country, nor preserve themselves, against a respectable force, tolerably well conducted, from being captured, without some powerful assistance.[16]

At this time the enrolled but untrained militia in the older settlements of the province of Quebec totalled 636 officers and 24,264 other ranks who were French-speaking and 63 officers and 982 other ranks who were English-speaking; there were a further 450 militiamen in the Gaspé Penin-

[12]C.O. 42/50, Sydney to Dorchester, April 5, 1787.
[13]Upton, *The Military Policy of the United States*, 68–74.
[14]*United States, Statutes at Large*, I, 2nd Congress, sess. I, c. 33, 1792.
[15]William H. Riker, *Soldiers of the States: The Role of the National Guard in American Democracy* (Washington, 1957), 18–21.
[16]C.O. 42/51, Dochester to Sydney, Nov. 8, 1787.

sula and 842 at Detroit. There were also the loyalists and former regulars: 996 were settled along the shore of the upper St. Lawrence River, 843 were around Kingston and the Bay of Quinte, and 457 were in the Niagara Peninsula. Even though they were disgruntled at having to live under French civil law and at the delay in having their land claims settled, the loyalists could be depended upon to join the British regular troops in the defence of their own immediate settlements.

When the provincial Militia Ordinance was renewed in April, 1787, a provision was inserted for the embodiment of detachments for two-year periods of training and service. Dorchester wanted to believe that such action would "afford the means of teaching the people that the Defence of this Country is their own immediate concern, a truth important for them to learn, and for us to teach."[17] He argued, in his letter to Lord Sydney of November 8, that the further step of embodying one battalion of loyalists and two battalions of French-speaking Canadians on regular establishments, and with himself as colonel, would provide employment as officers for "residents of distinction."[18] However, Lord Dorchester became somewhat concerned about the attitude of the *habitants*, who continued to be embittered by the way the *corvée* was administered, so he did not attempt to embody the detachments authorized by the latest Militia Ordinance.

Undoubtedly his viewpoint was coloured by the diplomatic tension in Europe occasioned by Pitt's firm attitude during 1787 towards French interference in Dutch affairs. The British Government decided to reconstitute the 3rd and 4th Battalions of the 60th (or Royal American) Regiment of Foot, which had been disbanded in 1783, and to increase each of the regular battalions of infantry on the British establishment from eight companies of 42 men to ten companies of 60 men, plus a depot company. A letter dated September 29, 1787, directed that the 1st and 2nd Battalions of the 60th Royal Americans, stationed at Halifax and Montreal, respectively, should be augmented locally; officers should be found from the half-pay list. The crisis being soon resolved, recruiting was suspended for all but the additional battalions for the 60th Royal Americans, which obtained most of their men in Germany. These battalions were consigned to garrison duty in the fever-ridden West Indies where they were joined in the following year by the young Canadians for whom Dorchester had managed to obtain commissions.[19]

[17]*Ibid.*, June 13, 1787.
[18]*Ibid.*, Nov. 8, 1787.
[19]J. W. Fortescue, *A History of the British Army* (London, 1911), III, 523–4; see also correspondence on C/930.

During the summer of 1788 the Commanding Royal Engineer, Captain Gother Mann, made a survey of the western posts. Their fortifications were now in a state of ruin.[20] This situation was anything but unexpected, however, and had been considered almost inevitable in view of the parsimonious attitude adopted by the British Government towards the defences of Canada. As might have been expected, no action was taken to remedy the conditions reported by Captain Mann. Experience had long demonstrated that the simplest fort, consisting of a palisade of vertical logs, was capable only of withstanding attack by Indians or other assailants who lacked artillery. Consequently, the original forts on the frontier had been rebuilt with walls made from timber cribbing and filled with earth. Such walls could withstand considerable bombardment, but they were bound to collapse if the timber facing was not replaced before it rotted. Deterioration could be prevented by facing the walls with stone, but there was not sufficient money to maintain the forts in this fashion; moreover, there was no way of knowing how long it would be before the British Government would be compelled to turn the disputed posts over to the United States. Strengthening them might be a wasteful measure.

Dorchester, in a despatch of March 8, 1790, again brought up the question of the western posts, expressing concern for their immediate safety in the face of possible attack. Because of the isolated position of each fort, no plan for mutual support was possible and an aggressive enemy could reduce them one by one. In order to wage a defensive campaign successfully at least 4,000 additional regular troops were necessary.[21] But Dorchester did not bother to explain that the bulk of such additional troops would be held as a central reserve to counter-attack an invading army which might either follow the route of Montgomery's expedition of 1775 or keep away from Montreal and head more directly for Quebec City. Nor did this letter explain how the weak American Government could suddenly produce a large expeditionary force. Dorchester also ignored the obvious: as long as the British were in possession of all the existing forts on the Great Lakes and the only vessels plying them belonged to either the Provincial Marine or Montreal fur traders, his own forces could move much more readily to a threatened point than an enemy advancing overland from the nearest American settlements.

On September 25, 1790, Dorchester returned to the idea of embodying a portion of the militia in an effort to "revive a spirit of national

[20]C.O. 42/88, Mann to Dorchester, Oct. 29, 1792.
[21]C.O. 42/67, Dorchester to Grenville, March 8, 1790.

defence."[22] One-third or one-half might be discharged annually and replaced either by volunteers or by ballot from the remaining personnel of the sedentary militia. Something had to be done, his despatch continued, to jar the *habitants* from their lethargy before an emergency fell upon the province: "The people are now enervated, few of them bring their arms to the parade, when they assemble for exercise, although it is imagined, every house has at least one gun, and some two or three, they are however tolerably punctual in attending these parades with very few refractory exceptions." A copy of this proposal was sent to the Lieutenant-Governors of New Brunswick and Nova Scotia. No one, however, took any action.

By this time the province of Quebec had a population of approximately 140,000 men, women, and children. In thirty years the number of French-speaking Canadians had almost doubled. About two-thirds of the 20,000 English-speaking inhabitants were living in the settlements southwest of the Ottawa River. The British Government decided to divide the province along the line of the Ottawa, leaving the seigniory of Longueuil in Lower Canada, a predominantly French-speaking province. Regardless of racial and religious complexities both new provinces would receive the institutions of representative government earlier granted to Nova Scotia, St. John's Island, and New Brunswick.

Section XLVI of the so-called Constitutional Act of 1791 reaffirmed the pledge given in the Declaratory Act of 1778 that

. . . the King and Parliament of Great Britain will not impose any Duty, Tax or Assessment whatever, payable in any of his Majesty's Colonies, Provinces, and Plantations, in *North America* or the *West Indies*, except only such Duties as may be expedient to propose for the Regulation of Commerce, the net Produce of such Duties to be always paid and applied to and for use of the Colony, Province, or Plantation in which the same shall be respectively levied, in such Manner as other Duties collected by the Authority of the respective General Courts or General Assemblies of such Colonies, Provinces, or Plantations are ordinarily paid and applied.[23]

Thus, apart from the upkeep of a militia, defence expenditure in each of the provinces of British North America was to be financed by a substantial military chest filled by the British taxpayer. This willing assumption of the cost of colonial defence, however, had an obvious corollary: control of defence policy must reside solely in the King and Parliament at Westminster.

[22]C.O. 42/69, Dorchester to Grenville, Sept. 25, 1790.
[23]31 Geo. III, c. 31.

The actual division into provinces of Upper and Lower Canada was effected by an Order in Council while Lord Dorchester was on leave in England. Colonel John Graves Simcoe was appointed Lieutenant-Governor of Upper Canada. One of his first actions on arrival at Quebec was to agree with Sir Alured Clarke, Lieutenant-Governor of Lower Canada, that a more realistic attitude must be taken towards settlement. Immigration had declined to a trickle except for the New Englanders who were crossing the border from Vermont and squatting in the area deliberately reserved in Lower Canada by Haldimand for future occupation by French-speaking Canadians. The obvious answer was settlement by loyal English-speaking immigrants, but the British Government did not foster emigration from the British Isles. However, it was commonly believed that the United States contained thousands of people now disgusted with a republican form of government and that they looked back with fond memory to life under British rule.[24] On February 7, 1792, Clarke and Simcoe issued almost identical proclamations, which offered 200-acre farms to individuals who would take up residence within six months, and large blocks of land to enterprising land speculators who would act as developers. The only safeguard deemed necessary was the following simple declaration: "I [A.B.] do promise and declare that I will maintain and defend to the utmost of my power the authority of the King in His Parliament as the supreme Legislature of this Province."[25]

There proved to be all sorts of plausible excuses for not having been an active loyalist during the American Revolution, and even for having fought on the wrong side. Most of the earlier loyalist settlers welcomed the newcomers from the United States into Upper Canada, which attracted the larger number. Simcoe especially encouraged the immigration of Quakers, Mennonites, and Dunkers, who were excellent farmers, even though they had conscientious objections to military service. The immigration was thus of doubtful value for the defence of Canada.

As long as land in the new Eastern Townships of Lower Canada and in Upper Canada was cheaper than that held by land speculators in northern New York State, was more accessible than that in the Old Northwest, and was not menaced by hostile Indians, the migratory movements in North America would be to British-controlled territory. Few of the newcomers cared whether they lived under the American or British flag as long as they were permitted to live in peace. Officials seemed to forget, for the moment at least, that war was always a possibility.

[24]Burt, *The United States, Great Britain and British North America*, 178–181.
[25]Copies in C.O. 42/89 and *Quebec Gazette*, Feb. 9, 1792.

(4)

THE DEVELOPMENT OF A DEFENCE PLAN

The events of these years in North America all took place against a background of turmoil in France. By 1792 war with Revolutionary France had become inevitable. The British could not have acquiesced for long while the French absorbed the Low Countries even if they had been willing to accept the execution of Louis XVI and the further spread of the doctrine of *"liberté, égalité et fraternité."* Yet Great Britain was far from ready when France declared war on February 1, 1793. A decade of economy and neglect had undermined still further the efficiency of the small British Army that had hardly excelled during the American Revolutionary War. The military machinery was outwardly identical to that outlined in the first chapter, but the appointment of Commander-in-Chief had remained vacant since 1783, and the reappointment of General Lord Amherst, now seventy-six and enfeebled, was not a wise decision. Reform of the Army would have to wait two more years until he could be replaced by George III's second son, Frederick Duke of York.

The Board of the Admiralty was more fortunate. One of the greatest administrators of its history, Sir Charles Middleton (later Lord Barham), had served as Comptroller of the Navy from 1778 to 1790. The Prime Minister, William Pitt, who had formed his first ministry in 1783, was interested in having the Royal Navy as strong as when his illustrious father had directed the successful campaigns of the Seven Years' War. Therefore, the Royal Navy was functioning efficiently, and its several squadrons were ready to engage an enemy in 1793.

On March 1, 1793, a small British contingent—three battalions from the Brigade of Guards—reached the Low Countries as a first reinforcement for the Austrian and Prussian armies which had been unsuccessfully opposing the ragged soldiers of the French Revolution. But the British Government soon decided that its main effort should be directed against

French colonial possessions, particularly those in the West Indies where the great powers had done most of their fighting during the previous war. Direction of this strategy was left to Henry Dundas, who was Secretary of State for the Home Department. (On July 11, 1794, he would relinquish this portfolio to become Secretary of State for War. Because the conduct of overseas military campaigns resulted in an increasing involvement in colonial matters, Dundas' successor in 1801 logically became the first Secretary of State for War and the Colonies.)

Three of the four British regiments of foot garrisoning Nova Scotia and its Dependencies were ordered to the West Indies in March, 1793, to take part in expeditions against French islands there.[1] Brigadier-General James Ogilvie was instructed to embark the remaining 4th Regiment of Foot at Halifax and, in co-operation with the Royal Navy, to seize the French fishing colony of Saint-Pierre-et-Miquelon before it could become a base for enemy naval activity. This action was accomplished without bloodshed on May 14, and a small garrison was left to occupy Saint-Pierre.[2]

The French navy was temporarily crippled by the loss of many of its better officers as *émigrés* from the Revolution. As a result the Royal Navy was not seriously challenged in its control of the North Atlantic, and the maritime provinces of British North America were in no immediate danger. Yet in order to reassure the populations of New Brunswick and Nova Scotia, their Lieutenant-Governors were authorized to raise provincial corps not exceeding 600 rank and file for local service.[3] The Lieutenant-Governor of St. John's Island was told that a similar corps was unnecessary. However, arms and ammunition were to be sent to his untrained militia, which should then be capable of repelling any purely predatory raid.[4]

Meanwhile the Lieutenant-Governors of Upper and Lower Canada had been plagued by fears that a French expedition might be sent up the St. Lawrence River or that American forces might attempt to seize the two provinces. The fears proved groundless, but Canadian forces would have been too meagre to defend the borders. Lower Canada had only four understrength battalions of regular infantry of the line, totalling about 1,600 effectives among the rank and file. In Upper Canada there were the 5th and 24th Regiments of Foot with few more than 700

[1]C.O. 42/93, Dundas to Clarke, May 1, 1793.
[2]J. Mackay Hitsman, "Capture of Saint-Pierre-et-Miquelon, 1793," *Canadian Army Journal*, XIII (July, 1959).
[3]C.O. 42/93, Dundas to Clarke, May 1, 1793.
[4]C.O. 226/13, Dundas to Fanning, Aug. 10, 1793.

rank and file, and the 350 members of the revived Queen's Rangers. Four small companies of Royal Artillery provided detachments for the forts in both the Canadas.[5] Fortunately there was also the small Provincial Marine. Although not particularly efficient, as long as the British garrisons hung on to the disputed western posts, its armed schooners could sail unopposed on Lakes Ontario, Erie, and Huron and carry reinforcements and supplies to them.

Militia Acts were hurriedly passed by the Legislatures of both Lower and Upper Canada in June, 1793. The Militia Act of Upper Canada provided that units could not be compelled to serve beyond the limits of their own county unless there actually was a war or state of emergency.[6] In the more populous Lower Canada the Militia Act approved by the Legislature's special wartime session went much further to include the following proviso:

> . . . it shall not be lawful to order the Militia nor any part thereof, to march out of the Province, except for the assistance of the Province of Upper-Canada, when the same shall actually be invaded; and except in pursuit of an enemy, who have invaded this Province; and except also for the destruction of any vessel or vessels, built or building; or any depot or magazine, formed or forming; or for the attack of an enemy who may be embodying or marching for the purpose of invading this Province; or for the attack of any fortification, which may be erecting to cover an invasion thereto.[7]

As long as the militia of both provinces were neither properly armed nor trained, however, they would be best employed transporting supplies, building roads and fortifications, and guarding prisoners.

As early as March 5, 1792, the Congress of the United States had passed legislation for the better protection of the frontier. This led to the creation of a mixed force of cavalry, artillery, and infantry known as the Legion of the United States. Its commander, Major-General "Mad Anthony" Wayne, planned to pacify the Old Northwest and avenge American defeats suffered earlier by Generals Harmar and St. Clair at the hands of the Indians.[8]

In Upper Canada there was a widespread fear by September, 1793, that Wayne was actually planning an invasion of the province. Simcoe had received a small reinforcement from Lower Canada, but he still had only 1,325 regulars, including his own Queen's Rangers who were

[5]W.O. 17/1504 contains relevant monthly strength returns.
[6]33 Geo. III, c. 1.
[7]34 Geo. III, c. 4.
[8]Maj.-Gen. Emory Upton, *The Military Policy of the United States* (Washington, 1904), 80.

employed primarily as military pioneers. On September 20, Simcoe wrote
Lord Dorchester that "little is to be expected from a people who have
already suffered severely for their loyalty, & too many of whom poor &
dispirited, are more apt to regret what they have lost than to remember
what they have received."[9] There was no possibility of augmenting his
regular troops by local enlistment as "no Recruits can be raised in this
province, so very high is the price of wages."

On October 7 Dorchester replied that the dearth of regular troops—
he now had only 1,490 all ranks in Lower Canada—would make it impossible to defend the long frontier of Upper Canada in the event of war
with the United States. He was responsible for the defence of the whole
of British North America, not merely of a single province like Simcoe,
and his letter continued with advice about possible local action:

> . . . the War cannot be confined to Upper Canada, and the greatest part of the
> Forces may eventually be drawn from thence whatever may be the inconvenience
> to that province: I shall therefore recommend, that after securing the established
> and direct communication as well as circumstances will permit, you keep the rest
> of the Troops free to act, where the occasion may require. You will, no doubt,
> pay great attention to the Militia, and make such arrangements as shall enable
> them to bring forth their whole Strength, and employ it to the best advantage;
> for it may so happen, that on their Strength alone they must depend for their
> defence.[10]

Dorchester's reasoning, as Simcoe well knew, was based on the proposition
that so long as the Royal Navy controlled the North Atlantic and Quebec
was held by an adequate garrison, any American attempts to conquer the
provinces must be "impotent and abortive."[11] No invading army would
have time to capture both Montreal and Quebec before the approach of
a long, cold winter put an end to active campaigning. Spring would bring
a British fleet up the St. Lawrence River with an army capable of regain-
ing all that had been lost—a repetition of what had occurred in 1776.

Dorchester, in a despatch of October 25 to Dundas, gave a thoroughly
realistic appreciation of his situation. Were American plans to establish
posts on Lake Ontario and Lake Erie merely a corollary to the westward
movement of settlement, he asked, or were the Americans bent on causing
trouble while Great Britain was fully occupied by a war with France?
"Independent of the French Intrigue, the Canadas alone cannot stand the
contest," he wrote, and "Nova Scotia & New Brunswick can give no

[9]C.O. 42/317, Simcoe to Dorchester, Sept. 20, 1793.
[10]C.O. 42/318, Dorchester to Simcoe, Oct. 7, 1793.
[11]C.O. 42/318, Simcoe to Dundas, Feb. 23, 1794.

assistance."[12] The 400 regulars of the 4th Regiment of Foot were divided among Saint-Pierre-et-Miquelon, Newfoundland, and Halifax, while the recently organized provincial corps—the Royal Nova Scotia Regiment and the King's New Brunswick Regiment—had only about 240 recruits each. Therefore he requested 4,000 or 5,000 additional regular infantrymen for service in Canada, plus large quantities of naval stores, an allocation of ship's carpenters, and 700 or 800 seamen to expand the Provincial Marine. Dorchester felt that a further 6,000 British regulars should be sent to Halifax to act on either the defensive or the offensive, as circumstances might dictate. Nevertheless Dorchester showed an appreciation also of over-all strategy and possibilities of action.

I am aware that this will change the present plan for carrying on the War, it will necessarily draw all the Infantry which can be spared from home to the American Service, or to attack the French Possessions out of Europe; but without it I consider these Provinces as incapable of making any defence provided an attack is conducted with common sense either by the Americans or by the French.

The extraordinary naval preparations for the Lakes may indeed be spared when a firm peace is concluded with America & part of the Reinforcement required for the Canadas may be sent to Halifax, & enable us to act more powerfully against the French possessions, combined always with a proper attention to Nova Scotia and to the River St. Lawrence.

At the same time that I point out the Precautions necessary to put this country in a proper state of defence I must acknowledge that the Interests of the King's American Dominions require Peace: and I think the Interests of the States require it still more, though their Conduct both to us & the Indians has created many difficulties.

In the natural course of things the People from the States will overspread all the Country south of the Lakes, from the Atlantic to the Mississippi and beyond: the treasures & People of Europe are already employed to forward this purpose, and it would have been still more advanced at this hour but for their own impatience, to say nothing worse.

Because of the slowness of communications, even between Lower and Upper Canada, Simcoe did not reply to Dorchester's letter of October 7 until December 2. Simcoe then wrote that the Queen's Rangers had been concentrated at York as a mobile reserve: defence of his advanced posts would be left mainly to invalids (personnel with low medical categories) or older soldiers of his regular regiments and to veterans who were settled in Upper Canada. Simcoe was afraid, however, that if all the regular troops were withdrawn to Lower Canada his province might not be able to continue as part of the British Empire.[13] On December 15 he

[12]C.O. 42/97, Dorchester to Dundas, Oct. 25, 1793.
[13]C.O. 42/31 J, Simcoe to Dorchester, Dec. 2, 1793.

complained directly by letter to Dundas that he could not lay Dorchester's instructions before the Executive Council of Upper Canada. Nor could he encourage his miltia in any forlorn hope. He considered it absurd to have enticed settlers to Upper Canada if they were now to be left to fend for themselves.[14]

Simcoe pursued this question in a long despatch to Dundas dated February 23, 1794. He argued that Dorchester's views on Canadian defence were unduly pessimistic. A well-constructed and garrisoned fort at the rapids on the Richelieu River would hold up an American army advancing from Lake Champlain. British warships could carry reinforcements and supplies from Quebec to Montreal and harass an enemy who got as far as the south bank of the St. Lawrence River. Communication between Lower and Upper Canada could not be seriously threatened because, although the St. Lawrence was interrupted by formidable rapids between Montreal and Oswegatchie, loyalists were settled all along the northern bank, and there was as yet no American settlement on the south side of the river. The Provincial Marine's unopposed control of Lake Ontario also meant British control of the St. Lawrence above Oswegatchie. The only possible weakness was Kingston, the harbour and fortifications of which were indefensible with the forces likely to be available, particularly during the winter months when Lake Ontario was frozen from shore to shore, and an enemy could cross on the ice and destroy the vessels immobilized there. The shores of the Bay of Quinte were settled by loyalists who could furnish some supplies for the more westerly portions of the province. The next settlement was York, which Simcoe regarded as being "the most important and defensible situation in Upper Canada, or that I have seen in North America."[15] York would be a much better base for the Provincial Marine's activities, and only the commercial transshipment depot should remain at Kingston. He regarded the settlement around Niagara as the "Bulwark of Upper Canada." His policy, he explained, had been to fill up these settlements before granting land to settlers elsewhere. He had made no land grants west of Fort Erie because he wanted first to be able to garrison Long Point for use as a naval base. Simcoe's preference was to remove the existing Detroit settlement to the nearer shore of that river and eventually settle a large population in the Thames valley. Until the United States was able to establish a naval force and bases on the Great Lakes, the several Canadian harbours on Lakes Ontario and Erie could be adequately protected by log blockhouses, manned by local militia.

14C.O. 42/318, Simcoe to Dundas, Dec. 15, 1793.
15*Ibid.*, Feb. 23, 1794.

Dundas, however, had in January already provided his views in an answer to Lord Dorchester's despatch of October 25, 1793. He hoped that the Americans would settle their differences with the Indians of the Old Northwest and he agreed with Dorchester that continued peace was essential for both Canada and the United States. The militia and a naval force on the Great Lakes he regarded as most important:

. . . it becomes exceedingly necessary, that the most conciliatory and friendly Disposition, consistent with the Safety and Preservation of the Posts in His Majesty's Possessions, should be demonstrated in all matters of dispute and Discussion with the Americans collectively, or individually. . . .

As it is very likely that the Americans . . . may think the present moment affords a favourable juncture to press forward their claims in a more urgent manner than heretofore, it becomes a matter of still greater moment, to allay, or keep back, by every possible means, all such matters of Dispute, as may intervene between the present moment, and that of a final arrangement between this Country & the States, which I trust, is at no great distance. Should the King's Service in the West Indies be crowned with that Success; which may reasonably be expected, the Strength & Situation of His Majesty's Land & Sea Forces in that Quarter will strongly counteract any Ideas that may be entertained in America, that the present is a favourable juncture for pressing matters on their side of the question, which ought to be the objects of a mutual and final arrangement. It is not however on these, or any other accounts, the less necessary, that your Lordship and Lieut. Govr. Simcoe should exert your utmost endeavours to put the militia of the Provinces of Lower and Upper Canada upon as respectable a footing as possible: for the use of which militia, a proper supply of arms, ammunition and accoutrements will be sent from hence to Quebec, by the earliest ships of the ensuing Season.

From the Dispatches which I have received from Lieut. Govr. Simcoe, I look upon a Naval Force, properly constructed for the Lakes, as a matter of great future Import and Consequence, as tending to form the most natural & efficient, as well as the cheapest mode of defence for the Province of Upper Canada. I therefore think, that immediate attention should be paid to the gradual formation of a Naval Force on the Lakes.[16]

A subsequent letter directly to Simcoe himself suggested that his militia should be made liable for shipboard service on the Great Lakes.[17] This suggestion was incorporated into the Supplementary Militia Act passed by the Legislature of Upper Canada at its next session.[18]

On May 11, 1794, Dundas wrote Simcoe again, remarking that there had been no need for Dorchester to suggest that Upper Canada might have to be abandoned.[19] Dorchester had been authorized to increase the strength of each of his regular regiments to 600 rank and file, by local

[16]C.O. 42/97, Dundas to Dorchester, Jan. 8, 1794.
[17]C.O. 42/318, Dundas to Simcoe, March 16, 1794.
[18]34 Geo. III, c. 7.
[19]C.O. 42/318, Dundas to Simcoe, May 11, 1794.

enlistment since none of the men being recruited for the Army in the British Isles could be spared as reinforcements. He was also to raise two battalions of a provincial corps of Royal Canadian Volunteers for service in the Canadas only, each battalion to consist of 750 men organized in ten companies.[20] In the event, since the more substantial settlers were not interested in a humdrum military existence, neither battalion ever got within 300 men of its authorized strength. Lieutenant-General Peter Hunter was to report gloomily to Dundas in 1799 about the difficulties of securing men for military service:

In both Battalions there are a very considerable number of old men, and many others too feeble to undergo the fatigue of Military Service.

From what I have observed of their discipline, but little can be said in their favor, this arises principally from a want of experience and Military knowledge in their Officers.

. . . notwithstanding the advantages of being officered, without exception by native Canadians, or Gentleman resident in the Country, and having received a bounty of ten guineas per man, exclusive of the privilege of being enlisted for three years only or during the War, such is the dislike the Canadians have to a military life, that it will (in my humble opinion) be impossible to complete them; another circumstance operates very strongly against their ever being completed; the very high price of labour in both the Canadas, particularly in the Upper Country, where a common labourer seldom receives less than a dollar a day, and at some seasons of the year, often more.[21]

Long before 1799, however, crises had been faced in Anglo-American relations. Rumours reaching Montreal that an American invasion of Lower Canada was scheduled to coincide with the arrival of a French fleet in the St. Lawrence River in the spring of 1794 caused Dorchester to order 2,000 militia to be ready on four days notice to move to assembly points. The English-speaking element in Quebec and Montreal "came forward with great alacrity," but the French-speaking *habitants* again evinced their unwillingness to be involved in someone else's quarrel.[22] Yet Dorchester quickly recovered confidence when no enemy appeared and reverted to his favourite theme of crediting the attitude displayed by French-speaking militiamen to "a long disuse of Military Services, rather than to a spirit of discontent or disloyalty."[23]

On February 10, 1794, Dorchester had made an inflammatory speech to an assembly of western Indians at Quebec, and this soon led to a tense situation in the interior. He had convinced them that they would

[20]C.O. 42/98, Dundas to Dorchester, Feb. 15, 1794.
[21]C.O. 42/324, Hunter to Dundas, Oct. 25, 1799.
[22]C.O. 42/101, Dorchester to Dundas, May 24, 1794.
[23]*Ibid.*

have British support in any forthcoming war against the Americans, and his order that Fort Detroit's communication with Lake Erie should be protected by the construction of a new Fort Miami at the rapids on the Maumee River further encouraged the Indians to fight for the Old Northwest.[24] An alarmed Simcoe learned early in August that Major-General Wayne, with his Legion of the United States and several hundred militia, was advancing into Indian country; he ordered the Canadian militia of Detroit to reinforce the small British garrison of Fort Miami and he called out a further 200 militia in the Western District of Upper Canada.[25] On the morning of August 20, however, Wayne defeated the Indians at the Fallen Timbers, within gunshot sound of Fort Miami, the garrison carefully remaining within its walls. Wayne could easily have captured Fort Miami, but he knew that President George Washington did not want war and that Chief Justice John Jay was even then in London to negotiate a settlement of all outstanding Anglo-American differences.

Jay's Treaty, signed on November 19, 1794, provided for the British surrender of the disputed western posts by June 1, 1796. The Indians now had no alternative but to accept the terms of the Treaty of Greenville offered them by Wayne on August 3, 1795. They withdrew from the Ohio country, which became available for American settlement. As far as Canada was concerned, the possibility of attack from the United States seemed to be at an end. Consequently the two regiments of foot were withdrawn from Upper Canada, leaving less than 500 rank and file of Queen's Rangers and Royal Canadian Volunteers to garrison Kingston, York, Fort Erie, and the replacement forts that were to be constructed on Canadian territory: Fort George, across the river from Fort Niagara; Fort Malden, at Amherstburg on the Detroit River; and Fort St. Joseph, on the island of that name in the mouth of the St. Mary's River.[26]

During the early summer of 1794, the British garrison and French inhabitants of Saint-Pierre-et-Miquelon had been evacuated. This made it possible to spare a regular detachment of one officer and fifty other ranks for the protection of Cape Breton.[27] Lieutenant-Governor Edmund Fanning of St. John's Island was busy trying to recruit a belatedly authorized two-company corps for local defence against possible predatory raids, but he could never manage to recruit more than half the

24A. L. Burt, *The United States, Great Britain and British North America* (Toronto, 1940), 133–7.
25C.O. 42/318, Simcoe to Portland, Oct. 24, 1794.
26C/1206, Russell to Prescott, Aug. 20, 1796.
27C/245, Ogilvie to Dorchester, May 5, 1794.

authorized 200 other ranks.[28] The King's New Brunswick Regiment had managed to secure 400 men.[29] Despite the fact that the Royal Nova Scotia Regiment was fated to remain about 230 rank and file below its newly authorized strength of 800 other ranks, H.R.H. Edward Duke of Kent, who had succeeded Brigadier-General Ogilvie in the military command at Halifax during the summer of 1794, considered it to be a useful corps.[30]

Rumours originating in New York that a French fleet was being assembled for an attack on Halifax prompted this enthusiastic younger son of George III to undertake extensive improvement of its harbour defences. Since the local labour force was inadequate for the needs of the Commanding Royal Engineer, the Duke of Kent persuaded the Lieutenant-Governor of Nova Scotia to embody two regiments of Halifax militia and a detachment from the volunteer artillery company to work on the new fortifications.[31] During May, 1795, another 600 militia were embodied for six months' work as labourers, at Army rates of pay. Naturally the more prosperous citizens selected by ballot exercised their right to hire substitutes from among the city's casual labourers.[32] For the summer season of 1797, fewer than 500 militiamen could be provided. A disgusted Duke of Kent reported on November 7 that the average regular soldier did as much work as three militiamen and suggested that the best way to hasten completion of the fortification programme would be to reinforce his troops from Great Britain. Never again, this letter continued, did he want to have to employ militiamen as labourers,

. . . for on the one hand, the Country is by far too new, and too thinly settled to admit of even so small a number as that called upon this season to be absent from their homes, without their families being materially injured by the measure; while on the other, the laws by which they are governed when embodied, are so totally inefficient, that it is next to an impossibility to enforce any kind of control or subordination, which they are not willing to submit to. In fact, had I not indulged them in almost every point and overlooked almost every irregularity, it would have been impracticable to have got them to do, even the little we were able to effect. The expense attending the measure of embodying them is certainly far from being attended with that proportionate good which it ought to produce.[33]

---

[28]C.O. 226/14, Dundas to Fanning, Feb. 5, 1794; C.O. 226/15, "A detail of Various Transactions at Prince Edward Island, and in particular the Conduct of Certain persons Entrusted with the Affairs of Government on that Island submitted to Mr. Vansittart at the Treasury and Mr. Sullivan at the Secretary of State's Office by J. Hill, a Proprietor," n.d.
[29]C.O. 188/6, Carleton to Portland, Sept. 10, 1795.
[30]C.O. 217/71, Wentworth to King, April 1, 1795.
[31]C.O. 217/71, Wentworth to Portland, Dec. 20, 1794.
[32]*Ibid.*, April 18 and June 24, 1795.
[33]C.O. 217/71, Kent to Portland, Nov. 7, 1797.

Fortunately his situation was soon eased by the arrival at Halifax of the 6th Regiment of Foot.

There were other rumours of French activity. Excitement had been created in Lower Canada by reports that a French fleet was cruising off the coast of Newfoundland. In December, 1796, a British warship had captured a French vessel carrying Ira Allen, of the famous Vermont family, and a cargo of 20 light field guns and 15,000 muskets for the Vermont militia. At Quebec it was naturally believed that an invasion of Lower Canada was being contemplated. Spies and hostile agents were thought to be infesting the province, and alarm lessened only after the public execution of David McLane at Quebec on July 21, 1797, for treason.[34]

A year later Lieutenant-General Robert Prescott, Governor-in-Chief and Commander of the Forces, was still nervous. His three regiments of British infantry in Lower Canada totalled only 2,034 rank and file; the 424 rank and file of the 1st Battalion of Royal Canadian Volunteers were mostly French-speaking Canadians and thus not to be relied on. "Quebec must be taken care of," Prescott wrote to the Home Secretary in August, 1798, "and at Montreal a considerable Force must necessarily be stationed to awe the *Habitants* of that vicinity who have in more than one Instance evinced a refractory Spirit."[35] Yet shortly thereafter a French royalist agent advised Prescott that, although the *habitants* generally were anxious to have Canada restored to France, they were inclined to continue their passive attitude. The last French republican spy had been withdrawn pending a reconsideration of policy by the Directory in Paris.[36]

General Napoleon Bonaparte, who overthrew the Directory on November 9, 1797, was too busy as First Consul of France to give Canada more than a passing thought. A new Lieutenant-Governor of Lower Canada, Sir Robert Shore Milnes, must have impressed the French-speaking *habitants* by his attendance at militia musters throughout the province. In any event, enough of them came forward willingly during October, 1801, when one-eighth of the militia was embodied and armed in response to further reports from Vermont of an impending invasion. There was even a considerable number of volunteers.[37]

The peace treaty signed at Amiens on March 27, 1802, between France and Britain ended the French threat to the widespread British Empire. The British Government promptly reduced the strength of the regular regiments in North America and ordered the several provincial corps to

[34]Burt, *The United States, Great Britain and British North America*, 170–7.
[35]C.O. 42/111, Prescott to Portland, Aug. 22, 1798.
[36]*Ibid.*, Oct. 1, 1798.
[37]C.O. 42/117, Milnes to Hobart, Oct. 28, 1801.

be disbanded. The special corps of Queen's Rangers in Upper Canada was also disbanded. This action reduced the garrisons in Nova Scotia and its Dependencies to a total of 43 officers and 1,177 other ranks, organized as two artillery companies and two regiments of foot.[38] The 6th and 41st Regiments of Foot in Lower Canada had about 1,000 rank and file. The widely scattered posts in Upper Canada were garrisoned by detachments of the newly arrived 49th Regiment of Foot. Royal Artillerymen serving in both the Canadas were still organized in four small companies.[39] Here it might be noted that the regular army of the United States had been reduced somewhat earlier: its actual strength was now only 248 officers and 3,749 enlisted men.[40]

Peace in Europe proved to be only a breather since, in spite of British protests, Napoleon persisted in a policy of piecemeal aggrandizement. Great Britain therefore declared war on France on May 16, 1803. Because of the impossibility of reinforcing the British troops in North America from home, Field-Marshal H.R.H. Frederick Duke of York, Commander-in-Chief of all His Majesty's Forces, authorized the organization of fencible regiments for each of Newfoundland, Nova Scotia, New Brunswick, and Canada.[41] During earlier wars the British Army had raised fencible regiments of cavalry and infantry for local defence duty, chiefly in Scotland which had no militia prior to 1797, but the fact that certain of these units volunteered to replace overseas garrisons of regular troops created a precedent. Recruits for the new fencible regiments were enlisted for service anywhere in the whole of North America. Since Prince Edward Island and Cape Breton were defenceless, except for a "small and disper'd Body of unarm'd and undisciplin'd Militia," an officer and 22 other ranks of the 5th Battalion, 60th (or Royal American) Regiment of Foot were sent to each from Halifax to prevent their seats of government being "insulted" by privateers or other enemy raiders.[42]

Danger to the maritime provinces did not materialize because the Royal Navy had a considerable strength in North American waters; as a consequence of the victory over combined French and Spanish fleets at Trafalgar in 1805 and the capture of the Danish navy at Copenhagen in 1807, the Royal Navy had no serious competitor on the high seas.[43] Therefore it did not greatly matter that none of the fencible regiments

[38]C.O. 217/78, Bowyer to Hobart, Aug. 16, 1803.
[39]C.O. 42/122, Milnes to Hobart, June 24, 1803.
[40]Upton, *The Military Policy of the United States*, 89.
[41]C/718, York to Hunter, Aug. 1, 1803.
[42]C.O. 217/78, Bowyer to Hobart, Aug. 16, 1803.
[43]Captain S. W. Roskill, *The Strategy of Sea Power: Its Development and Application* (London, 1962), 82–3.

in British North America was able to recruit its authorized 1,070 rank and file.

The Regiment of Canadian Fencible Infantry was able to recruit only 124 men in three years and thus could not be placed on the Army establishment as an effective corps.[44] Lieutenant-Governor Milnes managed, however, to form a total of seven volunteer militia companies—at Montreal, Quebec, and Trois-Rivières—for use in a possible emergency.[45] Milnes realized that it would be wishful thinking to expect the French-speaking *habitants* to remain loyal to George III in the event that a French fleet should appear in the St. Lawrence River. Yet the anti-clerical policies of Revolutionary France towards the Church of Rome were causing a great deal of anxiety in Lower Canada. An alarmed Canadian clergy was now doing its best to convince the *habitants* that God had made possible the British Conquest in order that the Church in Canada should be spared the horrors and abuses that had accompanied the Revolution in France. The *habitants* therefore should be good subjects of the King. Members of the seigniorial class had more mundane and mercenary reasons for continuing to support the *status quo*, as have the privileged groups in any society. How much attention the *habitants* paid to the opinions of their priests and seigneurs was another matter. Carleton had been overly optimistic in 1775, and Milnes had no intention of making the same mistake. Thus he merely reported that the *habitants* were much more "reconciled" to British rule than at any former time, and that they would fight against Americans should there be a renewed threat from the south.[46]

This threat was revived after H.M.S. *Leopard* attacked U.S.S. *Chesapeake* at sea on June 22, 1807, for refusing to permit a search for British deserters. The death of three Americans, the wounding of eighteen others, and the removal of four alleged deserters from a crippled *Chesapeake* united American public opinion in a demand for war against Great Britain. American sea power was, however, slight. A United States Navy had been authorized by Congress in 1794 and there had been seafights during an undeclared naval war with France (1798–1800) and the war with Tripoli (1801–05), but there were now only two frigates and four sea-going war vessels in commission. This was because President Jefferson

[44]C/795, Castlereagh to Brock, April 25, 1807; Calvert to Shank, April 28, 1807.

[45]C.O. 42/121, Milnes to Hobart, June 10, 1803.

[46]C.O. 42/122, Milnes to Hobart, June 24, 1803; see also Michel Brunet, "The British Conquest: Canadian Social Sciences and the Fate of the *Canadiens*," *Canadian Historical Review*, XL (June, 1959).

was enamoured of the idea that gunboats could provide a more satis-factory defence of the American coast and harbours than ships of the line and frigates, and at a fraction of the cost.[47]

Vice-Admiral of the White the Hon. George Cranfield Berkeley, R.N., commanding the North American Station with his headquarters at Halifax, was convinced that a British show of force in North America would bring the Americans to their senses and would put an end to the widely reported preparations for war. Should war materialize, however, a "flying army of 5,000 men" should be added to an augmented fleet to harry the American coast. These raids would deter the enemy from con-centrating an army to advance overland into either Canada or New Brunswick. In a letter of August 13, 1807, addressed to the President of the Board of Trade in London, then Lord Bathurst, Berkeley further suggested that destruction of the 1,200 to 1,400 American fishing boats as they returned home from the coasts of Newfoundland and Labrador would prevent their seamen from subsequently becoming privateers.[48] A second letter, dated August 17, suggested a naval attack on New York City: destruction of its harbour and shipping would be a crippling blow to the American economy and put an end to any ideas of waging suc-cessful war against Great Britain.[49]

During this alarm the youthful Colonel Isaac Brock was temporary Commander of the Forces in the Canadas. He requested the elderly Administrator of the Government of Lower Canada, Thomas Dunn, to call out sufficient of the militia to repair the defences and train for any emergency. Dunn and the other members of the Executive Council remembered the disorders that had accompanied previous attempts to embody the militia, and delayed action as long as possible. Finally, on August 20, Dunn ordered that one-fifth of the militia, or about 10,000 men, should be drafted by ballot and hold themselves in readiness for actual service. Bishop Plessis of Quebec issued a *mandement* that was read in all the Roman Catholic churches of his diocese. What followed was graphically described in the *Quebec Mercury* of August 31:

The first draught was, in consequence, made, on the Esplanade, from the first battalion, of the Canadian militia, on Tuesday [25th August], from the second battalion on Friday, and from the British battalion, by ballot, yesterday. We should be wanting in justice to our compatriots did we say less than that, never,

---

[47]Harold and Margaret Sprout, *The Rise of American Naval Power 1776–1918* (Princeton, 1939), 33–62.

[48]Historical Manuscripts Commission, *Report on the Manuscripts of Earl Bathurst, preserved at Cirencester Park* (London, 1923), 64–5.

[49]*Ibid.*, 65.

on a similar occasion, could there be manifested more cheerfulness, alacrity and zeal, than were shewn on these occasions, as well by the Canadians as by the British. Numbers volunteered their services. The Artillery company, the two flank companies, and Captain Burns' battalion company, who are the strongest and best disciplined of the British, have, to a man, formally tendered their services. Sums of money were offered by individuals, for prize-tickets, for such the tickets were called which, in ballotting, were for service. Some young batchelors procured prize-tickets from the married men, who had drawn for service; but the greater part of the latter insisted on keeping their tickets, notwithstanding that offers of exchange were made to them by other batchelors.

Too much praise cannot be given to the animating language of the field-officers and others, in their speeches, addressed to the different battalions and companies, on the occasion. The whole has been attended with much festivity and hilarity.

The only "gross instance of misbehaviour and insubordination" occurred in the parish of L'Assomption of the Montreal district.[50] This was immediately suppressed and the culprits sentenced by a Montreal court to twelve months imprisonment and fines ranging from five to ten pounds.[51] A laudatory Militia General Order was issued on September 9 to thank the men for "coming forward in the Cause of a justly beloved Sovereign, and in support of a Form of Government, which has been proved by Experience to be the best calculated for promoting the Happiness and securing the Liberties of Mankind." A disgusted Colonel Brock pointed out, however, that nothing had actually been done:

The men thus selected for service being scattered along an extensive line of four or five hundred miles, unarmed and totally unacquainted with every thing military, without officers capable of giving them instruction, considerable time would naturally be required before the necessary degree of order and discipline could be introduced among them.[52]

Lieutenant-Governor Francis Gore of Upper Canada had hastened down to Montreal to consult Brock, but all he could get was a promise that 4,000 stand of arms would be sent forthwith from Quebec. In the meantime there were practically no muskets available in Upper Canada for his untrained militia.[53] On October 7 Gore wrote Lord Castlereagh, Secretary of State for War and the Colonies, that he was refraining from calling out any part of his militia, "that the Americans may not be made acquainted with our weakness."[54]

---

[50]*Quebec Gazette*, Sept. 10, 1807.
[51]*Ibid.*, Nov. 10, 1807.
[52]Ferdinand Brock Tupper, ed., *The Life and Correspondence of Major-General Sir Isaac Brock, K.B.* (London, 1847), 65.
[53]*Ibid.*, 66.
[54]C.O. 42/347, Gore to Castlereagh, Oct. 7, 1807.

On October 18 Lieutenant-General Sir James Craig arrived at Quebec
to assume the long vacant appointments of "Captain-General and
Governor-in-Chief in and over the Provinces of Upper & Lower Canada,
New-Brunswick, Nova-Scotia, and the Islands of Prince Edward and
Cape Breton, and their several Dependencies, Vice-Admiral of the same,
Lieutenant-General and Commander of all His Majesty's Forces in the
Provinces of Lower and Upper Canada, Nova-Scotia & New-Brunswick,
and in the Islands of Prince Edward, Cape Breton, Newfoundland and
the Bermudas." The 59-year-old Craig had been a junior officer with the
ill-fated Burgoyne expedition of 1777, but he had later fought with
distinction at the Cape of Good Hope, in India, and in the Mediterra-
nean. Craig brought no reinforcements with him, and none could be
expected from Britain. However, the 10th Royal Veteran Battalion had
arrived at Quebec, as earlier scheduled, and both the 98th Regiment of
Foot and the Royal Newfoundland Regiment of Fencible Infantry were
transferred from Halifax to strengthen Craig's position further.

Craig's secret instructions from Lord Castlereagh, dated September 1,
1807, were quite specific. There was no possibility that Craig might
misunderstand or misinterpret them. They commenced by expressing the
hope that the crisis might be resolved amicably. If not, the British
Government would adopt the "most vigorous & Energetic Measures" to
bring the Americans to their senses.[55] Possible American offensive action
was visualized as follows:

From the inferiority of the Americans in Naval Power & impossibility they must
find of contending with His Majesty's Arms at Sea, it may naturally be their hope
to make some compensation for the Maritime Losses they may experience by
attacking His Majesty's American Provinces;—and as under the circumstances of
extended Warfare in which His Majesty is engaged it will not be possible to send
a numerous Force across the Atlantic for their Protection, the extended Frontier
of these Provinces certainly presents an opening for a favorable invasion. It
appears however that there are only two Capital Objects which would fully repay
the Expence and Danger of an Expedition. One the Seizure of the Town and
Harbour of Halifax in Nova Scotia, which could deprive His Majesty's Fleets of
the most important Naval Station in the North American Continent; the other
the capture of the Fortress of Quebec which would place them in the Sovereignty
of His Majesty's Canadian Possessions.

Since Craig was to proceed directly to Quebec and might not be able
to communicate with Halifax that autumn, Lord Castlereagh wrote that
he was sending separate instructions for the Lieutenant-Governor of Nova
Scotia and the Commander of the Forces there to take "the best Measures
in their power for placing Halifax in a state of Defence." The militia of

55C.O. 43/22, Castlereagh to Craig, Sept. 1, 1807.

both Nova Scotia and New Brunswick were to be armed and trained. In the event that New Brunswick was invaded by an overwhelming American military force, the troops were to retreat into Nova Scotia with as many of the militia as possible in order to strengthen the landward defence of Halifax.

Craig's own conduct of the defence of the Canadas was spelled out clearly, in line with the strategy that had been evolving over the years and that placed ultimate reliance upon possession of the fortress of Quebec:

. . . your first object will be to preserve Quebec, to which all other Considerations must be subordinate; If the American States shall make a serious Effort to get entire possession of these Provinces and to enter them with a Force it may be impossible to detach from hence so large a Body of Regular Troops as would enable you to meet their army in the Field and entirely to defeat and expel it—It may however be a Measure beyond the power of the American States, to bring at an early period a sufficient Force properly appointed which could reduce the Fortress of Quebec if properly defended, before means of succour could be sent from England—and in this consideration of the Subject I am to satisfy to you His Majesty's Pleasure, that in the event of Hostilities with the United States you do not omit any Exertion by which the Situation of Quebec may be strengthened or secured & its defence protracted to the utmost.

In the event of No Hostilities taking place you will nevertheless take the most immediate Measures for having the Works completed which are necessary for enclosing the Body of the Place and constructing the Casements connected with them.

With regard to the building of a Citadel or carrying permanent Works to the heights of Abraham, there will be time to receive your Opinion respecting their necessity or propriety before the other and more necessary Works can be finished.

Respecting the Province of Upper Canada and the defence of it, as the Command of all its Military Means will be under your authority, I shall leave to your discretion the extent of the resistance you may think it prudent then to make in case the American States shall attack it in force.

Although the militia of Upper Canada would remain under the civil government unless Craig should actually be in that province, Lieutenant-Governor Gore was being instructed to defer to Craig's "Judgement and Instructions not only in what relates to the Militia but whatever may relate to the Defence of the Province, or the Intercourse of its Government with that of the United States."

In view of the reputation that Craig was later to acquire in Lower Canada, Castlereagh's remarks as to what action should be taken to breathe life into its militia are most relevant:

With regards to the British part of the Population there will be little difficulty, the inducing the French Canadians to embody themselves is a subject of much delicacy, as they have in general hitherto shewn themselves averse from taking any

active part. I must leave the arrangement of this nice subject to your powers of
Management and conciliation, and you will be particularly cautious as far as
possible to prevent any Jealousies arising between His Majesty's English and
French subjects.

When Craig reached Quebec he realized that it was too late in the season
for the Americans to attempt to invade the Canadas before the late spring
of 1808, and merely issued a Militia General Order on November 24,
1807, warning the inhabitants of Lower Canada to be on their guard
against strangers and directing that "the portion of the Militia, amounting
to one-fifth, directed to be balloted for . . . is to continue to hold itself in
readiness, to assemble on the shortest notice."

During December, 1807, the arrival in Upper Canada of the 4,000
stand of arms promised by Colonel Brock made it feasible for Lieutenant-
Governor Gore to order his militia to be balloted. A letter written by a
resident of Kingston on January 3, 1808, describes the muster:

Our militia has been mustered, and arms issued out to them, also every fourth
man draughted, which draughts are to keep themselves in Constant readiness, in
case Jonathan should attempt an invasion. We are now learning the Exercise and
are drilled twice a Week by a Sergeant from the Garrison—and are already much
improved Considering our Awkwardness.[56]

That same day Gore finally received a letter from Sir James Craig,
written a month earlier, detailing the defence plans to be followed:

[These] point out the preservation of Quebec as the object of my first and
principal consideration, and that to which all others must be subordinate. It is the
only Post, defective as it may be in many respects, that can be considered tenable
for a moment, nor is the preservation of it of less consequence to the Province
under your immediate direction, than it is to this, as affording the only door for
the future entry of that force which it might be found expedient, and which the
King's Government might be then able to send for the recovery of both or either
. . . for if the Americans are really determined to attack these Provinces, and
employ those means which they may so easily command, I fear it would be vain
for us to flatter ourselves with the hopes of making any effectual defence of the
open country, unless powerfully assisted from home.[57]

Craig suggested sending into Upper Canada the loyal militia of the
Montreal district and any regulars not required for the defence of
Quebec. These, and some of Gore's regulars and militia, might be
employed to harry the rear of the American invading army which, after

    [56]Richard A. Preston, ed., *Kingston before the War of 1812* (Toronto, 1959),
256.
    [57]C.O. 42/136, Craig to Gore, Dec. 6, 1807.

having occupied Montreal, would likely be moving down the St. Lawrence River to attack Quebec.

In his reply of January 5, 1808, Gore agreed that the whole disposable force in Upper Canada might be so employed. Since the Americans had no war vessels on the Great Lakes, Gore could retain naval supremacy there. There was no doubt that it would be impracticable to defend Upper Canada against anything except a "partial or sudden incursion," but "this truth must be carefully concealed from Persons of almost every description in this colony, for there are few People here that would act with Energy were it not for the purpose of defending the lands which they actually possess."[58]

In order to give effect to such a policy of co-operation with Lower Canada, the consolidated Militia Act approved by the Legislature of Upper Canada on March 16, 1808, provided a similar clause to that existing in the militia legislation of Lower Canada since 1793:

... it shall not be lawful to order the militia or any part thereof, to march out of this Province, except for the assistance of the Province of Lower Canada, (when the same shall actually be invaded or in a state of insurrection) or except in pursuit of an enemy who may have invaded this Province, and except also for the destruction of any vessel or vessels, built or building, or any depot or magazine, formed or forming, or for the attack of any enemy who may be embodying or marching for the purpose of invading this Province, or for the attack of any fortification now erected, or which may be hereafter erected, to cover the invasion thereof.[59]

By this time Craig had received Castlereagh's letter of January 22, 1808, which had been brought overland by courier from Halifax to Quebec. Lieutenant-General Sir George Prevost was being sent to Halifax with three regiments totalling almost 2,300 rank and file of the British Army. A further regiment of foot was being sent to reinforce the garrison of Bermuda, and whether or not further reinforcements should be sent to British North America would depend on how the situation developed. Castlereagh's letter emphasized that "a great proportion of the Effort should be made by the People of the Country themselves."[60] Six "unattached and intelligent" lieutenant-colonels were being sent to Quebec and four to Halifax to serve as Inspecting Field Officers of Militia. They were to supervise the training of 12,000 militia in the two Canadas and 8,000 in the maritime provinces and possibly command

[58]C.O. 42/136, Gore to Craig, Jan. 5, 1808.
[59]48 Geo. III, c. 1.
[60]C.O. 42/136, Castlereagh to Craig, Jan. 22, 1808.

militia brigades on active service. Craig was directed to "lose no time in establishing a concert with Sir George Prevost, by which, in the event of an attack being directed against the Canadas, a due proportion of the Force stationed in Nova Scotia may move to your Support, and *vice versa*, should the latter Province be the object of attack." The naval transports carrying Prevost's regiments to Halifax had orders to wait there until future troop dispositions were decided.

On April 23 Sir George Prevost reached Halifax and almost immediately assumed the appointments of Lieutenant-Governor of Nova Scotia and Commander of the Forces. Not yet forty-one years of age, Prevost was the eldest son of one of the original Swiss officers in the 60th (or Royal American) Regiment of Foot. He had distinguished himself fighting against the French in the West Indies and had served briefly as Governor of St. Lucia after it was captured. Successful defence of Dominica against a determined French attack during the winter of 1805 had brought promotion to the rank of major-general and a baronetcy. His appointment to Nova Scotia warranted promotion to the local rank of lieutenant-general.

Prevost immediately dismissed the 2,000 militia embodied in Nova Scotia during the previous autumn and reported that the militia placed on duty in New Brunswick would also be released as soon as the 101st Regiment of Foot reached there from Halifax. Companies of the New Brunswick Fencibles would then be sent to garrison each of Cape Breton and Prince Edward Island.[61] The seaward defences of Halifax were adequate, but the land fortifications to its rear still needed strengthening, and there still were only temporary works on Citadel Hill.[62]

Craig had not despatched any confidential reports to London because letters sent via the overland route from Quebec to Halifax during the winter months might be captured by American marauders.[63] So it was May 12 before he wrote to Castlereagh in a very disparaging manner about the defences of Quebec:

I should begin by observing that as a Fortress I found this place extremely deficient under almost every point of view, in which as such it was to be considered, especially as connected with its relative importance to the ultimate security of that part of His Majesty's Dominions. The situation is in itself highly unfavourable, the ground rising in front of the works so as to afford a very dangerous command on them, while on both flanks, on the opposite sides of the two Rivers, but particularly on the further bank of the St. Charles, positions

---

[61]C/178, Prevost to Craig, April 11, 1808.
[62]W.O. 55/1558(4) contains reports and drawings designed to correct this situation.
[63]C.O. 42/136, Craig to Castlereagh, Jan. 11, 1808.

present themselves from which they could be swept in flank & even in reverse. The Works in themselves, for the most part, are in a ruinous State—the masonry of the walls, however good it may originally have been, is from the nature of the materials employed now rotten, no ditch or any counterscarp, by which the foot of the wall can be protected, and no outworks except in front of Cape Diamond where even those that appear to me the most material are in a state of ruin.

There is not a casement or single spot which would afford security to the sick or men off duty.[64]

There was no point embarking on a programme of permanent and costly construction in the midst of a crisis, so the Commanding Royal Engineer had devised a minimum programme to cope with likely dangers. New construction was to be limited to four martello towers spread across the Plains of Abraham, and to similar towers erected on the far bank of the St. Charles River and on Point Lévis to prevent the existing defences being enfiladed by enemy batteries. A proper citadel for Cape Diamond would have to wait.

Craig's attempt to increase the Canadian Fencibles to a usable strength had to be approached negatively since he could not compel men to enlist. He merely ordered from the Canadas the recruiting parties of the New Brunswick Fencibles who were offering a larger bounty for recruits.[65] On June 14, 1808, approval was given at the Horse Guards for the Canadian Fencibles to be placed upon the establishment of the Army whenever there should be 400 rank and file, with the usual proportion of officers and sergeants.[66] This strength was met during the autumn.[67]

Meanwhile Congress had authorized an increase of five regiments of infantry and one each of riflemen, light artillery, and dragoons to the United States Army. These units, however, were never recruited to anything like their authorized strength because the widespread desire to fight Britain soon died down. President Jefferson and his Republican party supporters in Congress believed that both Britain and France could be coerced into leaving neutral shipping alone by purely economic measures. The Embargo Act, hurried into effect as early as December 22, 1807, put an end legally to virtually all American international trade but did not have the desired effect. Napoleon refused to revoke his Berlin and Milan Decrees and the British Government stood by its Orders in Council. American merchants and shipowners were presented with the choice of bankruptcy or smuggling, and the nearby provinces of British North America benefited from their decision to conduct an illicit trade. American citizens at Sackets Harbor forcibly prevented customs officers

[64]*Ibid.*, May 12, 1808.
[65]Correspondence on C/718.
[66]C/795, Gordon to Craig, June 14, 1808.
[67]C/795, Strength Return, Nov. 11, 1808.

and troops from interfering with the trade across Lake Ontario and the upper St. Lawrence River. Armed guards ensured the safety of lumber rafts, and provisions floated down Lake Champlain into Lower Canada. Unprecedented storms forced New England vessels to seek shelter in Nova Scotian ports, while Passamaquoddy Bay became an even better rendezvous for smugglers.[68]

Castlereagh soon became convinced, from his vantage point in London, that the Anglo-American crisis was blowing over,[69] but the men on the spot were more impressed by the rumours that came their way. Napoleon, although he had sold Louisiana to the United States in 1803, was again believed to be contemplating intervention in the New World. Craig began to have visions of French agents reviving old alliances and unloosing Indians upon the "defenceless frontier of Upper Canada."[70] Therefore he wrote to Gore that it was more imperative than ever to win back the Indians. Yet, he cautioned, "the means that are pursued should be such as are of general conciliation and attachment without any particular allusion for the present to any possible state of hostilities with Americans."[71]

That Craig had already strengthened the prejudice against French-speaking Canadians, which he had acquired during the years of the American Revolution, and that he considered Lower Canada a conquered province to be ruled for the benefit of its English-speaking minority, seems evident from his despatch of August 4 to Castlereagh. But the following extract indicates that Craig was looking at the situation much more realistically than Dorchester had done:

. . . whatever may have been the case in former times the Canadian of the present day is not warlike or at all accustomed to arms. Nothing indeed can exceed the prejudices and absurd ideas that prevail among them. The Militia Service is ever in their mouths, they bring it forward as a merit on every occasion and, they seem to wish to be thought proud of belonging to it; but they have not the most distant idea of being Soldiers, or the slightest desire of becoming such, they have indeed an invincible abhorrence for the subordination and restraint that would be necessary for training them, and I have strong doubts whether they will ever be brought to submit to them.[72]

As a result, Castlereagh's cancellation of the arms shipment earlier ordered to Quebec had been a convenient excuse not to call out the militia of Lower Canada for training during the summer of 1808.

[68]Burt, *The United States, Great Britain and British North America*, 259–260.
[69]C.O. 42/136, Castlereagh to Craig, June 3, 1808.
[70]C.O. 42/136, Craig to Erskine, May 13, 1808.
[71]C.O. 42/136,, Craig to Gore, May 11, 1808.
[72]C.O. 42/136, Craig to Castlereagh, Aug. 4, 1808.

That Gore was almost as pessimistic about the loyalty of the population of Upper Canada, but for an entirely different reason, is evident from the much quoted letter he had written to Craig on January 5, 1808:

I think I may venture to state that the generality of the Inhabitants from Kingston to the borders of the lower province may be depended upon, but I cannot venture, from the Industry that has been used by certain characters now and lately in this Province, to assert that the Inhabitants about the Seat of this Government [York], Niagara and Long Point are equally to be relied on. I have also to observe that excepting the Inhabitants of Glengarry and those Persons who have served in the American War and their Descendents, which form a consider- able body of men, the residue of the Inhabitants of this colony consist chiefly of Persons who have emigrated from the States of America and of consequence, retain those ideas of equality and insubordination, much to the prejudice of this government, so prevalent in this country.[73]

Since the immediate crisis was now deemed to be over, all attempts at training the Canadian militia as combatant troops came to an end. The six Inspecting Field Officers recently arrived at Quebec thus found them- selves with no active employment, a condition that was to continue and turn their appointments into sinecures.[74]

Craig's further military appreciation of his situation, dated February 13, 1809, dealt with possibilities rather than probabilities. "The Security of Quebec is unquestionably the first object in every point of view," he wrote; "while we retain possession of it, we have always a door open, by which we may be able to recover the Province altho' it affords no security against the loss of it."[75] Craig now suggested that it would be better and cheaper, in the long run, to make an initial attempt to defend both Canadas. The militia would try to defend their own homes in the interior, but they could not later be organized from outside to help recover it. Upper Canada's best defence was the Great Lakes where the Provincial Marine was still not faced by a naval adversary. Unfortunately war vessels could not similarly be placed on Lake Champlain to help guard the approaches to Montreal because there no longer was a fortified base at either Isle aux Noix or St. Johns. All the forts in both provinces had been "totally neglected", and to date Craig had been forced to limit new work to Quebec. In any case, his 5,500 regulars and fencibles were not nearly enough. He estimated his needs as 12,000 additional regulars—

[73]C.O. 42/136, Gore to Craig, Jan. 5, 1808.
[74]Robert Christie, *Interesting Public Documents and Official Correspondence, Illustrative of, and Supplementary to the History of Lower Canada* (Montreal, 1855), VI, 145.
[75]C.O. 42/138, Craig to Castlereagh, Feb. 13, 1809.

2,000 to garrison rebuilt forts in each of the Canadas and 8,000 to function as a field force.

As the British Army was now heavily committed in Portugal, and a military expedition was being prepared for a landing on the island of Walcheren in the Netherlands, Craig was forced to get along with what he already had. In any event, Jefferson's successor as President of the United States, James Madison, had persuaded a new Congress to repeal the Embargo Act and to pass a weaker Non-Intercourse Act. This Act of March 1, 1809, restored American trade with all nations except Great Britain and France and authorized President Madison to proclaim resumption of trade with either or both of these belligerents whenever they should cease to violate the rights of neutral ships. In view of this Castlereagh cautiously replied to Craig on April 8, 1809:

> The existing state of circumstances between Great Britain and the United States of America, tho' it presents hopes that a rupture may be prevented & all differences terminate in a peaceful adjustment; yet on the other hand prevents our desisting from those cautionary measures which the probability of a late favorable issue renders expedient.
>
> I am therefore, to recommend you to persevere in the measures you are taking for strengthening Quebec, and for enabling you to avail yourself of the Militia Force of the Country, and should affairs take a more threatening aspect, proper means will be taken to augment your Force.
>
> You will consider the judicious and conciliating line you have hitherto pursued and take the necessary care that the measures of Defence you advise or adopt shall not be misconstrued, and that any imprudence of Individuals be not made the ground of National misunderstanding or retaliation.[76]

Craig continued to do what he thought was best, but he was aging and in poor health. Convinced that no good could be expected from the French-speaking inhabitants of Lower Canada and that war with the United States was not far off, he requested permission to resign and make way for a younger man. Permission having finally been granted, he sailed for England on June 19, 1811. His successor, Lieutenant-General Sir George Prevost, who was still serving in Nova Scotia, did not reach Quebec until September 13, 1811. This time lag did not worry the British Government unduly, for unlike Craig, it discounted the danger of war and was certain that its Minister, who was on his way to Washington, would be able to restore amicable Anglo-American relations without the repeal of the Orders in Council aimed at neutral traders.

[76]C.O. 42/138, Castlereagh to Craig, April 8, 1809.

(5)

THE WAR OF 1812

Lieutenant-General Sir George Prevost was understandably perturbed by the situation he found in Canada and by the news that soon began to arrive from Washington. Danger seemed to be imminent.

There was no way of knowing whether the majority of the French-speaking inhabitants of Lower Canada and the American latecomers to Upper Canada would be loyal, indifferent, or actively disloyal in the event that the United States went to war with Great Britain. The forts astride the obvious invasion routes were still in a dilapidated state, and there were insufficient troops to conduct an active defence against concerted American invasions. Prevost knew, of course, that more British troops could not be tied up in an inactive theatre while Britain was engaged in a life-and-death struggle with Napoleon. The British regulars and fencibles immediately available in the Canadas totalled roughly 5,600 effectives, but about 1,200 were garrisoning widely scattered posts in Upper Canada.[1] Few of the 173 officers and 4,889 other ranks serving in Lieutenant-General Sir John Coape Sherbrooke's subordinate command of Nova Scotia and its Dependencies might be transferred in an emergency to the more vulnerable Canadas; individual garrisons were small, except for that of Halifax, and 300 all ranks of the 98th Regiment of Foot were as far away as Bermuda.[2] The militia of Upper Canada was calculated as 11,000 "of which it might not be prudent to arm more than 4,000"; that of Lower Canada numbered upwards of 60,000, "ill armed and without discipline." About 6,000 of the 11,000 militia in Nova Scotia had been issued muskets since the *Chesapeake* affair and given rudimentary training, but few of the 4,000 militiamen in the scattered

[1]W.O. 17/1516, Strength Return, Canada, Nov. 25, 1811.
[2]W.O. 17/2358, Strength Return, Nova Scotia & Its Dependencies, Nov. 25, 1811.

settlements of New Brunswick had received any training, and those in
Cape Breton and Prince Edward Island did not "amount to any considerable number deserving to be noticed."[3] Since none of the provinces
produced sufficient food for its own needs, there was a definite limit to
the number of men that could be withdrawn from agriculture, particularly
during the weeks of planting and harvesting crops. As it was, a good part
of the provisions normally consumed by the British Army in North
America was imported from the United States. The Provincial Marine
enjoyed naval preponderance on the Great Lakes and Lake Champlain
because the United States Navy's only war vessel on the Great Lakes was
the 16-gun brig *Oneida* on Lake Ontario. The Provincial Marine's
miscellaneous collection of corvette, brig, and five schooners was, however,
neither efficiently manned nor maintained. No longer could the Provincial
Marine compete for commercial cargoes with privately owned vessels, nor
keep its best seamen. But its elderly officers were determined on continuing to serve and thus to block promotion for their subordinates.[4]

President Madison, in his opening message to Congress on November 5,
1811, asked for increases to the regular army, the acceptance of volunteer
corps, an improvement in the Navy, and an augmentation of the already
satisfactory supply of cannon, muskets, and ammunition. The younger
Republicans in the House of Representatives, for the most part represent-
ing agrarian interests in the south and west, clamoured for war with
Britain and were quickly dubbed "War Hawks." Even the Federalists
were now less pro-British; Napoleon having claimed to have revoked his
Berlin and Milan Decrees, they felt that Britain should cancel its Orders
in Council aimed at neutral traders.

Prevost set himself to improving his situation as best he could. Politically, he wooed the French-speaking Canadians and achieved a measure
of personal success because he was conciliatory by nature and the son of
French-speaking (Protestant) Swiss parents. Three of the new members
he appointed to the Legislative Council and two newcomers to his
Executive Council were French-speaking Canadians. Prevost ensured the
co-operation of the Roman Catholic Church by giving greater public
recognition to Bishop Plessis' status as head of the Roman Catholic clergy
and procuring for him sufficient funds to secure his position. This last
action, however, angered Bishop Mountain of the Church of England and
caused him to become Prevost's implacable enemy. Nor were the leading

[3]C.O. 42/146, Prevost to Liverpool, May 18, 1812.
[4]Documents on C/373.

members of the English-speaking oligarchy in Quebec and Montreal persuaded by lavish entertainments to like Sir George and Lady Prevost as they had Sir James Craig.[5]

On the military side, Prevost obtained authority from London to continue the work of fortification which had not got very far during Craig's tenure of office. He sent two officers to investigate the possibility of moving regiments overland from New Brunswick via the St. John River and the Madawaska–Temiscouata portage route to Rivière-du-Loup on the south bank of the lower St. Lawrence River.[6] Without waiting for authority from London, Prevost revived the scheme to raise a fencible corps in Upper Canada; its recruiting parties also visited the Scottish and Acadian settlements in New Brunswick, Nova Scotia, and Prince Edward Island during the winter and spring of 1812, and there was thus little justification for deciding to call the corps the Glengarry Light Infantry Fencibles.[7] A new Militia Act, which Prevost persuaded the Legislature of Lower Canada to pass in April, 1812, provided for the selection by ballot of 2,000 bachelors aged eighteen to twenty-five and their embodiment for ninety days training in each of two successive summers or their retention for a maximum of two years service in the event of war.[8] These personnel were to be known as Select Embodied Militia. Prevost also decided to raise a volunteer Provincial Corps of Light Infantry, or Voltigeurs, to serve during the "apprehended war" with the United States.[9]

Isaac Brock, recently promoted to the rank of major-general, had less success with the Legislature of Upper Canada, of which he was now Administrator in the absence of Lieutenant-Governor Gore in England. Brock blamed the "great influence which the numerous settlers from the United States" possessed over the decisions of the Assembly and the prevalent belief that war was unlikely.[10] Supplementary clauses to the Militia Act did authorize the formation of flank companies of volunteers for each sedentary militia battalion,[11] and about 2,000 men were accepted,[12] but

[5]J. Mackay Hitsman, *The Incredible War of 1812: A Military History* (Toronto, 1965), 27–8.
[6]C.O. 42/143, Prevost to Liverpool, Sept. 23, Oct. 13 and 28, 1811.
[7]F. B. Tupper, ed., *The Life and Correspondence of Major-General Sir Isaac Brock* (London, 1847), 123, 132–3.
[8]52 Geo. III, c. I.
[9]W.O. 1/96, Prevost to Torrens, April 21, 1812.
[10]Tupper, *The Life and Correspondence of Major-General Sir Isaac Brock*, 153.
[11]52 Geo. III, c. 3.
[12]Historical Manuscripts Commission, *Report on the Manuscripts of Earl Bathurst* (London, 1923), 175.

a subsequent circular letter reduced the number of training days from six to three per month.[13]

Since October 9, 1811, when he had assumed the government of Upper Canada, Brock had become convinced that the existing defensive concept should be modified. He had had only a brief experience of active operations—in the Low Countries' campaign of 1799 and at Copenhagen two years later—before he brought the 49th Regiment of Foot to Canada, but he was extremely offensive-minded in his outlook. Brock disliked the possibility of having to abandon Upper Canada in the face of an American invasion. He argued, in a long letter written to Prevost on December 2, 1811, that a strong stand could and should be made. If the western Indians were supplied by the British and encouraged to make war, the Americans would be kept too busy to threaten Upper Canada. "But before we can expect an active co-operation on the part of the Indians," Brock went on, "the reduction of Detroit and Michilimackinac must convince that people, who conceive themselves to have been sacrificed in 1794, to our policy, that we are earnestly engaged in the War."[14] Continued naval supremacy on the Great Lakes was also essential for a successful defence of Upper Canada and could be assured only by the augmentation of the Provincial Marine on both Lake Ontario and Lake Erie. The only sector of Upper Canada vulnerable to attack would be along the Niagara River which the Americans could cross in small boats.

The instructions Prevost had received from the British Government in October had been specifically defensive: he was not to commence offensive operations "except it be for the purpose of preventing or repelling Hostilities or unavoidable Emergencies."[15] If an avoidable mistake were made, the British Government would hold Prevost—not Brock—responsible, and both these soldiers knew it. Prevost's reply to Brock agreed on purely military grounds that there would be advantages in attacking Detroit and Michilimackinac while they were held only weakly "rather than [in] receiving the first blow."[16] He added that at the moment there seemed to be a distinct divergence of opinion in the United States upon the question of peace or war; hence extreme care should be taken to avoid giving offence.

Before Prevost had a chance to visit Upper Canada and draw his own conclusions on the spot, he received a letter from the Secretary of State

[13]*York Gazette*, May 1, 1812.
[14]C/673, Brock to Prevost, Dec. 2, 1811.
[15]C.O. 43/23, Prince Regent's Instructions to Prevost, Oct. 22, 1811.
[16]C/1218, Prevost to Brock, Dec. 24, 1811.

for War and the Colonies requesting a detailed appreciation of the military situation in North America. Prevost's lengthy reply, based on the best intelligence available and dated May 18, is important enough to warrant summary in the following paragraphs.

The most westerly fort on St. Joseph's Island could be considered only as a "Post of assemblage for friendly Indians, and in some degree a protection for the North West Fur Trade."[17] Repairs were being hurried to Fort Malden at Amherstburg, which was the Provincial Marine's base on the upper lakes as well as being a "place of reunion" for Indians. Fort Erie, Chippawa, and Fort George protected the line of communication between Lake Erie and Lake Ontario but, upon the outbreak of war, it would be well to capture the opposing Fort Niagara. Nothing had yet been done to fortify York, but the broad expanse of Lake Ontario was between it and the United States. Kingston was "exposed to sudden attack, which, if successful, would cut off communication between the Upper and Lower Province, and deprive us of our naval resources." Yet its garrison consisted of only four companies of the 10th Royal Veteran Battalion, totalling less than 200 effectives. In view of the populous American settlements now spread along the eastern end of Lake Ontario and the upper St. Lawrence River, Prevost thought it would be advisable to establish well above the rapids, at Prescott, a strong post for regulars and militia.

Since the commercial centre of Montreal would likely be the first object of attack in Lower Canada, but lacked any means of defence, British troops would have to maintain an "impenetrable line on the South Shore, extending from La Prairie to Chambly, with a sufficient Flotilla to command the Rivers St. Lawrence and the Richelieu." The ruins at St. Johns and Chambly were not really defensible positions, but the field works at William Henry (or Sorel) were about to be improved as it was a rendezvous for naval vessels patrolling the St. Lawrence River. Farther down the river were excellent positions for holding up an enemy marching along either bank, particularly if he did not control navigation on it.

The next paragraphs of this appreciation, which are concerned especially with Quebec, so closely resemble the planning of Sir James Craig that copies of the earlier documents must have been in front of Prevost as he dictated to his military secretary:

Quebec is the only permanent Fortress in the Canadas:—It is the Key to the whole and must be maintained:—To the final defence of this position, every other

---

[17]C.O. 42/146, Prevost to Liverpool, May 18, 1812.

Military operation ought to become subservient and the retreat of the Troops upon Quebec must be the primary consideration:—The means of resistance afforded by the Fortifications in their present imperfect State, are not such as could justify a hope of its being able to withstand a vigorous and well conducted siege. It requires Bomb proof Casements for the Troops, as the Town is completely commanded from the South Shore at Point Levi, a position which it has been frequently recommended to occupy in force:—The Casements ought to be erected on Cape Diamond, a position that points itself out for a Citadel:—It is advisable that the whole circumference of the summit of this Hill should be occupied, being the only elevation within the Walls and commanded by the height of Land on the plains of Abraham:—Such a Work would essentially defend the extensive Line of Fortification, sloping from Cape Diamond to the Artillery Barrack, which is old and imperfect, is commanded from the high land opposite, and is besides seen in reverse and open to an enfilade fire from positions on the bank of the St. Charles River. . . .

In framing a general outline of Co-operation for defence with the Forces in Upper Canada, commensurate with our deficiency in strength; I have considered the preservation of Quebec as the first object, and to which all others must be Subordinate:—Defective as Quebec is, it is the only Post that can be considered as tenable for a moment, the preservation of it being of the utmost consequence to the Canadas, as the door of entry for that Force the King's Government might find it expedient to send for the recovery of both, or either of these Provinces, altho' the pressure of the moment in the present extended range of Warfare, might not allow the sending of that force which would defend both, therefore considering Quebec in this view, its importance can at once be appreciated.

If the Americans are determined to attack Canada, it would be in vain the general should flatter himself with the hopes of making an effectual defence of the open country, unless powerfully assisted from Home:—All predatory or ill concerted attacks undertaken presumptuously and without sufficient means, can be resisted and repulsed:—Still this must be done with caution, that the resources, for a future exertion, the defence of Quebec, may be unexhausted.

"The Province of New Brunswick and the peninsula of Nova Scotia present so many vulnerable points to an invading army," Prevost's despatch continued, "that it is difficult to establish any precise Plan for the defence of either." Consequently "much must depend upon Contingencies in the event of Invasion:—Their security very materially depends upon the Navy, and the vigilance of our Cruizers in the Bay of Fundy." Neither Fredericton nor Saint John were defensible against an American army advancing overland, while the land defences of Halifax were "so imperfect as to be undeserving of notice." The defensive works at Sydney on Cape Breton and at Charlottetown in Prince Edward Island, were "so insignificant, as to be unworthy of observation," but attackers would have to elude the Royal Navy before they could reach either or both. There were 3 ships of the line, 23 frigates, and 53 sloops, brigs, and smaller war vessels in North American waters, even though these were scattered between the West Indies, Halifax, and Newfoundland.[18]

This despatch did not actually leave Quebec until June 1, 1812, by which time the President of the United States had decided that further interviews with the British Minister in Washington would be pointless. The President then sent Congress a message requesting an immediate declaration of war. This was approved 79 to 49 in a vote in the House of Representatives on June 4, and 19 to 13 by the Senate on June 17. On the following day President Madison signed the bill.

The United States was unprepared for war. The Navy had only 5 frigates, 3 sloops, and 7 brigs ready to put to sea. There were only 6,744 officers and enlisted men serving on the regular establishment of the United States Army, and about 5,000 newly commissioned officers and recruits in recently approved units. This total strength was only slightly more than the number of British regulars and fencibles in North America. How many American volunteers and militia would actually be supplied by individual states against their quotas could only be a matter for conjecture, and they would be completely untrained. There were no detailed plans for an offensive campaign, and no proper staffs to plan them. Then, as now, the President was Commander-in-Chief, but there was no uniformed Joint Chiefs of Staff Committee to advise him. Yet President Madison and his political Secretary of War seemed satisfied with the elderly Major-General Henry Dearborn's suggestion that offensive operations could be launched simultaneously against Montreal, Kingston, and Niagara by troops of his Northern Department. The equally elderly Brigadier-General William Hull was confident that an advance by his independent North Western Army from Detroit into the Western District of Upper Canada would be welcomed by the inhabitants, most of whom were recent arrivals from the United States.[19] Dearborn and Hull had served during the American Revolution, but they had subsequently pursued political careers and had not been commissioned in the regular army until the early weeks of 1812. There were only 29 field officers in the regular army, many were old and inept, and none had commanded a whole regiment since their fighting had been against hostile Indians. The highest naval rank was captain and each captain reported directly to the political Secretary of the Navy in Washington.

The first news of war reached Montreal merchants from fur trade

[18]Adm. 8/100. Total strengths for stations in west Atlantic, July 1812, in G. S. Graham, *Empire of the North Atlantic: The Maritime Struggle for North America* (Toronto, 1950), 246–7n.

[19]Hitsman, *The Incredible War of 1812*, 41–3.

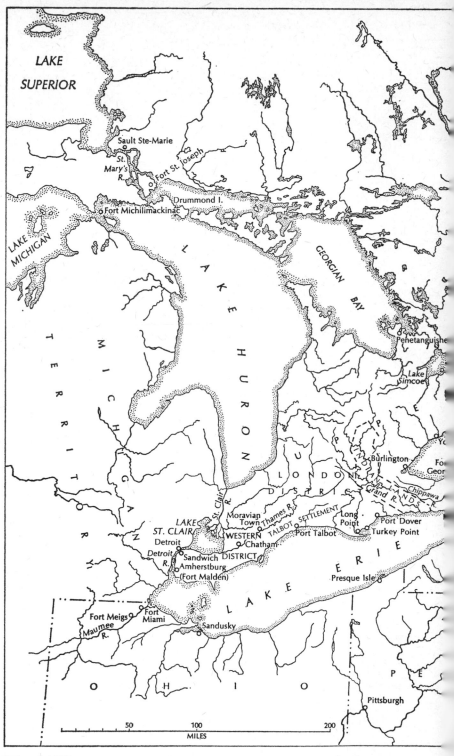

War of 1812.

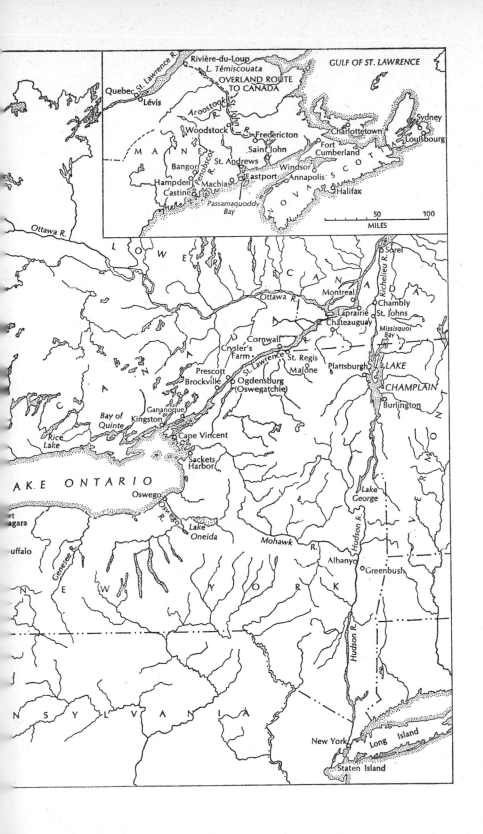

associates in New York City on June 24. Word was immediately relayed
to Quebec City, where Sir George Prevost began to implement his existing
plans. He cancelled the movement orders returning the 41st and 49th
Regiments to Britain because he had been told that he could treat the two
replacement regiments *en route* to Canada as a first reinforcement in the
event of war. He also held onto the 100th Regiment which had been
slated for transfer to Halifax. The flank companies of the regular and
fencible regiments in Lower Canada were formed into a flank battalion
to man an advanced line of posts stretching from St. Johns to Laprairie.
Most of their battalion companies and the available demi-brigade of field
artillery were shortly congregated forward of Montreal as a supporting
force. Command of the whole was entrusted to Major-General George
Baron de Rottenburg. This was, and would continue to be, Prevost's
principal troop concentration. Should this force be defeated by an
invading army of Americans, it would make a fighting withdrawal down
the left bank of the St. Lawrence River to Quebec, which would have to
be held safe throughout the long Canadian winter in the expectation that
the Royal Navy would bring succour as soon as the river was free of ice.
Garrison duty at Quebec and Montreal was temporarily left to volunteers
from the local sedentary militia units. After some rudimentary training,
the four battalions into which the Select Embodied Militia had been
recently organized joined the troops in front of Montreal.[20]

Tension eased when no invaders appeared on the borders of Lower
Canada. The instruction sent by the Secretary of War in Washington to
Major-General Dearborn on June 26 did not indeed suggest any need for
haste.[21] Refusal of the Governors of Massachusetts and Connecticut to
furnish militia quotas and slowness in recruiting resulted in there being
only 1,200 men at Albany when Dearborn arrived there a month later.[22]
Meanwhile the people of northern Vermont had let it be known in Lower
Canada that they wished to continue with the normal trade, obtaining
British manufactured goods in exchange for the agricultural products so
necessary to feed the British Army.[23]

Prevost was further heartened by reports from Nova Scotia and New
Brunswick. News of the American declaration of war had reached Halifax
on June 29, along with the encouraging information that the nearby

[20]C.O. 42/147, Prevost to Liverpool, June 29, July 6 and 15, 1812.
[21]RG 107, Letters sent by the Secretary of War, Military Affairs (M6), 5,
Eustis to Dearborn, June 26, 1812.
[22]RG 107, Letters received by the Secretary of War (M 221), 52, Dearborn to
Eustis, July 28, 1812.
[23]*Montreal Herald*, July 11, 1812.

inhabitants of New England were generally opposed to it and were desirous of continuing normal trade. Since New Brunswick was even more dependent on trade with New England, its Executive Council requested the newly appointed Administrator, Major-General G. S. Smyth, to permit the import of provisions in unarmed American ships.[24] After consulting his own Executive Council in Nova Scotia, Sir John Sherbrooke issued such a proclamation on July 3, 1812:

> Whereas every species of predatory warfare carried on against Defenceless Inhabitants, living on the shores of the United States contiguous to this Province and New Brunswick, can answer no good purpose, and will greatly distress individuals; I have therefore thought proper by and with the advice of His Majesty's Subjects under my Government, to abstain from molesting the Inhabitants living on the shores of the United States, contiguous to this Province and New Brunswick: and on no account to molest the Goods, or unarmed Coasting Vessels, belonging to the Defenceless Inhabitants on the Frontiers, so long as they shall abstain on their parts, from any acts of Hostility and Molestation towards the Inhabitants of this Province and New Brunswick, who are in a similar situation. It is therefore my wish and desire, that the Subjects of the United States, living on the frontiers, may pursue in peace their usual and accustomed Trade and occupations, without Molestation, so long as they shall act in a similar way towards the frontier inhabitants of this Province and New Brunswick.
>
> And I do hereby order and command all His Majesty's Subjects, within my jurisdiction, to govern themselves accordingly, until further orders.[25]

A week later Major-General Smyth issued a similar proclamation.

Smyth reported to London that he had not called out any militia, "as depriving the Country of its labour at this Season would occasion the most alarming scarcity, if not the total want of food, during the remainder of this year."[26] Sherbrooke had embodied 180 militiamen and had ordered guns to be mounted at the entrance of each principal harbour in Nova Scotia, but he also was aware of the importance of harvesting the local crops. There was no doubt in his mind that sufficient provisions could be imported from New England to meet local needs, so great was the American cry for British manufactured goods.[27] Prince Edward Island was such a quiet backwater that no unusual action was ever considered necessary.[28]

In Upper Canada, Brock's first reaction to the news of war had been to undertake offensive operations. But he had then to remember Prevost's

[24]C.O. 188/18, Smyth to Liverpool, July 4, 1812.
[25]C.O. 217/90, Sherbrooke to Liverpool, July 4, 1812.
[26]C.O. 188/18, Smyth to Bathurst, Aug. 31, 1812.
[27]C.O. 217/90, Sherbrooke to Bathurst, Aug. 7, 1812.
[28]C.O. 226/27, Smith to Bathurst, March 25 and Aug. 19, 1813.

repeated injunctions to adhere to the defensive strategy approved earlier. The militia in the Niagara Peninsula turned out cheerfully to the number of 800 men to supplement the 500 regulars of the 41st Foot garrisoning Fort George, Chippawa, and Fort Erie. Somewhat ironically, Brock's belief that a large enemy force was poised for attack on the opposite shore of the Niagara River was shared by the American commander of Fort Niagara who was literally screaming for reinforcements for his own tiny garrison. The militia of the loyalist settlements along the upper St. Lawrence River and at Kingston had also turned out to protect this vital line of communication between Lower and Upper Canada.[29] The lack of tents, blankets, kettles—and even muskets—was overlooked by most militiamen in their initial enthusiasm to do something,[30] Brock reported to Prevost.

As far as Prevost could judge, this unwanted war was not going badly, but his letter to Brock on July 10 emphasized caution:

Our numbers would not justify offensive operations being undertaken, unless they were solely calculated to strengthen a defensive attitude—I consider it prudent and politic to avoid any measure which can in its effect, have a tendency to unite the People in the American States.—Whilst dissension prevails among them, their attempts on these Provinces will be feeble;—it is therefore our duty carefully to avoid committing any act, which may, even by construction, tend to unite the Eastern and Southern States, unless by its perpetration, we are to derive a considerable and important advantage.[31]

Colonel Robert Lethbridge was despatched from Montreal to assume command at Kingston and to exercise a "vigilant general superintendence of the whole district," but to take orders from Major-General Brock.[32] Lethbridge was similarly warned not to stir up trouble by taking any offensive action. His most important task was to ensure that Kingston remain in British hands. *En route* Lethbridge was to ascertain the efficiency of the militia defending the river communication, along which a convoy system would be organized for the movement of supply boats.

Lord Bathurst issued a directive on August 10 approving the contents of the first wartime despatches from North America. Although the new Secretary of State for War and the Colonies hoped that war with the United States would be brought to a speedy end, once news reached Washington that a new British Government had conditionally repealed the controversial Orders in Council on June 23, Prevost was to do the

[29]Hitsman, *The Incredible War of 1812*, 52–5.
[30]C/676, Brock to Prevost, July 3, 1812.
[31]Brock Papers, Prevost to Brock, July 10, 1812.
[32]C/688A, Baynes to Lethbridge, July 9, 1812.

best he could with what men and munitions could be spared. There was no possibility of sending reinforcements from Great Britain, but two battalions of infantry were already *en route* from elsewhere, one to Quebec and one to Halifax, and 10,000 muskets were being diverted to the former and 5,000 to the latter. Prevost was warned to keep his Indian allies under close control so that there would be no excesses of barbarism. But the Indians must be retained as friends; otherwise they would certainly become enemies. Bathurst's letter then got to the crux of the matter, Quebec:

Your own Military Experience and local information will make you the best judge of the mode in which those means can be applied with the greatest Prospect of ultimate success. It is sufficient for me to express my concurrence in the general Principles upon which you intend to conduct operations, by making the Defence of Quebec paramount to every other consideration, should the Threat of Invasion be put into Execution.[33]

Sherbrooke in Nova Scotia and Smyth in New Brunswick were subsequently directed to continue "cultivating an amicable and liberal Communication with the neighbouring States, & of promoting any friendly disposition which may appear to you Best calculated to rensure its Continuence."[34]

Subsequent despatches from Canada were equally encouraging. As early as July 17, and using his own discretion, Captain Charles Roberts had led his small garrison of Fort St. Joseph and the local fur traders and Indians to a bloodless victory over the American garrison of Fort Michilimackinac. Receipt of this news at York persuaded Brock to lead 50 regulars and 250 militia to Amherstburg, which had been menaced since July 12 when Brigadier-General Hull had crossed the river from Detroit. In turn, receipt of these two items of news persuaded Hull to retreat back across the river to Detroit, and on August 16 he surrendered his army and Detroit without a shot being fired. Undoubtedly Hull had been influenced in his actions by Brock's hint that "the numerous body of Indians who have attached themselves to my troops will be beyond control the moment the contest commences."[35] Such a suggestion had earlier been enough to convince the American commander of Fort Michilimackinac of the wisdom of surrendering his defenceless position at once, and this veiled threat of an Indian massacre would be employed again by

---

[33]C.O. 43/23, Bathurst to Prevost, Aug. 10, 1812.
[34]C.O. 217/90, Bathurst to Sherbrooke, Aug. 10 and Sept. 30, 1812.
[35]Tupper, *The Life and Correspondence of Major-General Sir Isaac Brock*, 246.

British officers. Since the Americans had already abandoned Fort Dearborn, on the site of the present city of Chicago, the only remaining
American post in the Old Northwest was the tiny Fort Wayne on the
Maumee River. The western Indians were now convinced that the British
meant business, and the inhabitants of Upper Canada were encouraged
to think that a successful defence was possible. The most rabid of the
American-born settlers had already fled to the United States; the
remainder decided to keep their opinions to themselves.

Meanwhile, and upon receipt of word that the controversial Orders in
Council had been repealed, Sir George Prevost had sent his Adjutant
General, Colonel Edward Baynes, to arrange an armistice with Major-
General Dearborn. Agreement by Dearborn, on August 9, that the United
States was hardly likely to want to continue a needless war was
undoubtedly influenced by the fact that his own preparations had not
advanced sufficiently to make offensive operations feasible. Yet the best
he was empowered to do on his own authority was to order his
subordinates to confine themselves to defensive measures until President
Madison's pleasure should be known. This was good enough for Prevost,
who explained the advantages gained in a letter of August 24 to Bathurst:

> A suspension of hostilities . . . on a considerable portion of the extremely extensive
> line of Frontier which I have to defend has enabled me rapidly to strengthen the
> Flank attacked. The decided superiority I have obtained on the Lakes in conse-
> quence of the precautionary measures adopted during the last winter has permitted
> me to move without interruption, independently of the arrangement, both Troops
> & supplies of every description towards Amherstburg, while those for Genl. Hull
> having several hundred miles of wilderness to pass before they can reach Detroit,
> are exposed, to be harassed and destroyed by the Indians. Another consequence
> of the Mission of Col. Baynes and of the arrangement resulting from it, has been
> a Discovery of the inability of the Government of the United States to overrun the
> Canadas & of their unprepared state for carrying on the war with vigour; this has
> become so manifest that His Majesty's Subjects in both Provinces are beginning
> to feel an increased confidence in the Government protecting them, and as the
> means & resources which have been displayed appear to have far exceeded their
> expectations, so has it effectually secured their best exertions for the defence of
> their Country against any tumultuary force. In the mean time from a partial
> suspension of hostilities I am enabled to improve & augment my resources against
> an Invasion, whilst the Enemy distracted by Party broils & intrigues are obliged
> to remain supine & to witness daily the diminution of the Force they had so much
> difficulty in collecting.[36]

Brock received news of the ceasefire while returning to the Niagara
frontier from Detroit. "However wise and politic the measure must be
admitted to be," he wrote to Bathurst, "the Indians who cannot enter into

[36]C.O. 42/147, Prevost to Bathurst, Aug. 24, 1812.

our views, will naturally feel disheartened and suspicious of our intentions. Should hostilities recommence I much fear the influence the British possess over them will be found diminished."[37] Prevost's action was to be lauded by Carmichael-Smyth in a confidential submission to the Duke of Wellington in 1825:

It has been said that General Brock, after his return to the Niagara frontier, on the 24th August, might have immediately taken Fort Niagara, which would have had the happiest effects upon the war. General Brock's force was not more than 1,200 men upon the Niagara River, one-half of whom were militia. The Americans had 6,300. Offensive operations were, therefore, not likely to have been undertaken by the British. The capture of the fort at Niagara could not, moreover, at any rate, even if it had taken place, have prevented the Americans from passing the Niagara, above the Falls, between the Chippeway and Fort Erie, or below the Falls, from Lewis Town to Queen's Town. In fact, it would, in General Brock's possession, have been rather an inconvenience, compelling him to deprive himself of 300 or 400 men from his already too small disposable force for its garrison. In defensive warfare, delay is everything. The war was essentially defensive on the part of the British.[38]

President Madison, however, disallowed Dearborn's arrangement with Prevost. Hostilities were resumed on September 4, 1812.

Meanwhile the arrival of the 1st Battalion of the 1st Royal Scots at Quebec made it possible for Prevost to replace the 49th Regiment at Montreal and send it to Kingston during the month of August "for the preservation of the communication between Upper and Lower Canada, thereby securing in an extreme case of being attacked by an overwhelming force, a retreat for the Regulars, & Loyalists embodied" towards Quebec.[39] This movement was phased over several weeks, with the companies serving as armed escort for convoys of *bateaux* loaded with supplies. Colonel John Vincent of the 49th Regiment assumed the command at Kingston, and Colonel Lethbridge moved to Prescott whence he was to superintend the flank companies of militia stationed at the several convoy staging points along the upper St. Lawrence River.

Brock made an urgent request to Prevost on September 6 for reinforcements for the Niagara frontier, and Prevost's reply was not open to misinterpretation. "I have already afforded you reinforcements to the full extent of my ability," he wrote on September 14, "you must not, therefore, expect a further supply of men from hence until I shall receive from

[37]C.O. 42/352, Brock to Bathurst, Aug. 29, 1812.
[38]Sir James Carmichael, ed., *Précis of the Wars in Canada, from 1775 to the Treaty of Ghent in 1814. With Political and Military Reflections*, by the late Maj.-Gen. Sir James Carmichael-Smyth (London, 1862), 141–2.
[39]C/1218, Prevost to Brock, July 27, 1812.

England a considerable increase to the present regular force in this province [Lower Canada]; the posture of affairs, particularly on this frontier, requires every soldier who is in the country."[40] At the moment there were about 4,500 regulars, fencibles, and select embodied militia in front of Montreal. Should the situation continue to appear serious, Prevost suggested that Brock abandon Detroit and withdraw the greater number of Colonel Henry Procter's troops to the Niagara frontier "instead of taking them from Colonel Vincent, whose regular force ought not, on any account, to be diminished."

Vincent had, however, already answered a frantic request from Brock for reinforcements by sending forward from Kingston six companies of the 49th Regiment, the two flank companies of the Royal Newfoundland Regiment, and a detachment of the 10th Royal Veteran Battalion. By the time they arrived Brock was feeling more optimistic, so he sent the Royal Newfoundland Fencibles to Detroit, which he decided should be retained, and the 10th Royal Veterans to Michilimackinac.

American invasion of the Niagara Peninsula finally came on October 13. Brock was killed early in the ensuing Battle of Queenston Heights, but his successor, Major-General Roger Hale Sheaffe, successfully counter-attacked the enemy and forced the survivors to surrender. American failure had been virtually guaranteed by the refusal of the New York militia to cross the river and defend the United States by being outside it. Further American attempts at crossing the Niagara River were made on November 28 and 30, but neither officers nor men were ready to act in a determined manner and the result was ignominious failure.

Dearborn's much heralded advance against Montreal had fizzled out a week earlier, on November 23, because his militia refused to enter Lower Canada. The need for experienced officers and at least a nucleus of trained regulars might not yet be appreciated in Washington, but the British Government was well aware of their importance for Prevost's conduct of a successful defence of the Canadas. Bathurst's letter of November 16, 1812, had included a reference to the importance of the Army:

In estimating however the force under your Command as compared with that of the Enemy, I cannot so entirely confine myself to numerical Calculation, as to put out of the Question the vast superiority which the general composition & discipline of the British Army supported as it is by the good disposition of all classes of the inhabitants must give to any Military operation against an American Force acting beyond their frontiers.[41]

---

[40]Brock Papers, Prevost to Brock, Sept. 14, 1812.
[41]C.O. 43/23, Bathurst to Prevost, Nov. 16, 1812.

Unfortunately the naval situation on the Great Lakes was not nearly so satisfactory. The Provincial Marine's brig *Queen Charlotte* and schooner *General Hunter* had been usefully employed in Brock's operation against Detroit, but on the night of October 9 a small party of American sailors led by Lieutenant Jessie D. Elliott, U.S.N., had burned the brig *Detroit*, surrendered by Hull, and made off with the schooner *Caledonia* from under the guns of Fort Erie, placing in jeopardy its hitherto undisputed naval command of Lake Erie. The makeshift war vessels that Lieutenant Elliott was arming at Buffalo were, however, much less of a threat to the Provincial Marine than the squadron which Commodore Isaac Chauncey, U.S.N., was assembling at Sackets Harbor for service on Lake Ontario. On November 10 Chauncey's brig and six armed schooners chased the Provincial Marine's corvette *Royal George* into Kingston harbour and then exchanged fire with the shore batteries for over two hours. No damage of a serious nature was suffered by either side, but none of the Provincial Marine's vessels ventured out of Kingston for the balance of the navigation season, and Chauncey's blockading squadron must therefore be credited with having secured naval command of Lake Ontario.[42]

The emphasis placed by Prevost on the need for naval supremacy on the Great Lakes and Lake Champlain induced the British Government to put the Admiralty in charge of marine operations for 1813. The appointments of Commodore and Commander-in-Chief were given to Captain Sir James Lucas Yeo, R.N., who had spent twenty of his thirty years of life at sea and was a veteran of many small ship actions. Although Yeo was responsible directly to the Admiralty in London, he was to "cooperate most cordially" with Prevost and not undertake "any operations without the full concurrence and approbation" of him or his principal subordinates.[43] The Admiralty despatched nearly 500 officers and seamen to provide nucleus crews. Militarily Prevost's strength was scheduled to be almost doubled during the year by the addition of one cavalry and seven infantry regiments, companies of Royal Artillery, Royal Artillery Drivers, and Royal Sappers and Miners, and reinforcement drafts for the existing four companies of artillery and the regular battalions of infantry. A number of small corps of volunteers were recruited in each of Upper and Lower Canada for eighteen months' service or the duration of the war. The British Government also arranged that Admiral of the Blue Sir John Borlase Warren, Commander-in-Chief of the North American and West Indian Stations, should attempt a diversion in Prevost's favour by

[42]C. P. Stacey, "Commodore Chauncey's Attack on Kingston Harbour, November 10, 1812," *Canadian Historical Review*, XXXIII (June, 1951).
[43]C/729 contains a copy of Yeo's Commission, dated March 19, 1813.

harrying the American coast with a landing force of soldiers and marines from his fleet. It will be remembered that during the *Chesapeake* crisis of 1807, Vice-Admiral Berkeley had suggested such a course of action to Lord Bathurst who had then been President of the Board of Trade. The scene of operations now proposed was Chesapeake Bay and the Delaware River, the ports and harbours of which were placed under blockade "in a most strict and rigorous manner" by Admiral Warren on February 6, 1813.[44] Four days later, in far away Portugal, the Marquess of Wellington expressed his opinion of the over-all strategy being followed in a letter to Bathurst:

> I am very glad to find that you are going to reinforce Sir G. Prevost, and I only hope that troops will go in time; and that Sir George will not be induced by any hopes of trifling advantages to depart from a strong defensive system. He may depend upon it that he will not be strong enough either in men or means, to establish himself in any conquest he might make. The attempt would only weaken him, and his losses augment the spirits and hopes of the enemy, even if not attended by worse consequences; whereas by the other system, he will throw the difficulties and risk upon them, and they will most probably be foiled.[45]

Spring would be at hand, however, before all or even any of this information could reach Prevost at Quebec. Despatches had to travel across the Atlantic by sailing ship to Halifax, cross Nova Scotia and go up the St. John valley by sleigh, and finally be carried by a courier on snowshoes along the Madawaska-Temiscouata portage route to Rivière-du-Loup on the lower St. Lawrence River. This was also the route followed during February and March by the six companies of the 104th Regiment ordered from Fredericton to Quebec as an immediate reinforcement.

Meanwhile good news had arrived from Detroit, against which Brigadier-General William Henry Harrison had been advancing with 6,300 Americans of the new North Western Army. Before dawn on the morning of January 22, Colonel Procter's troops had surprised the American advanced guard at Frenchtown and had killed or captured more than 900. Harrison hastily retreated with his main force.

On February 21, when Prevost had got as far west as Prescott on his long postponed trip to Upper Canada, the garrison commander, Major

[44]Adm. 1/503, contains a copy of Warren's proclamation; see also C.O. 43/23, Bathurst to Beckwith, March 18, 1813.
[45]Lieut.-Col. Gurwood, comp., *The Dispatches of Field Marshal The Duke of Wellington, during his various campaigns in India, Denmark, Portugal, Spain, The Low Countries and France, from 1799 to 1818* (London, 1838), X, 108.

"Red George" Macdonell, sought permission to attack Ogdensburg, which had been the base for marauding American riflemen and militia for some months. Although American attempts to ambush supply convoys moving up river from Montreal had been beaten off by their armed escorts, fighting patrols from Ogdensburg had snatched not only several sentries from along the Canadian shore of the St. Lawrence for interrogation, but also a farmer and his team of horses; only a few days before a larger enemy force had crossed on the ice to nearby Brockville before dawn and surprised the whole Canadian militia garrison in bed. Prevost gave his qualified consent before departing for Kingston on the following morning. Macdonell immediately implemented an existing plan of attack and easily captured Ogdensburg. His force returned to Prescott that afternoon, but the American riflemen were too few in number to attempt reoccupation. For the balance of the war Ogdensburg was without a garrison, and there was no further serious American attempt to interfere with supply convoys of sleighs or boats travelling from Montreal to Kingston.

Northern New York State had elected members of the Federalist party to Congress, and most of its inhabitants were opposed to "Mr. Madison's War," as was the majority of New Englanders. In no time at all, residents of Prescott were shopping in Ogdensburg under the protection of a flag of truce, while the more affluent of the neutral-minded Americans crossed the river to dine with Macdonell. Other Americans came to Prescott to sell their beef, flour, and other provisions for the higher prices offered by William Gilkinson, a local merchant who had been appointed a purchasing agent by the British Army's Commissariat Department.[46]

Following his return to Montreal in mid-March, Prevost ordered a considerable troop movement to Upper Canada, because he now knew that he would begin receiving reinforcements as soon as the St. Lawrence River was free of ice. But, on April 26, while Kingston harbour was still ice-bound, Chauncey's squadron sailed across Lake Ontario with 1,700 of Dearborn's troops to attempt the capture of York. This was easily accomplished on the following morning because Major-General Sir Roger Sheaffe had withdrawn his outnumbered regular troops towards Kingston to avoid suffering unnecessary casualties which could not be readily replaced.[47] At Kingston Sheaffe was joined on May 15 by Lieutenant-General Sir George Prevost and Commodore Sir James Yeo who had

[46]J. Mackay Hitsman, "David Parish and the War of 1812," *Military Affairs,* XXVI (Winter, 1962–63).
[47]C. P. Stacey, *The Battle of Little York* (Toronto, 1963).

hurried there from Quebec as soon as the bad news had been received from York.

Yeo realized that Chauncey's naval squadron on Lake Ontario mounted more 32-pr. and 18-pr. long guns than the corvette and vessels of the Provincial Marine whose main armament was carronades which could fire cannon balls of equal size but only for lesser ranges of 400 to 600 yards. Once Chauncey's new corvette was completed and armed with 26 long 24-pr. guns, his squadron would be too strong for Yeo to attack. Therefore Yeo wrote to the Admiralty on May 26 that he would "put to sea" while the opposing navies were otherwise roughly even, "as the possession of Upper Canada must depend on whoever can maintain the Naval Superiority on Lake Ontario."[48] Prevost's letter to Bathurst was equally pointed about the fact that the holding of Upper Canada could never be entrusted to its population:

The growing discontent & undissembled dissatisfaction of the Mass of the People of Upper Canada, in consequence of the effects of the Militia Laws upon a population thinly scattered over an extensive range of Country, whose zeal was exhausted & whose exertions had brought want and ruin to the doors of many, & had in various instances produced a considerable Emigration of Settlers to the United States from whence most of them originally came, have compelled me for the preservation of that Province to bring forward my best and reserved Soldiers to enable me to support the positions we hold on the Niagara and Detroit Frontier. I have been also induced to adopt this measure from the further consideration that the Militia have been considerably weakened by the frequent desertion of even the well disposed part of them to their farms, for the purpose of getting seed into the ground before the short summer of this Country has too far advanced.[49]

When Prevost received intelligence at Kingston on May 26 that Chauncey's fleet was once again absent from Sackets Harbor the opportunity to create a diversion by a landing there was too good to miss. Had this landing of the British troops from Yeo's vessels not been delayed by an offshore breeze, success might have been achieved. As it was, the defenders of Sackets Harbor received some reinforcement and a doughty new commander in Major-General Jacob Brown of the New York militia. Prevost's decision that the attack against the forts could not succeed and that withdrawal was indicated is actually supported by Brown's own despatch: "Had not Prevost retreated most rapidly under the guns of his vessels . . . he would never have returned to Kingston."[50]

[48]Adm. 1/2736, Yeo to Croker, May 26, 1813.
[49]C.O. 42/150, Prevost to Bathurst, May 26, 1813.
[50]RG 107 (M 221), 51, Brown to Armstrong, June 1, 1813.

Meanwhile Chauncey's squadron had supported a successful American attack on Fort George on the morning of May 25. Brigadier-General John Vincent decided that there was nothing to be gained by risking heavy casualties. He ordered all the British garrisons along the Niagara frontier to retreat on Burlington and dismissed the local militia to their homes.[51] Commodore Yeo subsequently took his squadron to the head of Lake Ontario with reinforcements and supplies for Vincent's 1,600 regulars. On the night of June 5 Lieutenant-Colonel John Harvey led about half of these in a surprise attack on the American advanced guard encamped at Stoney Creek. The fighting was inconclusive, but two American brigadier-generals were captured, and the advanced guard retreated. The Americans soon voluntarily vacated the whole of the Niagara Peninsula except for Fort George.

Chauncey and Dearborn had certainly had operational successes. They had captured York, though they had abandoned it after burning the legislative and other public buildings, and they still held Fort George. In both instances, however, the British troops had managed to extricate themselves without suffering heavy casualties. Had Chauncey and Dearborn pursued the operational plan approved earlier in Washington, which called for the capture of Kingston as the first objective, the campaign of 1813 might have gone far differently. Nearly one hundred years later Admiral Mahan wrote, in his two volume study of this war, that the capture of Kingston would have solved "at a single stroke every difficulty" in the inland theatre of operations:

No other harbour was tenable as a naval station; with its fall and the destruction of shipping and forts, would go the control of the lake, even if the place itself were not permanently held. Deprived thus of the water communications, the enemy [i.e., British] could retain no position to the westward, because neither reinforcements nor supplies could reach them.[52]

Fortunately for the British, both Americans were timid commanders. Chauncey was an excellent organizer and had created a sizable squadron in an amazingly short time, but time would demonstrate that he was loath to endanger his creations in battle. The elderly Dearborn, forgetting his creditable days as a junior officer during the American Revolutionary War, had been encouraged to avoid positive action by his later success as a politician.

[51]C/678, Vincent to Prevost, May 28, 1813.
[52]A. T. Mahan, *Sea Power in its Relations to the War of 1812* (London, 1905), II, 30.

Prevost took advantage of the ensuing lull in the early summer of 1813 to switch his senior subordinates. A letter of June 23 to the Duke of York complained that they had not always measured up and proposed a new role for de Rottenburg:

The support I have received from the General Officers in Command since the death of Major-General Sir Isaac Brock, I am sorry to say has not always corresponded with my expectations. Circumstances indicating an insufficiency on the part of Major-General Sir R. H. Sheaffe to the arduous task of defending Upper Canada, have induced me to place Major-General De Rottenburg in the Military Comd and Civil administration of that province . . . except Sir John Sherbrooke [in Nova Scotia] the Major-General is the only General Officer of high character and established reputation serving in the Army in the North American Provinces, to whom I could entrust this important duty, without embarrassing myself with it to the prejudice of the other possessions of His Majesty committed to my care.[53]

Prevost still had high hopes for naval operations on Lake Ontario despite the advantage accruing to the Americans after Chauncey's new 26-gun brig was ready for action on July 20:

It is scarcely possible that a decisive naval action can be avoided, and I therefore humbly hope that His Royal Highness, the Prince Regent, will approve of it being courted by us, as a necessary measure for the preservation of the advanced positions of this army, which I have determined to maintain until the naval ascendancy on Lake Ontario is decided, convinced that a retrograde movement would eventually endanger the safety of a large proportion of the troops in Upper Canada and convert that province into the seat of war.[54]

Yet a decisive naval action *was* avoided: by Yeo who was unwilling to have his vessels blown out of the water at long range by Chauncey's long guns, and by Chauncey who was unwilling to face the British carronades at close quarters. In spite of Chauncey's loss of four schooners during the manœuvring on Lake Ontario in early August, nothing was settled. Yeo's inability to destroy Chauncey's squadron made it impossible for him to co-operate with Prevost's land forces who were making an attempt to reduce Fort George. Prevost was unwilling to risk the casualties, which a direct assault would otherwise incur,[55] and returned to Kingston late in August, leaving the inhabitants of the Niagara Peninsula and the rank and file of the army to think what they liked.

[53]C/1220, Prevost to York, June 23, 1813.
[54]C.O. 42/151, Prevost to Bathurst, Aug. 1, 1813.
[55]*Ibid.*, Aug. 25, 1813.

Naval command on Lake Erie went to the United States Navy as a result of the destruction at Put-in Bay, on September 10, of an ill-equipped and ill-manned squadron with which Lieutenant R. H. Barclay, R.N., had been hounded into battle by a newly promoted Major-General Henry Procter. Consequently, supplies could no longer reach Procter's army by water from Long Point, and he was forced to abandon the whole Detroit frontier. The lethargic manner in which this retreat towards Niagara was conducted enabled the American army of Major-General William Henry Harrison to overtake and rout the dispirited redcoats and Indians near Moravian Town on October 5, 1813.[56]

The first reports of the defeat to reach Kingston convinced Major-General de Rottenburg, administering the government of Upper Canada, that everything to the westward would have to be abandoned. However, news that Harrison's militia had insisted on returning home and that his regulars were back at Amherstburg soon persuaded de Rottenburg that York and Burlington should be held "so long as may be practicable with reference to supplies of provisions, &c."[57] Fortunately de Rottenburg's situation in November was strengthened by the failure of an American two-pronged offensive then being directed against Montreal. On August 8 the Secretary of War in Washington had spelled out a plan whereby Kingston should either be captured by direct action from Sackets Harbor or be cut off from communication with Montreal by an army moving down the St. Lawrence River and securing both its banks in the vicinity of the present town of Morrisburg. The rest of this American army could then continue against Montreal, joined by a lesser army advancing from the Lake Champlain region. Major-General James Wilkinson was as reluctant to attack Kingston as his predecessor, Dearborn, had been and opted for the alternative plan. On October 26, however, the advanced guard of Major-General Wade Hampton's lesser army was repulsed at Châteauguay, which proved to be a convenient excuse for him to retreat on Plattsburgh. Wilkinson descended the St. Lawrence River with his army in early November, but he insisted on going into winter quarters at French Mills after his rear guard had suffered a reverse at Crysler's Farm on November 11.

Since American strength along the Niagara frontier had been dangerously reduced to support Wilkinson's expedition, the Americans gave up Fort George on December 10. Unfortunately the American commander first took it upon himself to order the burning of Newark and most of

[56]Hitsman, *The Incredible War of 1812*, 148–57.
[57]C/681, de Rottenburg to Vincent, Nov. 1, 1813.

Queenston after turning out the inhabitants into a cold and snowy night. On December 16 a new Administrator for Upper Canada, Lieutenant-General Gordon Drummond, reached the Niagara Peninsula. Three days later he sent parties of British regulars across the river to capture Fort Niagara and to burn the village of Lewiston. On December 29 British regulars and Canadian militia burned Buffalo and Black Rock. Prevost issued a proclamation of January 12, 1814, deprecating the need for such action, but assuring the inhabitants of Upper Canada that they would be "powerfully assisted at all points by the troops under His Excellency's command, and that prompt and signal vengeance will be taken for every fresh departure by the Enemy, from that system of warfare which ought alone to subsist between enlightened and civilized nations."[58]

Prevost learned at the year's end that his efforts were still appreciated in London; but yet Bathurst's despatch of December 15, 1813, took him to task for complaining about having received no definite instructions. Distant campaigns could not be directed from London on the basis of intelligence that would be several months old by the time orders could get to Canada, so he had had to be given discretion as the obvious expedient

. . . to place at your disposal such means of defence as the Exigency of the Service required, & to leave their direction or distribution to your own discretion, more especially as the correct View which you expressed on the two points most essential to the Defence of the Canadas, the maintenance of a Naval Superiority on the Lakes, & the uninterrupted Communication with our Indian allies had at an early period received the Sanction of H. M. Government, & had been repeatedly called to your attention during the course of the preceding campaign.[59]

In view of what had happened as a consequence of the Battle of Lake Erie, Bathurst now approved Yeo's caution in husbanding his ships:

. . . the discretion of Sir James Yeo in not courting an action [on Lake Ontario] unless under circumstances which would afford a fair prospect of a successful issue. The preservation of the fleet under his Command is (next to the destruction of that of the Enemy) the object most essential for the Security of Canada. So long as it remains entire the Enemy are precluded from attempting with any hopes of Success the attack for which their means are preparing & their Troops collected—of the Numbers of the Enemy's force, tho' considerably increased, I confess that I feel but little apprehension, when I consider the Number & Composition of the force by which they will be opposed.

By this time Napoleon had been so badly beaten in Germany by the Allies that the end of the long European war was in sight. President

[58]*Quebec Gazette*, Jan. 13, 1814.
[59]C.O. 43/23, Bathurst to Prevost, Dec. 13, 1813.

Madison now agreed to a British suggestion that commissioners be appointed to negotiate a peace settlement. None of these events was yet known to Prevost, who knew only that he could not be reinforced from abroad until the St. Lawrence reopened for navigation. His 15,000 regulars and fencibles included many convalescents and all were weary from the previous campaign; only the 1,600 Royal Marines forwarded from Halifax during the previous autumn were in good condition. The 2/8th Regiment then marched overland from New Brunswick to Quebec, as a first reinforcement, following the route taken by the 104th Regiment of Foot during the previous winter. Commander Edward Collier, R.N., led 216 officers and men of the Royal Navy and Royal Marines on a similar march, but continued on to Kingston where they were needed to help man Yeo's new frigates H.M.S. *Prince Regent* and H.M.S. *Princess Charlotte*. These naval officers and men had been found by laying up four small war vessels at Halifax and by asking for volunteers from other vessels wintering there.

Once *Prince Regent* and *Princess Charlotte* were launched in mid-April, giving the Royal Navy undisputed superiority on Lake Ontario, Yeo and Drummond urged upon Prevost the desirability of attacking Sackets Harbor to destroy the larger frigate and brig under construction there. Prevost conceded that the proposal had merit but stated quite emphatically in a letter of April 30 that he could not risk so large a portion of his available regulars in any gamble:

... the force in this Country is insufficient to enable me to concentrate at any one point in Upper Canada, the number of regulars you require for this important Service, without stripping Lower Canada of nearly the whole of those that are at present in it, and committing its defence to provincials and Militia. The views of His Majesty's Government respecting the mode of conducting the war with America, do not justify me exposing too much on one shake. It is by wary measures and occasional daring enterprizes with apparently disproportionate means, that the character of the war has been sustained, and from that policy I am not disposed to depart.[60]

Yeo and Drummond thereupon quickly made up their minds to capture the less strongly held Oswego with their existing forces and seize the naval stores being held there until the Americans could move them in small boats along the American shore of Lake Ontario to Sackets Harbor. They experienced little difficulty capturing Oswego on May 6 and took back to Kingston with them large quantities of stores that were in short supply there, but the guns for Chauncey's new frigate and brig had eluded

[60]C.O. 42/355, Prevost to Drummond, April 30, 1814.

them because they were being held at the falls some twelve miles up the Oswego River. As a result, once the additions to Chauncey's squadron were seaworthy, the Americans would soon have undisputed command of Lake Ontario until such time as the monster ship of the line now under construction at Kingston for Yeo should be ready for action. The ship, which Yeo was able to construct in the comparative isolation of his command, would carry more guns than H.M.S. *Victory*, Nelson's flagship at Trafalgar.

A letter of June 21, 1814, from Drummond requested reinforcements to meet an American threat building up along the Niagara frontier; it also met with a curt refusal by Prevost. Drummond was correct in believing that American activity in the Plattsburgh area was not intended to lead to offensive action, but Prevost's announced policy was to continue the bulk of his force in front of Montreal. Prevost scribbled on the bottom of this letter: "Very much obliged to Genl. D. for his opinion; unfortunately for him it is not founded on fact as not one soldier intended for U.C. has been prevented moving forward by the Enemy's Demonstrations in the vicinity of Odle Town."[61]

By this time Prevost knew of Napoleon's abdication on April 11, 1814, and that it would make possible the transfer of large numbers of artillery and infantry from the Duke of Wellington's army to North America. He did not know, of course, what was being planned in London. As early as January 28 Bathurst had sought Wellington's opinion. The Duke had candidly admitted from the south of France on February 22 that he knew little about American affairs or topography. Yet his views were most cogent:

I believe that the defence of Canada, and the co-operation of the Indians, depends upon the navigation of the lakes; and I see that both Sir G. Prevost and Commodore Barclay complain of the want of the crews of two sloops of war. Any offensive operations founded upon Canada must be preceded by the establishment of a naval superiority on the lakes.

But even if we had that superiority, I should doubt our being able to do more than secure the points on those lakes at which the Americans could have access. In such countries as America, very extensive, thinly peopled, and producing but little food in proportion to their extent, military operations by large bodies are impracticable, unless the party carrying them on has the uninterrupted use of a navigable river, or very extensive means of land transport, which such a country can rarely supply.

I conceive, therefore, that were your army larger than the proposed augmenta-

---

[61]C/683, Drummond to Prevost, June 21, 1814.

tion would make it, you could not quit the lakes; and, indeed, you would be tied
to them the more necessarily in proportion as your army would be large.

Then, as to landings upon the coast, they are liable to the same objections,
though to a greater degree, than an offensive operation founded upon Canada.
You may go to a certain extent, as far as a navigable river or your means of
transport will enable you to subsist, provided your force is sufficiently large compared with that which the enemy will oppose to you. But I do not know where
you could carry on such an operation which would be so injurious to the Americans
as to force them to sue for peace, which is what one would wish to see.[62]

It was June 3 before Bathurst was able to send detailed secret instruc-
tions to Prevost, and they were not received until the second week in July.
They indicated that about 15,000 British regulars would be sent to
Canada, led by four of Wellington's best brigade commanders. The British
Government had two objects in mind: the first to guarantee the safety of
Canada; the second to secure the basis for a boundary rectification and
to enable the British peace commissioners being sent to Ghent to argue
uti possidetis. Bathurst's instructions, however, were intended to tell
Prevost only what he needed to know of the British grand strategy to
conduct his own campaign, for the first time as an offensive one:

. . . His Majesty's Government conceive that the Canadas will not only be protected for the time being against any attack which the enemy may have the means
of making, but it will enable you to commence offensive operations on the Enemy's
Frontier before the close of this Campaign. At the same time it is by no means the
intention of His Majesty's Government to encourage such forward movements into
the Interior of the American Territory as might commit the safety of the Force
placed under your command. The object of your operations will be; first, to give
immediate protection: secondly to obtain if possible ultimate security to His
Majesty's Possessions in America.

The entire destruction of Sackets harbour and the Naval Establishments on Lake
Erie and Lake Champlain come under the first description.

The Maintenance of Fort Niagara and so much of the adjacent Territory as
may be deemed necessary: and the occupation of Detroit and the Michigan
Country come under the second.

If our success shall enable us to terminate the war by the retention of the
Fort of Niagara, and the restoration of Detroit and the whole of the Michigan
Country to the Indians, the British Frontier will be materially improved. Should
there be any advanced position on that part of our frontier which extends towards
Lake Champlain, the occupation of which would materially tend to the security
of the Province, you will if you deem it expedient expel the Enemy from it, and
occupy it by detachments of the Troops under your command, always however
taking care not to expose His Majesty's Forces to being cut off by too extended
a line of advance.

---

[62]Gurwood, *The Dispatches of Field Marshal The Duke of Wellington*, XI,
525–6.

If you should not consider it necessary to call to your assistance the two Regiments which are to proceed in the first instance to Halifax, Sir J. Sherbrooke will receive instructions to occupy so much of the District of Maine as will ensure an uninterrupted intercourse between Halifax and Quebec.[63]

Four other regiments from Europe would be employed in direct operations against the Atlantic coast of the United States. A "considerable force" would also be concentrated at Cork for employment in "a more serious attack on some part of the Coasts of the United States" later in the year. "These operations," Prevost was advised, "will not fail to effect a powerful diversion in your favour."

On July 12 Prevost acknowledged receipt of these instructions but pointed out that some time must elapse before he could act on them. All that he could do at the moment was send three regiments to aid Drummond in Upper Canada.

Had reinforcements arrived a month or six weeks earlier, while Yeo's squadron still had the naval advantage on Lake Ontario, it would have been possible to prevent the American advance into the Niagara Peninsula and thus avoid the hard-fought engagement at Lundy's Lane on July 25 and the casualties incurred while trying unsuccessfully to recapture Fort Erie. Unless complete naval command was assured on Lake Ontario and Lake Champlain, however, Prevost had to remain on the defensive.[64] Prevost, in a despatch of August 14, explained that "the Naval Ascendency possessed by the Enemy on Lake Ontario enables him to perform in two days what our troops going from Kingston to reinforce the Right Division at Niagara require from Sixteen to Twenty of severe marching to accomplish; their Men arrive fresh whilst ours are fatigued, and with an exhausted equipment; the route from Kingston to the Niagara Frontier exceeds Two Hundred and Fifty Miles and passes in several places through a Tract of Country impenetrable for the conveyance of Extensive supplies."[65] No move could be made against Sackets Harbor as long as Chauncey was able to blockade Kingston harbour. Once Yeo's new ship was ready, in early September, naval command of Lake Ontario would change hands automatically because Chauncey would not risk battle against it. The 37-gun corvette being built at Isle aux Noix would be ready by September 15, by which date Wellington's veteran troops would be ready for an attack on Plattsburgh on Lake Champlain.

The North American Station was short 3,000 seamen, according to the

[63]C.O. 43/23, Bathurst to Prevost, June 3, 1814.
[64]C.O. 42/157, Prevost to Bathurst, July 12, 1814.
[65]*Ibid.*, Aug. 14, 1814.

Naval Chronicle, so none could be sent inland from Halifax to man the new British warships at Kingston and Isle aux Noix. Eventually, however, the Port Captain at Quebec was persuaded to order 400 seamen to Kingston from among the crews of the fifteen naval transports that had brought Wellington's veterans from Europe; a further 150 seamen were ordered to Isle aux Noix. Personnel of the 2nd Battalion of Royal Marines, disbanded for this purpose, and drafts from regiments of the line in Canada were also converted into seamen.[66]

Complete success attended the British diversions attempted against the Atlantic coast of the United States, which had been placed under strict and rigorous blockade by Vice-Admiral of the Red Sir Alexander Cochrane's proclamation of April 25, 1814. On the evening of August 24 a combined British military-naval force captured Washington and set fire to the Capitol and other public buildings. During the first two weeks in September a similar but smaller expedition occupied Maine as far as the Penobscot River. This made possible the resumption of the New England coastal trade with New Brunswick and Nova Scotia and ensured overland communication with Quebec by the shortest and most direct route.

In the Old Northwest there had been further Anglo-Canadian successes. On July 20 a small expedition forced the surrender of the American garrison of the trading post at Prairie du Chien on the Mississippi River, in what is now Wisconsin. On August 4 the garrison of Fort Michilimackinac defeated an American expedition sent from Detroit to effect its recapture. Two schooners which continued to blockade the island were captured by boarding parties during the first week in September, providing the Royal Navy with a makeshift force on Lake Huron.

All of the reinforcements from Wellington's army having arrived in Canada by mid-August to increase Prevost's effective strength to 29,437 other ranks, he prepared a division of 10,351 troops for an advance against Plattsburgh. This advance began on August 31, instead of a few days later when the new flagship of the accompanying naval squadron would have been ready for action. On September 11 Prevost goaded the much younger and junior Captain George Downie, R.N., into action for a supposedly combined operation against Plattsburgh. The military attack was delayed because the troops took the wrong road and was called off as soon as Downie's squadron was battered into submission at close range by a roughly comparable American squadron whose principal armament consisted of carronades. "Under the circumstances," Prevost reported to Bathurst, "I had to determine whether I should consider my own Fame

[66]Documents on C/733.

by gratifying the Ardor of the Troops in persevering in the attack, or consult the more substantial interests of my Country by withdrawing the Army which was yet uncrippled for the security of these Provinces."[67] A very disgruntled army began retreating into Lower Canada that night. Accustomed to victory, they must have realized instinctively what Wellington should have suggested to Bathurst: now that the tide had definitely turned and the British Army was strong enough in Canada to take the offensive, the defensively minded Prevost should have been provided with an aggressive senior officer to command his field army.

Prevost next visited Kingston. At long last Commodore Yeo had regained naval superiority on Lake Ontario with the completion of his 112-gun ship of the line, christened H.M.S. *St. Lawrence*, but so much of the stores tediously brought up the St. Lawrence River had been expended on her that there was not enough to equip an expedition to attack Sackets Harbor. Furthermore, Prevost's letter of October 11 to Bathurst suggested, the navigation season was drawing to a close. As a result the *St. Lawrence* merely escorted a convoy of schooners to Fort George with much needed supplies for Drummond's army.[68]

By this time the British Government was beginning to worry about the wisdom of prolonging the war in North America when the revival of hostilities in Europe was becoming a distinct possibility. The Prime Minister again sought Wellington's opinion. His reply of November 9 was very much to the point in his evaluation of the importance of the Lakes and the necessity of the holding operation which had been maintained successfully:

I have already told you and Lord Bathurst that I feel no objection to going to America, though I don't promise to myself much success there. I believe there are troops enough there for the defence of Canada forever, and even for the accomplishment of any reasonable offensive plan that could be formed from the Canadian frontier. I am quite sure that all the American armies of which I have ever read would not beat out of a field of battle the troops that went from Bordeaux last summer, if common precautions and care were taken of them. That which appears to be wanting in America is not a General, or General Officers and troops, but a naval superiority on the Lakes. Till that superiority is acquired, it is impossible, according to my notion, to maintain an army in such a situation as to keep the enemy out of the whole frontier much less to make any conquest from the enemy, which, with those superior means might, with reasonable hopes of success, be undertaken. I may be wrong in this opinion, but I think the whole history of the war proves its truth. . . . The question is, whether we can acquire

[67]C.O. 42/157, Prevost to Bathurst, Sept. 22, 1814.
[68]*Ibid.*, Oct. 11 and 18, 1814.

this naval superiority on the Lakes. If we can't, I shall do you but little good in America; and I shall go there only to prove the truth of Prevost's defence, and to sign a peace which might as well be signed now. . . .

Considering every thing, it is my opinion that the war has been a most successful one, and highly honourable to the British arms; but from particular circumstances, such as the want of the naval superiority on the Lakes, you have not been able to carry it into the enemy's territory, notwithstanding your military success, and now undoubted military superiority, and have not even cleared your own territory of the enemy on the point of attack [Fort Erie and Fort Malden]. You cannot, then, on any principle of equality in negotiation, claim a cession of territory [northern Maine, Fort Niagara and Fort Michilimackinac] excepting in exchange for other advantages which you have in your power.[69]

The American Government was now equally convinced of the desirability of concluding peace without further haggling by its peace commissioners at Ghent: trade was at a standstill; banks were failing and paper money was being heavily discounted; only a fraction of the latest war loan was subscribed; the regular army was declining in strength because there were not enough recruits to make good its wastage; and there was a growing movement in New England for secession from the United States and creation of a separate confederation.

On Christmas Eve, 1814, both parties signed the Treaty of Ghent based on the *status quo ante bellum*. On March 1, 1815, news reached Prevost at Quebec that this Treaty had been ratified in Washington. The following day, however, he learned that his commission as Governor-in-Chief had been revoked and that he was to return to London to explain his conduct of the Plattsburgh campaign. After issuing orders to put an end to hostilities and to disband the militia, Prevost took the overland route across New Brunswick to Saint John where he boarded a ship for England. He was succeeded in the government at Quebec by Lieutenant-General Gordon Drummond. The government of Upper Canada was temporarily assumed by Major-General Sir George Murray who had been sent to Canada in the local rank of lieutenant-general so that Prevost could be verbally advised of his dismissal. Shortly thereafter Yeo was replaced as Commander-in-Chief on the inland lakes of North America by Commodore Sir Edward Owen, R.N.

On both sides of the border there was a general sigh of relief at the coming of peace.

[69]*Supplementary Despatches, Correspondence, and Memoranda of Field Marshal Arthur Duke of Wellington, K.G.* Edited by his son, the Duke of Wellington (London, 1862), IX, 425–6.

(6)

DEFENDED FRONTIER

The Treaty of Ghent provided no answer for nor indeed did it even mention the causes that had brought about the War of 1812. It was perhaps natural for people on both sides of the Canadian-American border to assume that there would probably be another war at some time in the not too distant future. Planning was therefore put in hand by senior officers on both sides. But economics, as well as war weariness, soon dominated policy-making in political circles in London and Washington.

Proposals submitted by Lieutenant-General Gordon Drummond for new fortifications to defend Upper Canada were squelched by a letter from Lord Bathurst of October 10, 1815. He was directed to "abstain from undertaking them until His Majesty's Government shall have decided upon some general plan for the future defence of the Province; their attention has already been directed to this object and it is therefore desirable that no new Fortification shall be erected which might either interfere or impede the general measures of defence which upon a further survey may be considered most eligible."[1] A suggestion to provide an alternative water route between Montreal and Kingston by building canals on the Ottawa River and the Rideau waterway would, however, be considered, since it was now known that the Americans had proposed to cut the line of the St. Lawrence River had there been a military campaign in 1815.[2] Bathurst's letter of October 10 merely directed Drummond to get "estimates of expense of the Lachine Canal, and of the Ottawa and Rideau being made navigable, in order that His Majesty's Government may decide as to the propriety of undertaking these works, either separately or simultaneously."

Drummond had been loath to give up Michilimackinac because the

---

[1]C.O. 43/23, Bathurst to Drummond, Oct. 10, 1815.
[2]C. P. Stacey, "An American Plan for a Canadian Campaign," *American Historical Review*, XLVI (January, 1941).

Indian tribes of the region had not yet concluded peace with the United States and the Montreal fur traders were claiming that its sovereignty was a matter for settlement by the Boundary Commission authorized by the Treaty of Ghent. But the Americans, in retaliation, refused to return the much more important Fort Malden at Amherstburg, and Drummond was forced to yield. On July 18 the British garrison of Michilimackinac moved to Drummond's Island, which was considered preferable as a base to the former Fort St. Joseph.[3] A year later, on July 15, 1816, Lieutenant-General Sir John Sherbrooke, the newly appointed Governor-in-Chief of British North America, ruled that the western Indians must be told "distinctly and explicitly" that the British Government would neither assist nor countenance them in any hostilities against the United States.[4]

By this time the Duke of York's orders of February 1816[5] for the disbandment of the several fencible corps in British North America had been implemented. On February 5, 1817, Bathurst wrote Sherbrooke that the regular army establishment was being reduced for both Canada and Nova Scotia because no immediate trouble was anticipated with the United States.[6] Strength returns for December 25, 1819, showed 105 officers and 2,166 other ranks of the British Army actually serving in Nova Scotia and its Dependencies. The 15th, 2/60th and 62nd Regiments of Foot were at Halifax, and smaller detachments garrisoned Annapolis, Windsor, and Fort Cumberland; the 74th Regiment was divided between Fredericton, Saint John, St. Andrew's, Charlottetown, and Sydney. Royal Artillerymen were, of course, stationed at each fort.[7] Some 3,540 other ranks were actually serving in the Canadas, but 80 of their 173 officers seem to have been absent for the winter. Apart from gunners, there were the 1/60th and 76th Regiments at Quebec, the 37th Regiment at Montreal, the 70th Regiment at Kingston, and the 68th Regiment at Fort George; small detachments from these units were at St. Johns, Isle aux Noix, Coteau-du-Lac, Prescott, Fort Erie, Fort Malden, Penetanguishene, and Drummond's Island.[8]

Bathurst's letter of February 5, 1817, had also instructed Sherbrooke to improve his militia, but there is no evidence that he took any action.[9] About a year earlier, when opening the Legislature of Upper Canada on

[3]A. L. Burt, *The United States, Great Britain and British North America* (Toronto, 1940), 374.
[4]C.O. 42/167, Addison to McDouall, July 15, 1816.
[5]C.O. 42/168, York to Sherbrooke, Feb. 28, 1816.
[6]C.O. 43/24, Bathurst to Sherbrooke, Feb. 5, 1817.
[7]W.O. 17/2366, Distribution of the Troops serving in Nova Scotia & Its Dependencies, Dec. 25, 1819.
[8]W.O. 17/1523, General Monthly Strength Return, Canada, Dec. 25, 1819.
[9]C.O. 42/174, Sherbrooke to Bathurst, May 5, 1817.

February 6, 1816, Lieutenant-Governor Francis Gore had praised the wartime service of the militia: "Experience shows that the most disposable, and therefore the best form into which it can be moulded, so as to serve with a Regular Force, is that of Independent Companies, upon the principle on which the Flank Companies were formed in the year 1812."[10] Yet little was done in Upper Canada to continue flank companies on a volunteer basis, and the sections dealing with their organization and training were omitted from the Militia Act of 1823.[11] Since the whole United States Army now consisted of only 6,183 officers and enlisted men, and only 750 of them were stationed at posts along the Canadian-American border,[12] there was some basis for the general belief that an annual militia muster, even if it degenerated into a drunken brawl, was all the preparation for war that Canadians need make.

Congress had agreed to retain in peace time a properly balanced, if small, ocean-going navy,[13] but, as early as February 27, 1815, it passed an act authorizing President Madison to have the fresh-water navy laid up or sold, except for such vessels as he should deem necessary to enforce the revenue laws.[14] The unfinished ships at Sackets Harbor were housed over to protect them from the weather; the frigates and larger war vessels there and on Lake Champlain and Lake Erie were either laid up or dismantled.

Because there was a shortage of personnel and also for economic reasons the Royal Navy laid up its larger ships at Kingston and kept the rest in commission with only a few guns. Six small, armed schooners continued to handle transportation and other duties on the Upper Lakes. The gunboats of Lake Champlain were tied up at Isle aux Noix. Construction of ships and vessels at Isle aux Noix, Kingston, and Penetanguishene, which was being developed as the new naval base for the upper Great Lakes, was cancelled.[15] Nevertheless, the American Minister in London, John Quincy Adams, reported on August 29, 1815, that the British Government had determined "not only to maintain but to increase the British naval armament upon the lakes."[16] Presumably British newspapers had got wind of the fact that Commodore Sir Edward Owen was sending back from Canada reports which recommended strengthening the whole

---

[10]*York Gazette*, Feb. 10, 1816.

[11]4 Geo. IV, c. 5.

[12]*American State Papers Military Affairs* (Washington, 1832), II, 558.

[13]Harold and Margaret Sprout, *The Rise of American Naval Power* (Princeton, 1939), 88.

[14]*United States, Statutes at Large*, LXII 13th Congress, sess. 3, c. LXII.

[15]C. P. Stacey, "The Myth of the Unguarded Frontier," *American Historical Review*, LVI (October, 1950).

[16]Burt, *The United States, Great Britain and British North America*, 388.

line of the inland water frontier.[17] Naturally enough, this was much more exciting news than the fact that Owen had directed Lieutenant H. W. Bayfield, R.N., to undertake the first complete hydrographic survey and charting of the Great Lakes.

On November 15 the American Secretary of State, James Monroe, directed Adams to "propose . . . such an arrangement respecting the naval forces to be kept on the Lakes by both governments, as will demonstrate their pacific policy and secure their peace."[18] President Madison wished to limit the armed vessels to a fixed number, "and the smaller the number, the more agreeable to him; or to abstain altogether from an armed force beyond that used for the revenue."

Adams got a cautious reception from the Foreign Secretary, Lord Castlereagh, when he raised the subject on January 25, 1816. Castlereagh conceded that "keeping a number of armed vessels parading about the Lakes in time of peace . . . would be absurd,"[19] but he was well aware, as Adams knew he would be, that naval disarmament would benefit the United States far more than Great Britain and Canada. Upper Canada's only hope of survival in another war depended, as it had in 1812, on initial British naval superiority on the Great Lakes. Greater American local resources and population would permit a naval force to be built from scratch far more quickly than the Royal Navy could transport men and materials across the Atlantic and up the St. Lawrence River. Adams was wrong, however, to believe that Castlereagh's evasiveness meant rejection. He should have believed the prominent London banker, Alexander Baring, who had assured him earlier that the British Government would agree to mutual disarmament on the inland lakes as an economy measure. Fighting words were uttered in Parliament that winter, but the Marquess of Lansdowne was expressing a popular opinion in the House of Lords when on March 15, 1816, he questioned the need for a large naval force on the lakes of Canada as well as a large military garrison in British North America.[20] Adams therefore should not have been so surprised when he was called to the Foreign Office on April 9 to be told by Castlereagh that the British Government was prepared to accept reasonable American proposals for naval disarmament. It was then agreed that negotiations might be undertaken more conveniently in Washington.[21]

[17]C.O. 42/171 contains copies.
[18]Bradford Perkins, *Castlereagh and Adams: England and the United States 1812–1823* (Berkeley, 1964), 240.
[19]*Ibid.*, 241.
[20]Great Britain, House of Commons, *Debates*, 1816, XXXIII, 312.
[21]Burt, *The United States, Great Britain and British North America*, 389.

Since the British had more to lose, the American Government was
suspicious of the long delay before Charles Bagot, the British Minister in
Washington, received the necessary instructions. Undoubtedly objections
had been raised in Whitehall. Only on July 6, 1816, after Bagot had
begun his discussions, were the Admiralty's recommendations for the
naval defence of Canada sent to Lord Bathurst. This lengthy document,
and appendices, reflected the advice given by Commodore Sir Edward
Owen, who now had been replaced in Canada by his brother. The
Admiralty felt that the proposed Lachine Canal should be made wide
enough to admit a gunboat, and preferably a steam vessel. Some private
company should be encouraged to operate steam vessels on the St.
Lawrence River and Great Lakes; although designed for commercial
purposes they should be convertible into gunboats in an emergency. This
is a very interesting comment in view of the opposition that would be
made to the introduction of steam warships into the Royal Navy. Owen
believed that, in addition to maintenance of the existing naval establishment, the whole line of the water frontier should be strengthened by the
construction of further and better fortifications.[22] Sir James Yeo, writing
to the First Lord of the Admiralty on May 30, 1815, had similarly
recommended that if Upper Canada was to be defended at all a large
naval establishment should be authorized. "The preservation of Canada
by means of a Naval force on the Lakes, will, in my opinion," he had
added, however, "be an endless if not a futile undertaking."[23] Even if
the British people were willing to foot the bill for an expensive naval
race, there was agreement in Whitehall that the Americans could win
because of their greater local resources. Castlereagh was therefore ready
to recommend approval of the agreement reached by Bagot and Monroe
in early August when it finally arrived from Washington. Members of the
Cabinet were on holiday, however, and this was the excuse used to
account for the fact that it was January 31, 1817, before Castlereagh
could instruct Bagot to accept the American proposals.[24]

Agreement was formally effected by an exchange of notes rather than
a treaty. A note sent by Bagot to Richard Rush, acting head of the State
Department, on April 28, 1817, agreed that the naval force to be maintained on the "American Lakes" should henceforth be limited to the
following vessels on each side:

On Lake Ontario to one vessel not exceeding one hundred tons burthen and
armed with one eighteen-pound cannon.

[22]C.O. 42/171, Croker to Goulborn, July 6, 1816.
[23]Adm. 1/2738, Yeo to Melville, May 30, 1815.
[24]Burt, *The United States, Great Britain and British North America*, 390–4;
Perkins, *Castlereagh and Adams*, 242–3.

Arrival of a detachment of the 63rd Regiment at the temporary barracks, Peters-
ville, by E. J. Russell. *Illustrated London News*, London, March 29, 1862, 306.
Public Archives of Canada.

Royal Artillery,
1815, by
C. Hamilton
Smith, London,
1815.

Embarkation at Woolwich of the 4th Brigade of Royal Field Artillery on board the *Melbourne* for Canada. *Illustrated London News*, London, December 14, 1861, 607. *Public Archives of Canada.*

Field Officer of
Royal Engineers
and a private
sapper, by
C. Hamilton Smith,
London, 1815.

The Rideau Canal, Bytown, 1842, by W. H. Bartlett. *Public Archives of Canada.*

Storming Fort Oswego, 1814. *McCord Museum, McGill University.*

ABOVE Fort Garry, Rupert's Land, 19 March 1858, by G. Seton. *From a watercolour in the Public Archives of Canada.*

BELOW A view of Quebec from the southeast, by J. F. W. Desbarres. *From an aquatint in the Public Archives of Canada.*

The Citadel, Halifax. *Aerial photograph by the Canadian Government Travel Bureau.*

Commodore's house, Kingston, July 1815, by Emeric E. Vidal. *Royal Military College of Canada.*

ABOVE   Opening the first Welland
Canal 1829, by J. D. Kelly:
Confederation Life Collection.

BELOW   The first St. Lawrence Canal,
Coteau du Lac, 1781, by Rex Woods.
Confederation Life Collection.

Royal Engineers building the Caribou Road, 1862, by Rex Woods. *Confederation Life Collection.*

The founding of Halifax, 1749, by J. D. Kelly. *Confederation Life Collection.*

Fort Henry and Kingston. In the middle ground is Point Frederick and the site of one-time naval dockyard. *Aerial photograph by the Canadian Government Travel Bureau.*

ABOVE   Fort Henry from the air. *Canadian Government Travel Bureau.*   BELOW   The Citadel, Quebec City. *Royal Canadian Air Force, 1958.*

On the Upper Lakes to two vessels not exceeding like burthen each and armed with like force.

On the waters of Lake Champlain to one vessel not exceeding like burthen and armed with like force.

And His Royal Highness [the Prince Regent] agrees, that all other armed vessels, on these lakes shall be forthwith dismantled, and that no other vessels of war shall be there built or armed.[25]

The Rush-Bagot Agreement, an arrangement of no fixed duration, went into effect immediately, but could be abrogated by either side after giving six months' notice. Even before, on February 21, 1817, the Admiralty had ordered the Commander-in-Chief on the Canadian Lakes to strike his pennant as commodore and assume the duties of Commissioner of His Majesty's Navy in Canada.[26] Neither side bothered to maintain all of the permitted schooners, but the dockyards of both were continued on a reduced basis and large quantities of naval stores were held for possible use by what would now be called "mothball fleets." Considerable sums of money were spent annually on repair and maintenance. Yet Commodore Robert Barrie, R.N., hazarded the guess on October 31, 1819, shortly after his arrival at Kingston, that "the American ships are nearly as rotten as our own."[27]

Further negotiations resulted in the Anglo-American convention signed at London on October 20, 1818. Article II provided for the continuation of the international boundary from the northwest corner of the Lake of the Woods to the 49th parallel of latitude and along this to the Rocky Mountains. Article III made the territory westward to the Pacific Ocean free and open to both British and Americans for the next ten years. Meanwhile the British and American Commissioners appointed under the Treaty of Ghent were busy delineating the boundary from the 45th parallel through the St. Lawrence River and the Great Lakes and dividing up the disputed islands in Passamaquoddy Bay. They were, however, unable to settle the long-disputed boundary of northern Maine and both New Brunswick and Lower Canada.[28]

The British Government had in 1814 approved one relatively inexpensive measure which it hoped would further Canada's successful defence. This was a planned settlement of discharged soldiers, both those demobilized in North America and any who might wish to emigrate from the

[25]*Treaties and Agreements affecting Canada in force between His Majesty and the United States of America, with subsidiary documents, 1814–1925*, compiled in the Department of External Affairs (Ottawa, 1927), 12.

[26]Lake Service Letters Received 1815–1817, Commissioners of Admiralty to Hall, Feb. 21, 1817.

[27]Barrie Letters, Barrie to his mother, Oct. 31, 1819.

[28]Burt, *The United States, Great Britain and British North America*, 421–6.

British Isles with their families. The first soldier-settlers were a few men from the 10th Royal Veteran Battalion. With their wives and children, they were settled in scattered fashion along the overland route between Rivière-du-Loup and the settlements in northern New Brunswick during the late spring of 1814.[29] However, Bathurst's instructions that same year that soldier-settlements be established along the border of Lower Canada with the United States[30] were questioned by officers on the spot. In a letter of March 18, 1815, Sir George Prevost argued against filling up the border townships east of Lake Champlain:

The experience of the War with the United States, lately terminated has in more than one instance shown that an unsettled country immediately on the frontier affords a better defence than any population that could be placed there; and I am impressed with the firm persuasion that should the contrary plan be adopted, whatever may be the precautionary measures used, the object of His Majesty's Government for the protection and advancement of the colony, both in an agricultural and political point of view, would be frustrated.[31]

Later Lieutenant-General Sir Gordon Drummond objected with more success to the settlement of the still vacant border townships to the west of Lake Champlain. On July 1, 1816, Bathurst agreed that no further land grants should be made; existing settlers were not, however, to be dispossessed.[32] Elsewhere, blocks of land were set aside for members of the same unit, but only two of the locations were important militarily: the banks of the St. Francis River, settled by the Canadian Voltigeurs, and the route of the proposed Rideau Canal, where grants were made to officers and men of the 97th, 99th, and 100th Regiments of Foot and de Watteville's Regiment of foreign troops.

Despite the official help and supervision given, and in accordance with what Prevost had predicted,[33] many of the old soldiers did not become good farmers. The situation was well summed up in Robert Gourlay's *Statistical Account of Upper Canada*:

This has been the uniform issue of military settlements from first to last in Canada, and in some degree also in the United States of America. Soldiers, in general, choose their trade only to engage in idleness, and give reins to a roving disposition; and, after having spent 20 or 30 years in the profession of *gentlemen*, cannot easily train into the habits of sober and persevering industry. At the first

---

29C/621, MacPherson to Baynes, May 1, 1814; Bouchette to Prevost, June 30, 1814.
30C.O. 43/23, Bathurst to Prevost, July 12 and Sept. 8, 1814.
31C.O. 42/161, Prevost to Bathurst, March 18, 1815.
32C.O. 43/24, Bathurst to Sherbrooke, July 1, 1816.
33C.O. 42/161, Prevost to Bathurst, March 18, 1815.

settlement of Upper Canada, it was not uncommon for soldiers, to sell their 200 acre lots for a bottle of rum. Now-a-days, only 100 is granted, and settlers are prohibited from selling till after three years' residence, and the performance of certain easy duties. Still, I have been told since coming home, by a half-pay officer of the Perth settlement, that scarcely one soldier out of fifty now remains there for good.

The deserted lots have been for the most part filled up with emigrants from Britain and Ireland.[34]

Not long after the war the policy of keeping the area between Montreal and Lake Champlain in a state of nature had also proved to be a failure. Another Governor-in-Chief, Lord Dalhousie, reported on April 24, 1821, that this wilderness had become a haven for fugitives from both Canadian and American justice, that squatters were farming some of its excellent soil, and that Americans were illegally cutting its timber.[35] Approval for his request to open the districts to proper settlement meant that more definite steps would have to be taken to defend the Canadian border.

Such steps had already been proposed by the Duke of Richmond, in a long letter of November 10, 1818, addressed to Bathurst. A general in the British Army and a veteran of the Waterloo campaign, the Duke had made a personal trip along the Canadian border following his appointment as Governor-in-Chief in 1818. His proposals for the most part were based on long-accepted propositions, and only their wording differed from that of Simcoe, Craig, and Prevost. According to Richmond, too, the key points were clear:

> . . . the primary objects appear to be the preservation of Quebec, Kingston and Montreal; the first two as being the Keys of their respective Provinces & the last, as the Depot of the Arms & Ammunition of the Militia of that part of the Country: of those Stores which must be sent to Upper Canada, & as absolutely necessary to preserve the communication between the two Provinces.[36]

An American advance down the Lake Champlain route might again be anticipated and the best means of slowing it up would be to improve the defences of Isle aux Noix and to purchase the land on both banks of the Richelieu River to ensure that it would remain swamp and thus impassable for an army. New works at St. Johns, Chambly, and Sorel would also help to delay an enemy advance; a fortified depot on St. Helen's Island (as already recommended by Commodore Sir Edward Owen) would make it impossible for Americans to launch an attack against Montreal

[34]Robert Gourlay, *Statistical Account of Upper Canada: Compiled with a View for a Grand System of Emigration* (London, 1822), I, 550.
[35]C.O. 42/187, Dalhousie to Bathurst, April 24, 1821.
[36]C/1247, Richmond to Bathurst, Nov. 10, 1818.

from the south shore of the St. Lawrence River. Richmond renewed the recommendation for creating a line of communication between Lower and Upper Canada "independent of the St. Lawrence, the possession of which River above Cornwall for the conveyance of Reinforcements or Stores ought not to be ours for three Days after the commencement of hostilities." He thought that Sackets Harbor should be attacked as soon as war broke out. In summary, he proposed:

To strengthen Quebec, Isle aux Noix & Kingston;
To remove the Stores from Montreal to St. Helens & to place the Island in a state of defence;
To open the Navigation of the Ottawa & Rideau & construct a Canal from Montreal to Lachine;
To do enough on the Niagara Frontier to convince the Inhabitants that we do not intend to abandon them; and lastly
To place the Militia in some state of efficiency.[37]

This appreciation was referred to the Duke of Wellington, then serving as Master General of the Ordnance, an appointment which made him a member of the Cabinet. Wellington replied to Bathurst on March 1, 1819, that he agreed with Richmond's diagnosis. Quebec was still the key to a successful defence of Canada. The fact that it could not withstand a siege, as Richmond had emphasized earlier in a private letter to Bathurst,[38] was temporarily offset by another fact that no regular American army could advance against it using the wilderness route followed by Benedict Arnold in 1775.[39]

Wellington believed that not only would it be impossible to navigate the St. Lawrence River above Cornwall in time of war, but that, by planting a few heavy batteries along its own shore, the enemy could also prevent supply boats from navigating the Niagara, Detroit, and St. Clair rivers. Wellington's memorandum continued with a discussion of the Great Lakes:

. . . our use of each of them must depend upon our naval superiority upon it; and as everything which can enable us to acquire and maintain such naval superiority must come from England, and then by a difficult river navigation of nearly three hundred miles to Kingston and twelve hundred to Lake Huron, whereas the enemy have all they require upon the spot, it can scarcely be believed

---

[37]*Ibid.*
[38]Richmond to Bathurst, Aug. 21, 1818, in *Report on The Manuscripts of Earl Bathurst, preserved at Cirencester Park*, 454.
[39]*Despatches, Correspondence, and Memoranda of Field Marshal Arthur Duke of Wellington, K.G.*, edited by his son, The Duke of Wellington, K.G., in continuation of the former series (London, 1867–78), I, 39.

that we shall be able to acquire and maintain that naval superiority. The pains which [Commodore] Sir E. Owen has taken to survey these lakes and rivers, and to point out the places at which loaded boats and vessels might take shelter and might receive protection from works and troops, show the difficulty, nay, the impossibility, of executing such a system. Works must be constructed, armed, and manned at every point of the lakes; and, after all, the officers and men in them might and would have the mortification of seeing valuable cargoes carried off by a single gunboat, to which they should not be able to afford protection.

Rather than gamble on elaborate arrangements which might or might not ensure free navigation of the inland waterways in wartime, Wellington favoured the construction of canals along the Ottawa River and Rideau waterway to provide a safe water route to Kingston. To obviate possible American naval supremacy on Lakes Ontario and Erie, he suggested improving water routes across country from the Rideau River to Lake Simcoe, from Kingston via the Bay of Quinte and Rice Lake to Lake Simcoe, from Lake Simcoe to Lake Huron, and from the Grand River to the Thames River. By such means the head of the lower Lakes need not be isolated:

... we should be able to maintain an army upon the Niagara frontier notwithstanding that the enemy should be in possession of the navigation of Lake Ontario. We should likewise be enabled to concentrate our naval means in small craft upon lake Huron, lake Erie, and lake Ontario, upon whichever of the three we might see fit, and thus be enabled to be superior to the enemy on one of the three, notwithstanding that our operations on shore and the defence of the country could be entirely independent of such superiority.

Wellington admitted, however, that he was "perfectly aware" that it would be difficult, if not impossible, to convince the inhabitants of Upper Canada that they would be defended unless there was something tangible for them to see. Therefore it might be necessary to build a new fortress on the Niagara frontier, but on the Chippawa River rather than at either Fort George or Fort Erie.

Implementation of such a defence plan, the Duke of Wellington emphasized, would require a field force of 10,000 regulars and regular garrisons of 1,000 at Quebec, 500 at Montreal, 500 in forts along the Richelieu River, 500 at Kingston, 500 split between Niagara and Penetanguishene, and all the available militia. The left corps of the field force, 5,000 regulars and 3,000 militia, should be based on the juncture of Irish Creek with the Rideau River, near the village of Merrickville (which is 44 miles from the present city of Ottawa). From here it could move to Montreal in four days, to Kingston in two or three days, or to Lake Simcoe in from six to eight days. The right corps of similar size should be based between the headwaters of the Holland and Grand rivers (roughly the location of the present day Canadian Forces' Base Borden), whence it could move towards Niagara, York, or Kingston. As far as Wellington could judge from the experience of the War of 1812, the Americans would have difficulty forming army corps capable of taking on either of the defending corps, or even of advancing into and maintaining themselves on Canadian soil. Yet the Duke was quite emphatic about decrying any idea of the British taking the offensive:

> In considering this system I have laid aside, as impracticable, the notion of attacking the United States on their frontier. I have never yet seen any plan of attack upon that power which was at all likely to answer the purpose; but I am certain that an attack could not succeed made from this frontier, in which we are frozen up for five months of the year, and on which the enemy have, and must continue to have, the naval superiority.

Wellington's recommendations resulted in some money being made available almost immediately. Canalization of the Ottawa River began in 1819, the work being undertaken by a detachment of the Royal Staff Corps. A British subsidy of 12,000 pounds sterling towards the construction of the Lachine Canal, which had been authorized by the Legislature of Lower Canada as early as 1815, enabled work to be rushed to completion late in 1824. The only stipulation was that all boats and vessels carrying government stores should be permitted to use it without the payment of any toll or duty.[40] Work had also commenced in 1819 at Isle aux Noix, where a new Fort Lennox was to replace the rotting wooden defences. Only bomb-proof store houses were started on St. Helen's Island. During May, 1820, work was finally begun on a proper citadel at Quebec City, under the supervision of the Commanding Royal Engineer, Lieutenant-Colonel E. W. Durnford.[41] In each instance, the Inspector General of Fortifications in London had submitted the plans to the Board of Ordnance for approval.

On April 11, 1825, the Duke of Wellington judged it expedient to appoint a Commission, headed by Colonel Sir James Carmichael-Smyth, R.E., to visit British North America to report on what had been done to implement his recommendations of 1819 and what difficulties were preventing or impeding completion of that programme. Carmichael-Smyth, it should be noted, had been Chief Engineer of Wellington's army during

[40]Bathurst to Maitland, Sept. 30, 1826, in *Journal of the House of Assembly of Upper Canada*, 1826–27, 25.

[41]C. P. Stacey, "A Note on the Citadel of Quebec," *Canadian Historical Review*, XXIX (December, 1948), 389.

the Waterloo campaign. The importance of the Rideau waterway was stressed in the instructions given to Colonel Carmichael-Smyth and his two associates, Major Sir George Charles Hoste and Captain John B. Harris, but they were told to investigate all the water routes mentioned by Wellington in the appreciation he had made in 1819. They were also to report on the state of the various forts and of the overland route between New Brunswick and Lower Canada.[42] The Commissioners reached Quebec City on May 25 and after spending the summer and early autumn on their task, they returned to England and submitted a bulky report to Wellington. By this time Carmichael-Smyth had become a major-general.

The three Commissioners reported that, despite the nine hundred miles of frontier, American forces were likely to attack Canada by only three routes. The Lake Champlain–Richelieu River route was still the most probable; the Hudson River had now been joined to Lake Champlain by a canal which made it possible to move troops and stores all the way by water from New York City to within forty-five miles of Montreal. The Erie Canal, completed only on October 28, 1825, connected the Hudson River with Buffalo, to facilitate invasion of the Niagara Peninsula. An offshoot of this canal, being built to connect with the eastern end of Lake Ontario at Oswego, would facilitate an attack on Kingston.[43] Extension of settlement and an increase in the number of roads along the border of Lower Canada would make it possible for an American army advancing down the Lake Champlain route to bypass Isle aux Noix, but it could not avoid St. Johns at the rapids on the Richelieu River, nor could it safely proceed from its mouth down the St. Lawrence towards Quebec while a British garrison remained at Montreal. The report therefore recommended the construction of a major fortress on the island of Montreal and lesser works on St. Helen's Island, at St. Johns, Chambly, and the mouth of the Châteauguay River. Reconstruction of the fortifications at Kingston would afford protection for that naval base and the terminal of the proposed Rideau Canal. A new fortress was recommended for the Niagara frontier as were smaller ones for the mouth of the Ouse River, at Chatham on the Thames River, at Amherstburg, and at Penetanguishene. There was no need to relocate the garrison of Drummond's Island, which had

[42]*Despatches, Correspondence, and Memoranda of Field Marshal Arthur Duke of Wellington*, II, 436.

[43]*Copy of a Report to His Grace The Duke of Wellington, Master General of His Majesty's Ordnance &c. Relative to His Majesty's North American Provinces by a Commission of which M. General Sir James Carmichael-Smyth was President, Lieut. Colonel Sir George Hoste and Captain Harris were members* (London, Colonial Office, 1825).

Defences during the canal era.

been allocated to the United States by the Boundary Commission, since the dwindling number of Indians in the Old Northwest could easily travel to Amherstburg or Penetanguishene to get their annual presents. British garrisons would have to be placed throughout the Canadas, because the sedentary militia in both provinces was untrained and unarmed and no more suited for waging war than in 1812. Because the "great use of the Province of New Brunswick, is as a connecting link between Canada and Nova Scotia," the report also recommended the construction of a military road along the line of the existing portage route. The correct defensive line was the St. John River; thus the report suggested that settlement should be discouraged to the west of it so that there might continue to be a wilderness barrier bordering the State of Maine.

On the orders of Wellington the final section of the report was not lithographed for circulation because it dealt with "Vulnerable Points of America" and suggested British offensive operations to forestall American attacks on the outbreak of war. It proposed three possibilities: an advance down the Lake Champlain route to Waterford, where the Mohawk River joined the Hudson River; the damaging of the Erie Canal at Lockport; the landing of an army on Long Island or Staten Island while the Royal Navy blockaded New York City and the rest of the Atlantic coast.[44] Such proposals ran counter to Wellington's view that offensive operations against the United States were impracticable. Perhaps because of this Carmichael-Smyth submitted a confidential "Précis of the Wars in Canada, from 1775 to the Treaty of Ghent in 1814," intended to suggest that the Duke could be wrong.[45]

On December 6, 1825, Wellington forwarded a copy of Carmichael-Smyth's report to the Secretary of State for War and the Colonies. Wellington's personal endorsement of this report stressed that it was impossible for the British Government to withdraw from these dominions: "Whether valuable or otherwise, which can scarcely be a question, they must be defended in war."[46] Action would, however, have to be initiated ahead of time. "It is quite clear," his memorandum continued, "unless some system of communicating with Upper Canada besides the use of the river St. Lawrence should be carried into execution, such communication will be impracticable beyond Montreal in time of war." Uninterrupted communication between Lower Canada and New Brunswick would also

44J. J. Talman, "A Secret Military Document," *American Historical Review*, XXXVIII (January, 1933).
45Edited and published by his son in 1862, and described in chap. 1, n. 23.
46*Despatches, Correspondence, and Memoranda of Field Marshal Arthur Duke of Wellington*, II, 573.

be essential and justified a demand for the proper demarcation of the
international boundary with Maine. Fortifications were almost as important as communications, and Wellington added Halifax and Quebec to
those listed in the Carmichael-Smyth report. Wellington concluded that
execution of all recommendations would give some hope of success in time
of need:

As, on the one hand, I do not entertain the smallest doubt that, if the communications and works proposed by the Committee are carried into execution,
his Majesty's dominions in North America ought to be, and will be, effectually
defended and secured against any attempt to be made upon them hereafter by the
United States, however formidable their power, and this without any material
demand upon the military resources of the country; that if these, or some measures
of this description are not adopted, and if measures are not taken at an early
period to manifest the determination of the King's government to hold this
dominion, at all events we cannot expect the inhabitants, upon whose loyal and
gallant exertions we must in the end depend for their defence, will do otherwise
than look for the security of their lives and properties to a reasonable submission
to the United States.
Even by the greatest exertion of the military resources of his Majesty's government in war, these dominions could not be successfully and effectually defended
without the addition of the greatest part of the measures proposed; but if they are
all adopted, and attention is paid to the militia laws in these countries, and care
taken to keep alive a military spirit among the population, the defence of these
dominions ought not to be a more severe burthen upon the military resources of
the empire in war than such defence as was made proved to be during the
late war.

The enormous expense involved in these recommendations frightened
the British Government, which had to think of the taxpayers, and only
the Grenville Canal on the Ottawa River and the eighteen miles or so of
canals required to connect the lakes, rivers and "drowned land" on the
Rideau waterway were undertaken as new works in 1827.[47] The Rideau
waterway was completed by Lieutenant-Colonel John By, R.E., in May,
1832, but it cost more than one million pounds sterling and became the
subject of a parliamentary inquiry.[48] A very small subsidy was paid to the
private company which completed the Welland Canal for shipping in
1833; it was given on the understanding that the locks should be twenty-
two feet wide and that boats and vessels carrying public stores might use
it without paying a toll.[49]
During the spring of 1828 Wellington had told a Select Committee of

47*Ibid.*, III, 80.
48*British Parliamentary Papers*, 1830–31, III, no. 395; 1831–32, V, no. 570.
49*Journal of the House of Assembly of Upper Canada*, 1826–27, 25.

the House of Commons on Public Income and Expenditure that "if these communications be established, there is no doubt whatever that the Naval operations on the Lakes might be either abandoned altogether or might be carried on with every prospect of success."[50] Stated more bluntly, Wellington was suggesting that implementation of his own costly recommendations would guarantee the safety of Canada against American attack without the Admiralty having to spend any considerable sum of the British taxpayers' money there. It will be remembered that as early as March 15, 1816, the Marquess of Lansdowne had questioned the need for a naval force on the inland lakes when there was a sizable military garrison in Canada. Lansdowne could have been wrong, but no responsible person had the temerity to question the correctness of Wellington's military opinions to his face. His recommendations were never fully implemented, solely for economic reasons. Since there never was another Anglo-American conflict, no one will ever know whether the implementation of his proposals would have been good enough or whether they would have merely created the same false sense of security that the incomplete Maginot Line did for Frenchmen in 1939–40.

The Select Committee recommended the construction of new fortifications at Halifax and Kingston. Parliamentary approval having been obtained, work was commenced on a citadel for Halifax during the ensuing October.[51] The Treasury Board, however, baulked at the cost of the fortifications recommended for Kingston by the Carmichael-Smyth Commission, and further studies were undertaken by the Board of Ordnance. These suggested that insufficient thought had been given to the defence of the naval dockyard and that a complicated system of fifteen mutually supporting works—casemented redoubts, towers, and batteries—would be preferable, at an even greater cost. A displeased Treasury Board did nothing.[52] During 1831 the fortifications at Quebec were completed, at a cost of nearly 236,000 pounds sterling rather than the 70,000 pounds originally estimated, but this sum did include repair of the existing walls as well as construction of the new citadel.[53]

The Admiralty all this time had been debating the wisdom of continuing any naval establishment upon the lakes of Canada. In contrast, the United States Navy had in 1826 closed similar establishments and left the

[50]*British Parliamentary Papers*, 1828, III, no. 493.
[51]Harry Piers, *The Evolution of Halifax Fortress, 1749–1928* (Halifax, 1947), 37–41.
[52]John Dendy, "The Strategic Importance of Kingston: A Study of the Role played by the British Base at Kingston, Ontario in the Defence of Canada, 1778–1854" (unpublished M.A. thesis, Carleton University, Ottawa, 1965).
[53]Stacey, "A Note on the Citadel of Quebec," 390.

remaining two unfinished ships at Sackets Harbor in the charge of a sailing master.[54] On May 24 of the same year Sir Byam Martin, Comptroller of the Royal Navy, had sought an answer about the future of the British naval establishment on the lakes from the First Lord of the Admiralty. Lack of money and artificers was making it impossible to maintain the existing ships and vessels: Canadian oak of which they were built rotted so quickly that repair was almost synonymous with rebuilding. New construction was prohibited by the Rush-Bagot Agreement. Yet, Martin argued, "only by making use of the leisure of peace" could the British "hope to diminish the natural disadvantages [of distance from the scene] under which we are placed."[55] The First Lord of the Admiralty avoided answering the question, and it remained dormant until late in 1830 when there was a short-lived Anglo-American crisis over the still unsettled Maine-New Brunswick boundary.

On January 9, 1831, a new First Lord of the Admiralty, Sir James R. G. Graham, requested an opinion from Lieutenant-General Sir James Kempt, the new Master General of the Ordnance (but not one with membership in the Cabinet) who had just returned home from administering the government of Lower Canada and serving as Commander of the Forces in North America. According to Graham, there was no questioning the fact that after the outbreak of a war the Americans could build larger naval forces on Lake Ontario and Lake Erie than the Royal Navy could provide or that the Rideau Canal would be the only safe route to Kingston. However, if fortresses were completed at Kingston, St. Johns, Montreal, St. Helen's Island, and Châteauguay as recommended, and if the Canadians proved loyal, could the Canadas be defended without a naval force? Sir James Kempt was also asked to comment on Graham's misgivings:

If then the Ships now at Kingston be unfit for Service, their repairs expensive, their decay certain, their future use most doubtful, would it not be wise to follow the example of the Americans, & at once withdraw our Commissioner, & whole naval establishment from the Lakes? We keep up the semblance of a Fleet, and the only reality is the Cost, and at a moment of profound Peace when the jealousies between England and the United States are dormant, would it not be wise to seize the opportunity of ending a useless expense & of proving the sincerity of the pacific Policy of our Government?

At all events if defensive preparation be deemed necessary, the building of the Fortresses, especially at Kingston, is a matter of paramount importance, and our

---

[54]Stacey, "The Myth of the Unguarded Frontier," 14.
[55]C.O. 42/245, Martin to Melville, May 24, 1826.

Finance cannot bear in time of profound Peace a large Expenditure in a distant Colony both for Naval and Military Defence.

A doubt will arise, whether the moral effect in Upper Canada of withdrawing our Naval Establishment altogether from the Lakes may not be prejudicial, & give cause for suspicion to the Colonists that the Mother Country in case of need will not strenuously defend the Territory. The large outlay on the water communication between Montreal & Kingston, the conciliatory tone of our Colonial Government, and the growing importance of our North American Possessions in the general estimation of this Country with a view to the vital aid which Emigration may afford are all sufficient to dissipate such doubts, & to assure the Canadians of our zeal and readiness to defend them.[56]

Kempt naturally consulted the Duke of Wellington under whom he had served in the Peninsular War. Wellington had been Prime Minister until November 22, 1830, when his Government had been defeated by the Whigs, but he was still the leader of the Tories, so no policy that he recommended to the Government would be opposed in Parliament. The Duke agreed with Kempt that there was no point bothering further about the wooden warships rotting away at Kingston, but he insisted that its navy yard must be continued if Lake Ontario was to be utilized to ensure the safety of York and the Niagara Peninsula.[57]

Kempt's lengthy reply to the First Lord of the Admiralty in January suggested that never again could "any beneficial result" be expected from naval warfare on the Great Lakes, nor were large-scale offensive operations ever likely to be undertaken from Canada.[58] The best course, in the event of war, would be to create an armed flotilla for transportation duties by the conversion of commercial steam vessels. As Upper Canada prospered, the number of such vessels was bound to increase at no expense to the British Government. But even if the "mothball fleet" were abandoned, a small naval establishment would have to be continued at Kingston to look after the naval stores that would be needed to equip gunboats in an emergency and to assemble the frames of vessels shipped from Quebec via the Rideau waterway. He also recommended that a naval officer be retained at Kingston to take command of any emergency operations and to maintain public morale in the Canadas. Kempt, as Master General of the Ordnance, naturally placed his faith in the completion of fortresses, which would encourage a militia:

The real defence of Canada if seriously attacked, will chiefly depend upon having an efficient *Militia* composed of a contented & well disposed Population, sustained

---

[56]C.O. 42/245, Graham to Kempt, Jan. 9, 1831.

[57]*Despatches, Correspondence, and Memoranda of Field Marshal Arthur Duke of Wellington*, VIII, 397–8.

[58]C.O. 42/245, Kempt to Graham, Jan. 26, 1831.

by an adequate proportion of regular Troops to give confidence to the Inhabitants of the Country, and that confidence will, I think, be more completely secured by the construction of Works on proper lines of defence, protecting our communications and our Depots, than by attempting a Naval Defence by means of large Ships of War.

The Admiralty decided to follow Kempt's advice. No money was spent on ship repairs at Kingston during 1831,[59] and in the following year an attempt was made to sell the rotting hulks, after some of their guns and naval stores had been shipped down the St. Lawrence River for return to Britain.[60] A small staff was maintained at Kingston to look after the guns and stores housed in what was known as the "Stone Frigate," and Captain Robert Barrie remained as Commissioner of the Dockyard.[61] The smaller naval establishments at Isle aux Noix and Penetanguishene had already been closed, but military garrisons were left at each.

During January, 1832, Sir James Kempt managed to work out a compromise solution for the fortifications required at Kingston. He convinced the Secretary of State for War and the Colonies and the Chancellor of the Exchequer that a system of mutually supporting works could be constructed piecemeal as funds became available. On January 31 orders were sent authorizing the Commanding Royal Engineer in Canada to commence work at Point Henry. However, only the casemented redoubt known as Fort Henry and, somewhat later, an advanced battery were constructed; the rest of the plan was pigeon-holed.[62]

On December 3, 1833, the Second Secretary of the Admiralty, Mr. John Barrow, suggested in a letter addressed to the Permanent Under-Secretary of State for War and the Colonies that the continuing naval establishment at Kingston should be reduced.[63] No objection having been raised to this proposal, the dockyard was closed during March, 1834, and Captain Barrie left Kingston.[64] Only naval stores which would be needed to arm steam vessels for military transport duties were retained at Kingston, in the care of a warrant officer.[65] The reasoning behind this action had seemed irrefutable in British official circles. Completion of the

[59]*British Parliamentary Papers*, 1830–31, VI, no. 149.
[60]Richard A. Preston, "The Fate of Kingston's Warships," *Ontario History*, XLIV (June, 1952), 95–6.
[61]Richard A. Preston, "Broad Pennants on Point Frederick," *Ontario History*, L (Spring, 1958), 87.
[62]Dendy, "The Strategic Importance of Kingston," 72–3.
[63]C.O. 42/245, Barrow to Hay, Dec. 3, 1833.
[64]*Kingston Chronicle and Gazette*, March 15, 1834.
[65]Barrie Letters, Barrow to Barrie, Jan. 10, 1834.

Rideau Canal, Mr. Barrow had written on December 3, 1833, had
"greatly improved our defensive position, by securing an inland Communication between Quebec and Kingston; while the Completion of the
Works around Quebec and the progress of the Fortifications at Kingston
which form part of the line of Forts recommended by the Duke of Wellington, go far to place the future defence of the Canadas on a basis, which
the highest Military Authority has pronounced to be impregnable."[66]

[66]C.O. 42/245, Barrow to Hay, Dec. 3, 1833.

(7)

BORDER PROBLEMS

From a military point of view the rebellions which erupted in both Canadas during the late autumn of 1837 were minor police actions. They are only briefly discussed here as a prologue to the border defence problems that arose in their wake and are of more interest in the military context.

Lieutenant-Governor Sir Francis Bond Head of Upper Canada had had enough military experience during and after the Napoleonic Wars to know that no amount of drilling with homemade pikes could make up for a lack of muskets. Personally convinced that the majority of the inhabitants were loyal and would rally to his support whether or not they liked his government, Bond Head sent his single regiment of British regulars (24th Foot) to the assistance of the Commander of the Forces, Lieutenant-General Sir John Colborne, in Lower Canada. This left a large quantity of army muskets virtually unguarded at Toronto, but William Lyon Mackenzie's attempted march on Toronto turned into a fiasco on December 5. Two days later the loyal, but untrained militia who had responded to the Lieutenant-Governor's call to arms had no trouble in driving the rebels from Montgomery's Tavern and into exile. Bond Head's despatch of December 19, to Lord Glenelg, Secretary of State for War and the Colonies, was substantiation for his policy and included no words of false modesty:

On the day of Mr. McKenzie's defeat, as well as on the following morning, bands of militiamen, from all directions poured in upon me, in numbers which honourably proved that I had not placed confidence in them in vain.

From the Newcastle district alone 2000 men, with nothing but the clothes in which they stood, marched, in the depth of winter, towards the capital, although nearly 100 miles from their homes. . . .

The numbers which were advancing towards me were so great [10,000–12,000 men] that, the day after Mr. McKenzie's defeat, I found it absolutely necessary to print and circulate a notice declaring that *there existed no further occasion for the resort of militia to Toronto*; and the following day I was further enabled to issue a general order, authorizing the whole of the militia of the Bathurst, Johnstown, Ottawa and Eastern districts, to go and lend their assistance to Lower Canada.[1]

As seen by Lord Durham, the rebellion in Lower Canada was primarily a racial conflict; he also saw it as affecting the usefulness of the militia:

. . . every institution which requires for its efficiency a confidence in the mass of the people, or co-operation between its classes, is practically in abeyance in Lower Canada. The militia, on which the main defence of the Province against external enemies, and the discharge of many of the functions of internal police have hitherto depended, is completely disorganized. A muster of that force would, in some districts, be the occasion for quarrels between the races, and in the greater part of the country the attempting to arm or employ it would be merely arming the enemies of the Government.[2]

Volunteer corps of cavalry, artillery and rifles had been belatedly authorized by the Governor-in-Chief, Lord Gosford, to augment Sir John Colborne's 3,300 British regulars.[3] Actual insurrection, following Louis-Joseph Papineau's sudden departure from Montreal on November 16 and the consequent issuance of warrants for the arrest of the principal *patriotes*, was limited. Mixed columns of British regulars and Canadian volunteers were able to vanquish the ill-armed rebels with comparative ease, although Colonel Charles Gore's column suffered an initial reverse at St-Denis. On December 23 Lord Gosford felt justified in writing to the Secretary of State for War and the Colonies that "no further organized attempt is likely to be made to interrupt the public tranquillity."[4] He decided, however, to retain 4,128 volunteers of cavalry, artillery, and rifle corps on full-time, paid service until May 1, 1838, if necessary. Most of the volunteers, though not all, were English-speaking citizens. Fifty-two more small corps of unpaid volunteers continued to drill weekly.[5]

In London on the same December 23, 1837, however, the Military Secretary, Major-General Lord Fitzroy Somerset, addressed a memorandum to the Commander-in-Chief of the British Army based on the first

[1]C.O. 42/439, Head to Glenelg, Dec. 19, 1837.
[2]C. P. Lucas, ed., *Lord Durham's Report on the Affairs of British North America* (Oxford, 1912), III, 53.
[3]W.O. 17/1541, General Monthly Strength Return, Canada, Oct. 1, 1837.
[4]C.O. 42/274, Gosford to Glenelg, Dec. 23, 1837.
[5]W.O. 43/72, Paid Volunteers in Lower Canada during winter of 1837–38, n.d.

reports of insurrection received from Canada. Lord Fitzroy Somerset (later Lord Raglan) made several important observations about restoring tranquillity:

> The great object in Lower Canada is the possession of the Navigation of the River St. Lawrence; and of the Cities of Quebec and Montreal.
> These secured, the rest depends upon *la petite Guerre*. The Canadians will be tired of this before we shall, if we should secure the great points.
> The Army in Lower Canada and the Fleet should be reinforced at the earliest possible period of time.
> It would be very desirable to have an Army and a Fleet in the St. Lawrence as soon as the Navigation shall open.
> It is obvious that the operations of the War will depend upon the Communications, which must be by water; by the St. Lawrence and its Tributary Streams.[6]

Meanwhile the service companies of the 43rd and 85th Regiments were travelling the overland route from New Brunswick in sleighs. They were followed to Quebec during January, 1838, by the flank companies of these units, the 34th Regiment, and a detachment of Royal Artillery.[7] Colborne then ordered the 24th Regiment to return to Upper Canada, to be accompanied by the 32nd Regiment from Lower Canada.

With the arrival of William Lyon Mackenzie at Buffalo, New York, on December 11, 1837, recruiting had got under way openly for a "Patriot Army" which planned to invade the Canadas and establish republics there. There had been a precedent barely two years before: American newcomers to Texas had secured its independence from Mexico by force of arms. A considerable anti-British element in the northern states was reinforced by large numbers of labourers thrown out of employment by a current economic depression, and recruits flocked into the ranks of the patriots. The United States was obligated by its own Neutrality Act of 1818 to put a stop to any filibustering activities originating on its own soil, but Congress had passed no legislation that would permit federal officials to interfere with the warlike preparations of the "patriots." Furthermore, the greater part of the small American regular army was either momentarily campaigning in Florida or garrisoning forts west of the Mississippi River. Above all, no one was anxious to antagonize potential voters in a mid-term election year.[8] The preparations continued.

Border incidents were precipitated quickly, and by the Canadians. Colonel Allan MacNab's 2,000 militia and volunteers standing guard

[6] C.O. 537/25, Memorandum on Defence of Canada, Dec. 23, 1837.
[7] W.O. 17/2385, General Monthly Return, Nova Scotia, Jan. 1, 1838.
[8] Albert B. Corey, *The Crisis of 1830–1842 in Canadian-American Relations* (Toronto, 1941) is a definitive account of the border disturbances.

along the Canadian shore of the Niagara River had been ordered not to attack the patriots occupying Navy Island above the Falls, but in an attempt to alleviate boredom, MacNab on December 29 sent seven boat-loads of men to seize the American-owned steamer *Caroline* which was running supplies to the patriots. The *Caroline* was set on fire in mid-stream where she sank, but the attack had actually occurred when she was docked alongside the American shore, and an American citizen had been killed; the result was further cause for negotiation between the British and American Governments. At Detroit the patriots, who had been drilling openly, failed miserably in their ill-organized attempt to capture Amherstburg on January 7, 1838. A week later Major-General Winfield Scott, specially sent from Washington to maintain the peace, managed to persuade the socially prominent but militarily inept young Rensselaer van Rensselaer to withdraw his force of patriots from Navy Island.

Following the arrival of the 24th and 32nd Regiments in Upper Canada the Lieutenant-Governor felt justified in dismissing most of the volunteers and militia on duty, in a Militia General Order dated January 30, 1838. Only about 1,950 volunteers were incorporated into units as provincial troops to serve until July 1, 1838.

Three attempts by patriots to attack across Lake Erie on the ice were easily foiled. On February 22 van Rensselaer occupied Hickory Island in the St. Lawrence River near Gananoque but was quickly daunted by the bitter cold and returned to the warmth of the American shore. Robert Nelson's attempt to establish a republic in Lower Canada foundered on February 28, when Missisquoi County volunteers chased his *patriotes* back into Vermont, where they were disarmed by a detachment of American regular troops.[9] Colborne's letter of March 24 to Bond Head's successor, Sir George Arthur, stated the problem quite simply:

The American Government must be anxious to avoid a War; but if we should again have disturbances in either Province, we can only depend on our own force and exertions to defend the Colonies against the attacks which will be made upon us by the people of the adjoining states. It is my intention to send two Regiments to the Upper Province as soon as our reinforcements arrive.[10]

In May large British reinforcement reached Quebec. They included two battalions of Her Majesty's Foot Guards and two cavalry regiments, and increased the regular strength in the Canadas to 283 officers and

[9]*Ibid.*
[10]C. R. Sanderson, ed., *The Arthur Papers; being the Canadian Papers, Mainly Confidential, Private and Demi-Official of Sir George Arthur, last Lieutenant-Governor of Upper Canada* (Toronto, 1957), I, 155.

7,055 other ranks. The Foot Guards remained at Quebec City; the cavalry regiments were sent to Montreal, where there already were the 2/1st Royal Scots and the 85th Regiment. The remainder of Colborne's infantry regiments were disposed as follows: 66th at Trois-Rivières, 15th at Chambly, 43rd at Laprairie, 71st on St. Helen's Island, 34th at Merrickville, 83rd at Kingston, 24th at Toronto, and the 32nd at London.[11] Colborne specified that the regular troops in Upper Canada were to be kept concentrated and away from the border, except for detachments of 100 rank and file at each of Niagara and Amherstburg. This deployment would facilitate the launching of counter-attacks against any attempted invasion, lessen the danger of "incidents" involving American citizens, and provide less opportunity for desertion.[12] Volunteers and militia anxious to get back to their farms had already been released.[13] The remaining corps were progressively disbanded during June and July.[14]

By this time Captain Williams Sandom, R.N., who had reached Kingston late in April with a party of 25 seamen and artificers, had reopened the dockyard, had repurchased three vessels of the former naval squadron from their civilian owners, and was using the guns and naval stores still in the Stone Frigate to convert requisitioned steam vessels into gunboats.[15] Additional naval officers and seamen were sent to him from the squadron with which Vice-Admiral of the White the Hon. Sir Charles Paget, Commander-in-Chief of the North America and West Indies Stations, escorted Lord Durham to Quebec on May 27.[16]

Durham, unlike his predecessors, was in a full sense of the term Governor General of all the British North American provinces and not merely a formal Governor-in-Chief. An influential member of the British Whig party and son-in-law of the Lord Grey under whose leadership the First Reform Bill had been enacted in 1832, Durham was also appointed "High Commissioner for the adjustment of certain important questions pending in the provinces of Lower and Upper Canada respecting the form and future government of the said provinces."[17] Lieutenant-General Sir John Colborne, who had been administering the government of Lower Canada since February 27, was to continue as Commander of the Forces. Vice-Admiral Paget, who remained at Quebec for the summer

[11]W.O. 17/1542, General Monthly Return, Canada, June 1, 1838.
[12]*Arthur Papers*, I, 192.
[13]*Ibid.*, 173.
[14]W.O. 43/72, Paid Corps in Upper Canada during winter 1838, n.d.
[15]Adm. 1/2563, Sandom to Paget, April 21, 1838.
[16]C.O. 42/282, Durham to Glenelg, June 16, 1838.
[17]Chester W. New, *Lord Durham: A Biography of John George Lambton, first Earl of Durham* (Oxford, 1929) is still the definitive study.

with a considerable naval strength, was to accompany Lord Durham in his travels.

Only a few hours after Durham had taken his oath of office, a border crisis seemed possible. Early on the morning of May 30 a Canadian steam vessel, *Sir Robert Peel,* was attacked at Wells Island in the American channel of the St. Lawrence by river pirates under the leadership of a notorious Canadian scoundrel, Bill Johnson. The passengers were forced ashore in the Thousand Islands and then *Sir Robert Peel* was set on fire by the supposed allies of the patriots. On June 2 Durham issued a proclamation offering 1,000 pounds reward to anyone who should identify and bring to justice any of the miscreants. The proclamation assured the inhabitants that sufficient military force was available to protect the border from aggression and that Lord Durham would raise the issue with the President of the United States.[18]

Durham sent his brother-in-law, Lieutenant-Colonel the Hon. Charles Grey, commanding the 71st Regiment of Foot at Montreal, on the diplomatic mission to Washington. Grey was instructed to explain personally to President Van Buren "the impossibility that Lord Durham, with the ample force at his disposal, would allow the present insecure state of things on the frontier to continue without making use of that force for the protection of her Majesty's subjects, should the American Government not take effectual measures itself."[19] Grey arrived in Washington on June 12 and conferred with the British Ambassador, but he did not have a chance to speak privately with President Van Buren until June 15. The President then repeatedly asked him to assure Lord Durham of his "sincere wish to prevent a recurrence of late events."[20] The United States Army was very small and fully employed elsewhere, but a steamer carrying 50 American soldiers was about to be assigned to patrol Lake Ontario, and there was to be a similar patrol on Lake Erie; other troops would be ordered to Sackets Harbor, and the General-in-Chief, Major-General Alexander Macomb, would direct operations from there, co-operating fully with British officers commanding posts in Canada. Grey wrote from New York that President Van Buren had been most anxious to avoid further trouble:

He said that nothing could be more untrue than that the United States Government had the slightest wish to foment disturbances in Canada—much less that

---

[18]*Upper Canada Gazette,* Toronto, June 14, 1838.
[19]William Ormsby, ed., *Crisis in the Canadas; 1838–1839: The Grey Journals and Letters* (Toronto, 1964), 24.
[20]*Ibid.,* 41.

they had any views upon those Provinces for annexing them to the Union. On the contrary that it was against their interests to do so. That as the Northern States now protested about the annexation of Texas, the Southern States would equally be opposed to any increase of Territory in the north, and that they had already too many things on their hands not to wish to restore the peace of the frontier.[21]

It was widely suspected in British circles—and was possibly true—that the official American desire to co-operate most fully to prevent further unrest along the international border was prompted largely by the British display of force in Canada.

Britain was now prepared to reinforce the army establishment in Canada further. Lord Glenelg's letter of July 13 asked whether Durham was satisfied with the number of troops in Canada, or whether he would like two more regiments from Nova Scotia.[22] The British Government was also considering whether the Rush-Bagot Agreement should be modified or terminated[23] because Captain Sandom's naval strength now included two armed steam vessels and three armed schooners on Lake Ontario and action was being taken to place armed vessels on Lake Erie.[24]

Continued signs of discontent in Lower Canada were reported by military garrison commanders throughout the summer, and members of the Hunters' Lodges, a secret brotherhood that spread across the border from Vermont and New York, were talking openly of a "great hunt." Even though the British Army's effective strength was increased to 417 officers and 10,271 other ranks by the arrival of the 73rd and 93rd Regiments of Foot,[25] approximately 10,000 volunteers were embodied in Lower Canada for general or local service during the last days of October and first days of November.[26] Colborne resumed the administration of the government of Lower Canada on November 1, when Durham sailed for England to give an account of his mission, which he felt had been sabotaged by the British Government's lack of support. At Colborne's behest, Lieutenant-Governor Arthur of Upper Canada did his best to recruit upwards of 12,000 provincial troops.[27]

Robert Nelson's second attempt to proclaim a Republic of Lower Canada was frustrated at Napierville on November 4 by local volunteer corps. The continuing but dispirited rebels fled to the safety of Vermont, on

[21]*Ibid.*, 41–2.
[22]G. 1/39, Glenelg to Durham, July 13, 1838.
[23]*Ibid.*, July 20, 1838.
[24]C.O. 42/282, Durham to Glenelg, June 16, 1838.
[25]W.O. 17/1542, General Monthly Return, Canada, Nov. 1, 1838.
[26]Durham Papers/17, Return of Volunteer Forces, Oct. 30, 1838. Also Militia General Orders for Lower Canada.
[27]*Arthur Papers*, I, 293, 299, and 336.

November 9, as Colborne's column of regulars approached from Montreal. On the following day a last pocket of resistance at Beauharnois was easily dispersed by a detachment of the 93rd Foot, 200 volunteers, and a band of Indians from St. Regis. The Hunters who crossed the St. Lawrence River and seized a stone windmill east of Prescott stood off a sizable force—of regulars, transported from Kingston by steam vessel of Captain Sandom's flotilla, newly raised provincial troops, and local militia—for five days before surrendering on November 17. But the 200 Hunters from Detroit who landed near Windsor on December 4 quickly fled on the approach of two companies of provincial troops outfitted in red tunics, whom they imagined to be regulars. These events discredited the Hunters: the hitherto sympathetic Americans of the border states now lost interest in what was obviously a losing cause; the United States Government despatched additional regular troops to its border posts, and commanders were instructed to report every substantial rumour to the nearest British garrison; and the State of New York placed militia companies on duty at additional border points.[28] As the United States had not protested the growth of British naval strength on the Great Lakes, the British Ambassador in Washington suggested that it would be unwise for Britain to raise the question of the continuance of the Rush-Bagot Agreement with the American Secretary of State. Britain's Foreign Secretary, Lord Palmerston, agreed.[29]

Thus events stood at the end of 1838. During the winter of 1838–39 about 21,000 provincial troops remained on continuous service in the Canadas. Two further regiments of British infantry then made the overland trip from New Brunswick to increase Colborne's regular strength to almost 12,000 all ranks.[30]

A separate crisis now arose over the long-disputed northern portion of the Maine-New Brunswick boundary. Possession of 12,000 square miles of wooded country was desired by lumbering interests in both Maine and New Brunswick. Mounting pressure during 1838 had caused the New Brunswick Legislature to authorize the mobilization of 1,200 volunteer militia should there be an emergency. The Legislature of Maine had appropriated $800,000 for defence, and border incidents in early February, 1839, led the Governor of Maine to mobilize 10,000 militia. Thereupon Major-General Sir John Harvey, the Lieutenant-Governor of New Brunswick, ordered a detachment of the 36th Foot to the border town of

[28]Oscar A. Kinchen, *The Rise and Fall of the Patriot Hunters* (New York, 1956), 85–92.
[29]C.O. 42/286, Backhouse to Stephen, Dec. 10, 1838.
[30]W.O. 17/1543, General Monthly Return, Canada, March 1, 1839.

Woodstock and called out militia units for garrison duty at both Fredericton and Saint John. Four companies of the 11th Foot were subsequently
sent from Quebec to the Madawaska country, but while Harvey was
making elaborate plans to protect the vital overland military route to
Canada the crisis was resolved.[31] Major-General Winfield Scott arrived
from Washington and, as instructed by the United States Government,
arranged a *modus vivendi* with the Governor of Maine and Sir John
Harvey before any casualties occurred in this so-called "Aroostook War."
The agreement called for the withdrawal of all troops from the disputed
area. On March 27 orders were issued for the New Brunswick militia to
return to their homes. Two days later the detachment of the 11th Regiment of Foot began its march back to Quebec. However, because of
encroachments by American lumbermen into the Aroostook valley, two
companies of the 11th Regiment returned from Quebec during November, 1839. They built a fort overlooking Lake Temiscouata, where they
remained for six months without incident.[32]

During April, 1839, Colborne had reduced the number of provincial
troops on duty in Lower Canada to 300 cavalry and 700 infantry, who
would garrison a chain of frontier posts in the Eastern Townships.[33]
About 3,500 of those recruited in Upper Canada for eighteen months
service were retained on duty, organized as a troop of dragoons and five
battalions of infantry.[34] The six British infantry regiments assigned to
Upper Canada were now concentrated at Kingston, Toronto, London,
and Amherstburg. Colborne had very realistically put the need for
readiness in a letter to Sir George Arthur citing the disturbed condition
of the times:

We shall however be at the mercy of the Vagabonds, and a constant expense must
be incurred in maintaining a large regular force, and a well organized Militia,
prepared to concentrate at a short notice. The periodical alarms to which we are
opposed, and the dread of an attack from Pirates formidable from the uncertainty
as to the extent of their means, will be ruinous to Upper Canada, unless we have
a disposable force at all times ready to repel invasion, without calling the agricul-
turalists from their homes. A more expensive system could not be adopted than the
one to which we have been compelled to resort, in consequence of the menaces of
the American population on our frontier. The same game may be continued with
little inconvenience to the Patriots for many years. If we were to diminish our

---

[31]C.O. 188/64, Harvey to Normanby, April 25, 1839.
[32]Corey, *The Crisis of 1830–1842 in Canadian-American Relations*, 112.
[33]*Arthur Papers*, II, 121.
[34]W.O. 1/536, Arthur to Thomson, Feb. 15, 1840.

force in this district, there can be no doubt that the hatred towards us, and the virulence which has been demonstrated by the conduct of the adjoining States, would be again demonstrated by the borderers.[35]

Despite Colborne's fears of provocation there were no more incidents along the Canadian border, and the vessels leased as gunboats were returned to their owners, leaving the Royal Navy with only the four vessels actually purchased for further service on the Great Lakes.[36] During October, 1839, Sir John Colborne returned to England and was raised to the peerage as Lord Seaton. His opinion of the Canadian situation was set forth in a memorandum of January 1, 1840, addressed to the Secretary of State for War and the Colonies, recommending there should be permanent forts at the border points where he had found it desirable to have blockhouses erected in 1838. Such forts, garrisoned by provincial troops, would reassure the inhabitants that all was well and also make it possible to keep the bulk of the British troops concentrated at central locations for use as counter-attacking forces. Filibusterers were, he felt, most likely to congregate along the American shore of the St. Clair, Detroit, and Niagara rivers and along the sector of the St. Lawrence River between Brockville and Prescott. He assumed that the "American Patriots, with an irregular force, would not venture to cross at any other points, aware of the difficulty of returning to their own shores, in case of failing to establish a communication with the disaffected."[37]

His successor as Commander of the Forces, Lieutenant-General Sir Richard Downes Jackson, viewed the over-all situation differently. Jackson sensed that the political climate of the United States was changing rapidly. Danger did not lie in fringe groups but in the fact that Americans in all walks of life were becoming convinced that it was the "manifest destiny" of the United States to extend the American Revolution over the whole continent. Jackson believed that any future threat to British North America might thus well come from the armed forces of the United States. The largest element of the small American regular army was still in Florida fighting the Seminole Indians, but the number of troops along the Canadian border from Sault Ste Marie to Eastport had now quadrupled to about 3,000 officers and enlisted men.[38] In 1839 Congress had

[35]*Arthur Papers*, II, 43.

[36]K. R. Macpherson, "List of Vessels employed on British Naval Service on the Great Lakes, 1755–1875," *Ontario History*, LV (September, 1963).

[37]W.O. 1/536, Seaton to Russell, Jan. 1, 1840.

[38]Frank Paul Prucha, "Distribution of Regular Army Troops before the Civil War," *Military Affairs*, XVI (Winter, 1952).

voted money to renovate existing forts and work was immediately commenced at Fort Niagara and Oswego. Recommendations made later by a Board of Engineers led to considerable expenditure on new forts near Detroit and Buffalo and at Rouse's Point on Lake Champlain.[39] Jackson felt it wise therefore to make a submission on February 25, 1840, to the new Governor General, Charles Poulett Thomson (soon to become Lord Sydenham), urging the construction of permanent defensive works in front of Montreal, as well as the continuance of a large force of British regulars in North America. He laid great stress on communications:

> The provinces of Upper and Lower Canada must support each other, and the defence of Nova Scotia and New Brunswick should also be based upon the same principle, indeed this system of general succour should be extended throughout British America, and it has been partially provided for, by the Lieut. Governor and Legislature of New Brunswick [which had agreed during the brief Aroostook War scare that 1,200 militia might be embodied for one year's continuous service].
>
> It is obvious that a purely defensive force should be restricted to what may be deemed strictly necessary, but in the Provinces of North America (and particularly in the Canadas) it should be available for purposes of general defence, so as to afford support to, or supply the want of, the Regular Troops according to circumstances. If this principle be correct, and it has been advantageously acted upon in Great Britain and Ireland, an extensive reduction in one Province of the Canadas does not warrant the inference that a proportional reduction may be expedient in the other although equally quiet.[40]

The Governor General had himself received instructions emphasizing the need to implement certain of Lord Durham's recommendations as soon as possible, particularly the political union of the two Canadas. This was accomplished by the Act of Union of 1840. No publicity was given to his instructions concerning military matters. He was enjoined "not to permit Maine to occupy or possess Land to the North of the St. John's and to maintain in perfect security, the communication by the Madawaska between Fredericton and Quebec" and to do whatever was "indispensable" for that purpose.[41]

Economy continued a vexing problem. The Board of Ordnance in London protested to the Secretary of State for War and the Colonies against the cost of maintaining even the existing sixteen fortified posts in Canada, and Lord John Russell sent a letter of inquiry to the Governor

[39]C. P. Stacey, "The Myth of the Unguarded Frontier," *American Historical Review*, LVI (October, 1950), 16.
[40]W.O. 1/536, Jackson to Governor General, Feb. 25, 1840.
[41]C.O. 42/312, Sydenham to Harvey, Nov. 23, 1840.

General. He replied on August 24, 1840, that the geography of Canada precluded any idea that these forts were occupied only because of the late rebellions, but had a possible enemy to the south in view:

The stations at Lake Temisquata, at the Dégété, at Philipsburg, at Prescott, at London, at Chippawa, at Drummondville, at Port Colborne, at Queenston, at Waterloo Ferry, at Chatham, Sandwich & Windsor, *thirteen* out of the sixteen places enumerated, have no more to do with any revolt than they have with the Irish Rebellion. They are all protective and precautionary measures, whether well or ill judged it is not my purpose to determine, against aggression from the United States.[42]

The makeshift gunboats Captain Sandom had put in service—*Traveller* and *Experiment* on Lake Ontario and *Toronto* on Lake Erie—were adequate to cope with filibustering activities but not with any true war vessels the United States Navy might place on the inland waters. The Admiralty was having a paddle-sloop, H.M.S. *Minos*, built at Chippawa for service on Lake Erie, but in a letter of October 12, 1840, Sydenham requested Lord John Russell to try and secure a similar war vessel for Lake Ontario. "It is of the utmost consequences," he wrote, "to have a force on which we can call there. We *could* hold that Lake—not so Lake Erie, out of which the Yankees would drive us at once."[43] As a result two paddle-sloops were built at Kingston and were named H.M.S. *Cherokee* and H.M.S. *Mohawk*.

During November, 1840, Jackson provided Sydenham with a much more detailed memorandum on defending Canada. The Commander of the Forces took for granted that Sydenham was aware Quebec was the key to any successful defence, but he reiterated what he had written earlier about the need for permanent fortifications in the Montreal area. Then he elaborated on the Duke of Wellington's comments respecting the fortifications recommended by the Carmichael-Smyth Commission of 1825:

. . . without works of one kind or another, the Canadas cannot be considered safe. Well disciplined troops may defend a land frontier against a very superior number of troops of inferior quality, when the communications are sufficiently good to admit of concentration with celerity and accuracy of time; but the Canadian frontier resembles a maritime frontier, and our communications cannot be depended upon.

---

[42]W.O. 1/536, Sydenham to Russell, Aug. 24, 1840.
[43]Paul Knaplund, ed., *Letters from Lord Sydenham, Governor General of Canada, 1839–1841, to Lord John Russell* (London, 1931), 97.

The proposed works would be bulwarks, behind which our small but superior force might move and act with promptitude and energy.

This frontier resembles at present a long weak line of battle, liable to be pierced or turned, and overwhelmed at points decisive of the struggle.

The works proposed by the United States are evidently calculated to form a basis of offensive operations. What have they to apprehend from us on this frontier?

If permanent works on this border were proscribed on either side by treaty, or regulated as to number and quality, like the vessels of war on the lakes, the advantage would be wholly on their side; defensive works are absolutely necessary for the weaker party against such disparity of force.

I have scarcely mentioned the important subject of interior communications, or the postions (according to the ordinary acceptation of the term) because the former are changing every year, in an improving country, and postions vary with them. Neither have I adverted to the assistance to be derived from the Indians. It is a description of assistance that, from all I have heard of it, ought not, if possible, to be employed; but I understand that the Indian will not be quiet in war, and we may be obliged to submit to this necessity.[44]

The Board of Ordnance countered that not even the most elaborate fortifications would guarantee successful defence against a rapidly growing United States. According to the letter its secretary addressed to Lord John Russell on February 18, 1841, only the inhabitants of the country could really preserve it, along with troops in the field.

The successful defence then of the Canadas must, after all depend on the spirit, the loyalty, and the exertions of the people of that country (in conjunction with the army in the field). If they are heart and hand with us, it may fairly be hoped and expected, that any attempt at invasion would be defeated, as such attempts already have been. If, on the other hand, the inhabitants are not disposed to join us in endeavouring to repel an invading force, no extent of fortification would afford a certain security.[45]

Wellington's opinion, after he had read all the correspondence, was that the British Government had an obligation to defend people who had willingly continued within the British Empire. Unless it was agreed that the provinces of British North America would be properly defended if attacked, however, it would be "more wise, beneficent and fair" to abandon them now and let them make the best possible bargain with their American neighbours.[46]

Sir Richard Jackson's request in February, 1842, that 2,329 provincial

[44]W.O. 1/536, Memorandum upon the Canadian Frontier, November, 1840.
[45]W.O. 1/536, Vivian to Russell, Feb. 18, 1841.
[46]W.O. 1/537, Memorandum on the Defence of Her Majesty's Dominions in North America, March 31, 1841.

troops be continued on duty in Canada after their existing engagements expired in April was approved by Sydenham's successor, Sir Charles Bagot.[47] Anglo-American matters in dispute were, however, resolved on August 9, 1842, when Lord Ashburton (the former Alexander Baring) and Daniel Webster, the U.S. Secretary of State, signed a compromise treaty in Washington. The United States received the largest portion of the disputed territory along the northeastern international boundary, but Webster had initially accepted Ashburton's contention that British retention of the Madawaska-Temiscouata route was essential for maintenance of all year round communication between Halifax and Quebec.[48] This stipulation had been made by the Master General of the Ordnance, General the Rt. Hon. Sir George Murray, when his opinion had been sought by the Foreign Secretary.[49] Murray, it will be remembered, had travelled this route early in 1815 to inform Sir George Prevost that he was suspended from duty and he had next spent a few months governing Upper Canada.

During the month of September, 1842, the two battalions of Foot Guards returned to England, followed shortly by the 7th Hussars. Sir Charles Bagot, in the January following, recommended the disbandment of all the provincial troops, except an infantry company of 100 Negroes and three troops of cavalry totalling 120 all ranks. He also recommended a considerable reduction in the strength of the British garrison.[50] The coloured troops were recommended for retention because they had no love for the United States, where they or their parents had lived as slaves, and because they were less likely than British troops to suffer from the malaria which was then prevalent in certain of the border districts of Upper Canada. The provincial cavalry continued to patrol the open country along the 45th parallel of latitude and to watch for British deserters trying to make their way to the United States and a new life. Bagot's successor, Sir Charles Metcalfe, explained in a letter of June 22 why regular cavalrymen could not be trusted to serve along the land frontier:

. . . in addition to any other motives that may account for desertion, the Regular Cavalry would have the temptation of selling Her Majesty's Horses and Appointments in the neighbouring States; whereas the Provincial Cavalry, being mounted

---

[47]W.O. 1/538, Bagot to Stanley, Feb. 7, 1842.

[48]Correspondence with Special British Mission is printed in *United States Senate Documents*, 27th Congress, 3rd Session, no. 1, 1842, 34–52.

[49]W.O. 80/11, Aberdeen to Murray, March 5, 1842; Murray to Aberdeen, March 6, 1842.

[50]W.O. 1/539, Bagot to Stanley, Jan. 24, 1843.

on their own Horses, have no such temptation, and are altogether of a class that have no inducement to desert.[51]

The temporary barracks hired during the emergency were vacated and the British regular army strength was reduced to 7,474 all ranks, as compared to a peak strength of 12,452 all ranks in early 1842.[52]

In May, 1844, Sir Richard Jackson decided to appoint a commission to study the military situation in Canada, because of the ominous slogan of "Fifty-four Forty or Fight" that James K. Polk was using in his campaign to win the American presidential election. This slogan aptly expressed the American demand for the whole of the disputed Oregon territory where an uneasy *modus vivendi* between Britain and the United States had continued since 1818. Polk was also making no secret of the fact that the admission of the Republic of Texas to the federal union as a slave state would be offset by the annexation of British North America which was "free" soil. The chairman of Jackson's commission was the Commanding Royal Engineer, Colonel W. E. Holloway. Members were: Captain Edward Boxer, R.N., who was employed by the Canadian Government as Harbour Master at Quebec; Mr. David Taylor, late Master Attendant of the Kingston Dockyard; and Lieutenant H. C. B. Moody, R.E.[53] Working separately, Boxer and Moody visited all the America ports on the Great Lakes and estimated their capabilities in the event of war. Detailed maps of key areas were compiled.[54]

Many Americans in these years were disturbed by the continued presence of British war vessels on the Great Lakes.[55] The American Government had recognized the British need to convert local steam vessels into gunboats during the crisis of 1838, but the paddle-sloops *Minos, Cherokee,* and *Mohawk* were proper war vessels; hence, the United States Navy launched a larger iron, side-wheel war vessel, U.S.S. *Michigan,* at Erie, Pennsylvania, in 1843. The British Foreign Secretary, Lord Aberdeen, protested this American action on July 23, 1844, but neither the British nor American Governments was convinced that the Rush-Bagot Agreement applied to steam vessels. On September 5, the Secretary of State for War and the Colonies, Lord Stanley, suggested to the Prime Minister, Sir Robert Peel that something would have to be done. His memorandum, however, referred to the opinions about strategy for the Lakes previously

[51]W.O. 1/552, Metcalfe to Stanley, June 22, 1843.
[52]W.O. 1/552, Jackson to Stanley, May 14, 1845.
[53]W.O. 1/552, Boxer to Higginson, June 4, 1845.
[54]Adm. 7/625, Cathcart to Stanley, Dec. 11, 1845.
[55]*The Times*, London, Oct. 21, 1841.

expressed by the Duke of Wellington and others and to the Duke's plans never yet implemented:

. . . that in the event of war, it would be hopeless to attempt to maintain the Naval superiority of the Lakes, with the local advantages possessed by the United States: and a large and expensive Establishment at Kingston was consequently put down. It was however intended to provide for the *Military* defence of Canada, according to a plan laid down by the Duke of Wellington in 1826; but for one cause or another, though much has been said about these works, I am afraid little or nothing has been done. . . . The whole plan involved an expense, if I remember right, considerably exceeding a Million Sterling: and I own that I should very much hesitate about spending such a sum on such an object, in the present state of our connexion with Canada. Still some course ought to be decided on, and acted on, by the Cabinet: and I doubt whether the measure suggested by Aberdeen, of building up their present force, and then making a new agreement will be sufficient or advisable.[56]

Two days later Peel returned a considered reply, and brought forward the familiar arguments about defences:

A great expenditure on fortifications and Military defences by land might be a protective measure against the hostile disposition and hostile preparations on the Lakes, of the Americans. But the cost of them is not only useless but money thrown away so far as Canadian feeling is concerned. The progress of such defences too is so slow—that which is done is so liable to be questioned by Military Men— may perhaps be so inapplicable to purposes of defence, some years hence, against novel methods of attack—that I do not see much prospect of controlling effectually the American tendencies to hostility by costly outlays on land fortifications.[57]

Matters came to a head with the election of Polk as President of the United States and the emphasis he gave to the new doctrine of "manifest destiny." The British Government had no desire to go to war over "miles of pine swamp" in the Northwest when some sort of settlement could be negotiated. The Pacific Squadron of the Royal Navy was a trump card that could be played at any convenient moment especially since President Polk's inaugural address of March 4, 1845, indicated quite clearly that he was not yet willing to arbitrate.[58]

Those charged with the defence of Canada continued to try to find ways and means. General Sir George Murray's memorandum of September 27, 1844, had suggested that Kingston could not withstand attack

[56]Paul Knaplund, "The Armaments on the Great Lakes, 1844," *American Historical Review*, XL (July, 1935), 232.
[57]*Ibid.*
[58]James O. McCabe, "Arbitration and the Oregon Question," *Canadian Historical Review*, XLI (December, 1960), 308.

by combined military and naval forces during the next summer's campaigning or a winter military attack across the ice.[59] Lord Stanley had therefore requested the Board of Ordnance on January 23, 1845, to plan better defences for the Kingston dockyard and the entrance to the Rideau Canal.[60] On April 4 Stanley wrote directing Metcalfe to accept an offer made by the Niagara Harbour and Dock Company to construct three steam vessels which could be appropriated for naval service on the lakes of Canada if required.[61] A few weeks later he directed Metcalfe to check the quantities of naval stores and ammunition in Canada. He suggested that Captain Boxer might be given leave from his civilian duties as Harbour Master to do some naval spying in the United States, as there were rumours that the Americans were stockpiling munitions close to the border.[62] The arrival in Canada of a civilian employee of the Admiralty to supervise the possible conversion of commercial steam vessels into gunboats caused rumours to spread in turn in the United States. On May 31, 1845, Niles' *National Register* carried a report that "the dockyard at Kingston is forthwith to be put on a full establishment and an admiralty commissioner will assume command, under whose superintendence three steam frigates of the largest class are to be built."

With the dispute in Oregon in mind, the Commander of the Forces in British North America ordered two young officers, Lieutenants H. J. Ware and M. Vavasour, to accompany Governor Sir George Simpson of the Hudson's Bay Company on his journey by canoe to the Red River colony and then continue westward to make a military appreciation of the Oregon country.[63] They set out, dressed as civilians, on May 5, 1845. Gone more than a year, they sent back reports from time to time, the first, from Fort Garry, stating that it would not be practicable for regular troops to travel the canoe and portage route they had just traversed.[64]

Early in June, 1845, Lieutenant-General Sir Richard Jackson died suddenly of apoplexy, and the spread of Sir Charles Metcalfe's cancerous growth soon indicated that he also had not long to live. Therefore General Lord Cathcart was appointed both Governor General and Commander of the Forces.[65] He immediately began familiarizing himself with the historical background of Canadian defence policy and went on to study

[59]W.O. 80/11, Memorandum on Defence of Canada, Sept. 27, 1844.
[60]G. 1/109, Stanley to M.G.O., Jan. 23, 1845.
[61]G. 1/109, Stanley to Metcalfe, April 4, 1845.
[62]*Ibid.*, April 17, 1845.
[63]W.O. 1/552, Metcalfe to Stanley, May 19, 1845.
[64]*Ibid.*, July 26, 1845 and enclosure.
[65]Sir Arthur G. Doughty, ed., *The Elgin-Grey Papers 1846–1852* (Ottawa, 1937), I, 3.

the recent reports by Colonel Holloway, R.E., and Captain Boxer, R.N.
He set forth his own views in a long letter of December 11, 1845,
addressed to the Secretary of State for War and the Colonies. Again
striking power on the Lakes is a preoccupation:

> There can be no doubt that the Americans must possess great advantages at the
> commencement of a War, from their resources being so near at hand that they
> can be brought immediately to bear upon any point, or in any direction in which
> they may be required, through the facilities afforded by their extensive lines of
> Inland Navigation or Railroad; Whereas all our means whether for defence or for
> aggression, must be transported across the Atlantic.
>
> If Canada is to be defended with success this can only be looked for in our being
> able from the very earliest moment to acquire and to maintain the command of
> the Navigation of the Lakes. This must at all hazards be done with reference to
> Lake Ontario, and our utmost endeavours must also be exerted to put afloat as
> respectable a Force upon Lakes Erie and Huron as means and circumstances will
> admit of, for the same object; and if that is not to be effected so completely, in
> consequence of the difficulty of obtaining access to them by large vessels owing to
> the defects in the Locks of the Welland Canal and to other local causes; this
> Force should at all events be sufficient for the protection of our own Coasts from
> Invasion or insult.
>
> Without being prepared with a sufficient Naval Force upon the Lakes, or the
> means of creating one at the moment when it may be wanted, the opportunity
> must be lost which perhaps might never be regained, of striking the only blow
> which would be calculated to paralyze the enemy's measures, and to retard their
> operations until time were afforded for the arrival from England of the reinforce-
> ments of all descriptions, which would doubtless be sent out as soon as possible.
>
> In my estimation the whole success of the War would in a great measure depend
> upon our being able to take the initiative upon the first commencement of hos-
> tilities, instead of waiting until the enemy were fully prepared to act upon the
> offensive; for by a combined naval and military attack we might succeed in
> capturing or destroying the vessels in the American Harbours on the Lakes, and
> disposing in the same manner of their Military or Naval Stores before they would
> have time to strengthen their defences, or to reinforce the Garrisons of their Forts,
> which from their having few Regular Troops, are kept up upon the lowest possible
> scale.
>
> Every moments delay must add to the difficulty of such operations, and render
> the prospect of their success less certain, and therefore I cannot too strongly
> support the views which have been expressed by Captain Boxer . . . that Her
> Majesty's Government should cause to be sent out immediately to this country the
> means of arming & equipping a sufficient number of Steamboats or Propellors
> [i.e., screw rather than paddle-wheel steamers]; that is to say, the machinery
> required for their fittings which might be applied either to Boats built or put
> together expressly for the purpose; or to the schooners or other vessels of the
> Country which might be of a size and description, capable of being converted into
> Vessels of War. . . .
>
> Without the command of the Lakes, or having at least a Force upon them that

might make itself respected, I am satisfied that no Military positions that could be taken up to protect the exposed Frontiers of Canada West, could be maintained without the risk of their being turned by the enemy effecting a landing in their rear, at the same time that they might be attacked by a superior Force in front.[66]

The Canals were a strong link in this chain of defence. Unfortunately the enlargement of the Lachine Canal would not likely be completed until 1847; no steps had been taken to enlarge the Grenville Canal; and work on the Welland Canal was being hindered by local jobbery.

On December 22 the Commanding Royal Engineer issued instructions that contracts were to be awarded for the construction of four martello towers at Kingston, the plans for which had been recently approved by the Master General of the Ordnance. The contracts were awarded without advertisement to "trustworthy persons" so as not to create alarm in the United States,[67] and Cathcart approved them himself on January 28, 1846, as an emergency measure.[68]

On March 26, 1846, Cathcart reverted to the theme that next to nothing had been done about fortifications, despite all the surveys and plans made. His letter to the young William Ewart Gladstone, who had succeeded Lord Stanley as Secretary of State for War and the Colonies, emphasized that the approaches to Montreal should be strengthened. He was not convinced, however, that fortresses with large garrisons were necessary in Canada where climate and topography would make lengthy sieges improbable.[69] The elderly Duke of Wellington, once again serving as Commander-in-Chief of the British Army, was inclined to agree when his opinion was sought,[70] and as a result the strength of the British Army in Canada was not increased.

Wellington also agreed that the Hudson's Bay Company's request for regular troops to garrison Fort Garry in the Red River colony might be granted on other than purely military grounds.[71] The request had been prompted by rumours of American troops at Pembina, only about fifty miles from Fort Garry, during the summer of 1845, and the Hudson's Bay Company was sufficiently alarmed to offer to pay the whole cost of the expedition, including the military stores which would be needed at both Upper and Lower Fort Garry.[72] Since the only information about the

---

[66]Adm. 7/625, Cathcart to Stanley, Dec. 11, 1845.
[67]C/455, Holloway to the Respective Officers, Dec. 22, 1845.
[68]W.O. 44/49, Cathcart to Holloway, Jan. 28, 1846.
[69]W.O. 1/554, Cathcart to Gladstone, March 26, 1846.
[70]W.O. 1/555, Wellington to Gladstone, April 29, 1846.
[71]Ibid., March 28 and May 2, 1846.
[72]W.O. 1/552, Simpson to Metcalfe, Nov. 6, 1845. See also Alvin C. Gluek, *Minnesota and the Manifest Destiny of the Canadian Northwest: A Study in Canadian-American Relations* (Toronto, 1965), 60ff.

Red River Colony to reach England was from the Hudson's Bay Company, it is possible, as is suggested in Alvin Gluek's recent study based on Company records, that Governor Simpson had deliberately magnified the danger, hoping that the presence of British troops in the colony would frighten away the free traders who were ignoring the Hudson's Bay Company's monopoly rights. In any event, during the summer of 1846 Major J. Crofton of the 6th Regiment of Foot travelled by ship from Ireland to Hudson Bay with 16 officers, 364 other ranks, 17 wives, and 19 children. The final stage of the journey was made in York boats.[73]

The situation of Nova Scotia and New Brunswick in these years was greatly different because of British naval superiority over any and all possible adversaries in the North Atlantic. The Lieutenant-Governor of Nova Scotia, Lord Falkland, was not nearly as impressed as many of the inhabitants by American boasts that, in the event of war, strong enemy forces would invade the province, march inland, and destroy its coal mines, but he did remark in a despatch of March 2, 1846, that the mines at Sydney, Cape Breton, were close to the sea and utterly defenceless.[74] Gladstone agreed, after discussion with the Admiralty, that an enemy privateer or frigate might cause serious damage to the coal mines at Sydney. His reply suggested that half a company of infantry might be detached from the British garrison of Halifax for duty at Sydney and that 1,000 miners might be issued with arms, if and when the Commander of the Forces considered such action necessary.[75] There were about 8,000 obsolescent flintlock muskets stored at Halifax that could be issued to the Nova Scotia militia,[76] but, as Falkland had pointed out earlier,[77] it was completely untrained, and neither he nor the British military commander had ever seen it:

It was perhaps natural that a disinclination should exist on the part of the Rural population to abandon, in a time of profound peace, their ordinary avocations, for the number of days necessary to keep the different Corps in a high state of discipline; and this feeling having been participated in, or yielded to, by the members of the Local Legislature, the periods for exercise were by degrees diminished or curtailed, until they became so infrequent as to be ineffectual for the purpose for which they were established, and were in 1844 altogether abolished.[78]

---

[73]C/831, Crofton to D.Q.M.G., Sept. 13, 1846; also W.O. 1/557, Crofton to Somerset, Sept. 15, 1846.
[74]W.O. 1/543, Falkland to Gladstone, March 2, 1846.
[75]W.O. 1/543, Gladstone to Falkland, April 3, 1846.
[76]W.O. 1/543, Minute on Falkland to Gladstone, March 2, 1846.
[77]W.O. 1/542, Falkland to Stanley, Nov. 1, 1845.
[78]W.O. 1/543, Falkland to Stanley, Jan. 2, 1846.

The Legislature of New Brunswick and most of its inhabitants had become equally uninterested in its militia, following successful settlement of the Maine–New Brunswick boundary. However, the militia artillery, commanded by a half-pay officer of the Royal Artillery, was reasonably proficient, and there were still a few enthusiastic members of cavalry and infantry units.[79] During the summer of 1845, the Lieutenant-Governor, Sir William Colebrooke, had encouraged the formation of rifle companies and yeomanry to act as bush rangers and protect the line of communication with Canada.[80] Gladstone wrote Colebrooke in March, 1846, that flintlock muskets would be made available in an emergency,[81] as in Nova Scotia, but the Legislature refused to take any action because of the widespread belief that there would not be a war with the United States.[82]

Despite military preparedness on both sides of the border common sense prevailed, and President Polk consented to arbitration of the Oregon dispute.[83] On June 15, 1846, an agreement was reached that the international boundary would continue to the Pacific coast as the 49th parallel of latitude and then be deflected so that Vancouver Island would be British territory. Ten days later Sir Robert Peel's Government was defeated and replaced by a Whig Ministry. The new Prime Minister, Lord John Russell, and his Secretary of State for War and the Colonies, Lord Grey, soon decided that Cathcart should be replaced by someone who was less war-minded and more capable of introducing responsible government, now a pressing issue, in Canada.[84] Their choice was Lord Elgin, a son-in-law of the late Lord Durham and a capable parliamentarian. Elgin assumed his new appointment on January 30, 1847.

With the pressure for war lessened military programmes were modified. Construction of the four martello towers at Kingston and of lesser works under progress at Quebec was carried to completion, Lord Grey told a Select Committee of the House of Commons on Army and Ordnance Expenditure in 1849, "because they could not be arrested without an entire sacrifice of the outlay previously incurred."[85] During December, 1846, however, he had decided that "all new works which had not at that time been commenced, should be deferred."[86] Orders to withdraw

[79]W.O. 1/543, Colebrooke to Gladstone, Feb. 23, 1846.
[80]W.O. 1/542, Colebrooke to Stanley, Sept. 26, 1845.
[81]W.O. 1/543, Gladstone to Colebrooke, March 18, 1846.
[82]W.O. 1/543, Colebrooke to Gladstone, March 27, 1846.
[83]McCabe, "Arbitration and the Oregon Question," 308.
[84]Doughty, *The Elgin-Grey Papers, 1846–1852*, I, 266.
[85]*British Parliamentary Papers*, 1849, IX, no. 499, lvi.
[86]*Ibid.*, lvii.

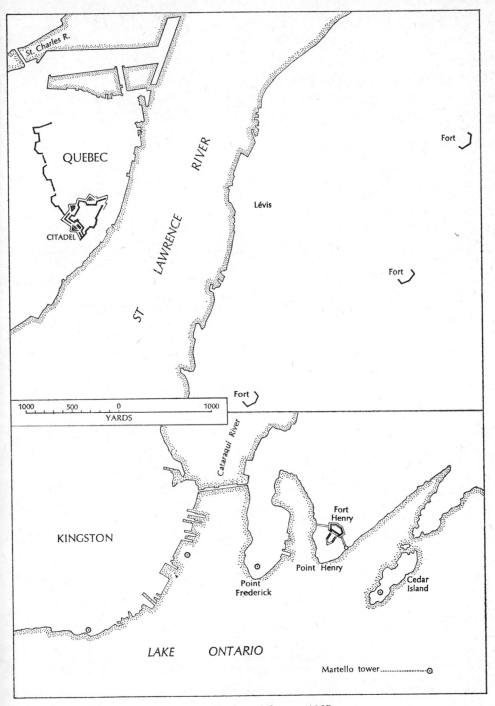

St. Charles R.

QUEBEC

CITADEL

ST LAWRENCE RIVER

Lévis

Fort

Fort

Fort

1000 500 0 1000
YARDS

Cataraqui River

KINGSTON

Fort
Henry

Point Henry

Point
Frederick

Cedar
Island

LAKE ONTARIO

Martello tower..................⊙

ABOVE Quebec defences, 1867.
BELOW Kingston defences, 1846.

the British garrison from Fort Garry had arrived too late in the summer of 1847 to be implemented until the next spring,[87] but during the summer of 1848 the garrison sailed for Great Britain in the ships that had brought out a company of 70 army pensioners whom the Hudson's Bay Company had agreed to maintain as soldier-settlers at Red River. With them were 45 wives and 37 children. These old soldiers were to serve the Company's interests on a part-time basis for seven years, but they proved to be as drunken and incompetent as their commander, Major William B. Caldwell, was inept as Governor of what was now called Assiniboia.[88]

By this time responsible government was being introduced in Canada, and Lord Grey was arguing that "now the Canadians have self Govmt. so completely granted to them they ought also to pay all its expenses including military protection. . . ."[89] The *laissez-faire* theories of the Manchester School had gained wide acceptance in Great Britain: although there should be no unseemly haste in granting complete independence to colonies, it was considered to be inevitable and their inhabitants should get used to the idea of bearing the cost of defence forces in peace time.[90] Lord Elgin, in a long private letter to Grey of December 6, 1848, however, objected to asking Canadians to bear any share of the cost of its British garrison. "Canada has a special claim for protection beyond any other Colony," he wrote, "because it is the fact of her connexion with Great Britain which exposes her to hostile aggression—She has no enemy to dread but the States, and they would cease to be dangerous to her if she were annexed."[91] Personally he did not think there would be any widespread protest in Canada against the number of British troops being reduced if the winter passed quietly and without any cause for alarm. There could, of course, be no reason to expect British troops to perform purely police duties in a self-governing colony. Thus the defence situation, as Elgin saw it, had become quite simple:

What You really want then is a sufficient body of troops to occupy the forts, to form a nucleus around which a great force mainly composed of militia may be gathered in case of regular warfare, and to give the peaceful residents on the frontier, who have the misfortune to dwell in the vicinity of a population combining the material force of high civilization with the loose political morality & organization of barbarous hordes, a reasonable security against marauding incursions.

---

[87]C/831, Wellington to Officer Commanding at Fort Garry, June 4, 1847.
[88]Documents on W.O. 43/89; see also Gluek, *Minnesota and the Manifest Destiny of the Canadian Northwest*, 71–2.
[89]Doughty, *The Elgin-Grey Papers, 1846–1852*, I, 126.
[90]C. P. Stacey, *Canada and the British Army, 1846–1871: A Study of the Practice of Responsible Government* (rev. ed.; Toronto, 1963) is the definitive account of the reasons why the British Army left Canada.
[91]Doughty, *The Elgin-Grey Papers, 1846–1852*, I, 267.

There are two ways in which America may give us serious annoyance here and occupation for our troops—either by going regularly to war with the view of wresting Canada from England, or by permitting bands of citizens under the denomination of fox hunters, buffalo hunters,—sympathisers, or what not, to invade this territory—If she prefers the former game I trust it will be played out by Her Majesty's fleets off New York and Boston, and by my old friends the West Indian Regiments in Florida & South Carolina, as well as here by Regulars and Militia—And, as to the other species of desultory warfare, I must own that I have little apprehension that it will be attended with any material or permanent results unless there be widespread disaffection in the Colony itself—Although, unquestionably, if we were to do nothing to defend the Colonists against such attacks, the borderers might conceive a just indignation and listen to the suggestions of those who whisper to them that the honour of being subjects to Her Majesty is hardly worth the cost.[92]

The size of the British Army in Canada was thus a political rather than a military question, but senior officers in Canada were obsessed by the experiences of the past decade and were intent only on keeping their forces on a war footing at all times. Was invasion possible, Elgin asked, with the small United States Army dispersed over so immense a territory? Were enough Canadians sufficiently disgruntled with their present form of responsible government to encourage American filibusterers to enter Canada?

Grey's continued suggestions for the adoption of a policy of "cautiously proceeding to throw more of the Military expenditure upon the Colonies" were prompted by the criticism directed at the Government by Cobdenites in the House of Commons at Westminster.[93] Elgin, however, was by now going through a much more trying time. A Tory mob had pelted his carriage with stones and rotten eggs and burned the Parliament Buildings in Montreal because he had signed the Rebellion Losses Bill and provided evidence that responsible government was a reality. During October, 1849, the frustrated Tories issued an Annexation Manifesto in the mistaken belief that British adoption of free trade made it pointless for Canadians to remain within the Empire: more would be gained by joining the United States. Elgin and his ministers, however, continued resolute, and the militia officers and other holders of Crown appointments who had signed the Manifesto were dismissed. On December 19, 1849, Elgin replied to Grey's suggestions that some reduction in the regular force might be possible though no officer would admit it:

I have always told you that if you would do it quietly you might reduce yr garrison—You are just as little able to cope with the power of the States with

---

[92]*Ibid.*, 268.
[93]*Ibid.*, 448.

5000 men as with 3000—You may therefore if you please largely reduce the staff and more moderately the men—leaving the remainder in the best barracks—I think you may do this without in any material way increasing the tendency towards annexation—provided always that you make no noise about it—You must do this however if you attempt it on the authority of the home Govt. If you wait till Doomsday you will never get a military man here to agree to such a course.[94]

The appointment of Commander of the Forces had been abolished a few months earlier, and completely separate, lesser commands were then created for Canada and Nova Scotia.[95] The last of the provincial troops, three troops of cavalry, were disbanded on April 30, 1850;[96] the company of coloured infantrymen had been paid off two years earlier.[97]

Grey's despatch of March 14, 1851, followed the line suggested by Elgin: except for a number of enrolled pensioners who would be settled on Crown lands,[98] on the understanding that they would be available to assist in the maintenance of law and order as was the practice in Great Britain,[99] "the troops maintained in Canada should be confined to the garrisons of two or three fortified posts of importance, probably only Quebec and Kingston."[100] Should the Canadian Government desire to have British troops continue to garrison other existing posts, this could be arranged "if the actual cost thus incurred were provided for by the Province." Canada was requested to assume the cost of maintaining the canals built by Britain "at a very heavy cost, chiefly with a view to the military defence of the Province." Yet Grey's despatch made it quite clear that the British Government still fully acknowledged responsibility for defending any of its colonies against any foreign aggressor.

The strength of the British Army was soon reduced by about 1,400 rank and file, and the military posts at Trois-Rivières, Sorel, Chambly, La-prairie, Brockville, Chatham, Amherstburg, and Penetanguishene were abandoned.[101] By January 1, 1852, there were only 4,742 rank and file in Canada and 2,319 in the whole Nova Scotia command.[102] During that year the Royal Navy's paddle-sloops *Minos, Cherokee,* and *Mohawk* were paid off. The dockyard at Kingston was closed late in 1853, Lord Grey having agreed earlier with the Admiralty opinion that there was no point

[94]*Ibid.,* II, 560.
[95]W.O. 1/559, Grey to Elgin, June 14, 1849.
[96]W.O. 1/560, Grey to Elgin, Dec. 22, 1849.
[97]W.O. 1/560, Falkland to Elgin, Dec. 30, 1848.
[98]Documents are on W.O. 4/287.
[99]F. C. Mather, "Army Pensioners and the Maintenance of Civil Order in Early Nineteenth Century England," *Journal of the Society for Army Historical Research,* XXXVI (September, 1958).
[100]G. 5/37, Grey to Elgin, March 14, 1851.
[101]G. 12/66, Elgin to Pakington, Oct. 27, 1852.
[102]Relevant monthly strength returns on W.O. 17/1556 and W.O. 17/2399.

in maintaining an inland naval establishment in peace time when the United States might, if it so desired, establish at any time a larger one with the greater resources that it had immediately available.[103] As Elgin had predicted, none of these reductions caused more than mild expressions of regret, and no effort was expended by the provinces in improving the militia. The vast majority of the inhabitants were not interested in military affairs at a time when they were enjoying friendly relations with the United States and so much money and energy were necessary for the internal development of their provinces.

The British people were, on the whole, almost as lacking in interest in military matters. British troops had not appeared on a European battlefield since Waterloo, and none of the many colonial campaigns fought in the far corners of the Empire had been serious enough to give the Government cause for concern. What had been good enough for the Duke of Wellington once must still be adequate; Britain's greatest soldier had not suggested any serious military change or reform during all the years he had been Master General of the Ordnance, Prime Minister, or Commander-in-Chief.

A serious situation was revealed following the outbreak of war with Russia on March 28, 1854. It was soon realized that the Duke of Newcastle had too many responsibilities as Secretary of State for War and the Colonies, and on June 10 Sir George Grey was appointed Secretary of State for the Colonies; Newcastle continued in office as Secretary of State for War. During August, 1854, the British Government ordered the withdrawal of units required for war service, including two companies of artillery and three battalions of infantry from Canada and a single company of artillery and a regiment of infantry from Nova Scotia.[104] This transfer left in Canada only the 26th Regiment at Quebec City, the Royal Canadian Rifles, split between Montreal and Kingston, and two companies of Royal Artillery.[105] Moreover, the Royal Canadian Rifles, consisting of older men not likely to desert from border posts because of their service towards a pension, was not as fully combatant a corps as regiments of the line. A battalion of infantry remained at Halifax, less companies at Fredericton and Saint John, and there were detachments of the continuing company of Royal Artillery at each. The token garrisons were no longer maintained in Cape Breton and Prince Edward Island.[106]

[103]Doughty, *The Elgin-Grey Papers 1846–1852*, I, 266; IV, 1604.
[104]Newcastle to Rowan, Aug. 18, 1854, in *British Parliamentary Papers*, 1856, no. 289.
[105]Monthly strength returns on W.O. 17/1558.
[106]Monthly strength returns on W.O. 17/2401.

These military reductions were possible largely because the United States Senate had approved the Reciprocity Treaty negotiated by Lord Elgin on behalf of the several provinces of British North America during the hectic ten days he spent in Washington late in May and early June, 1854.[107] Elgin's instructions had directed him to persuade all his provinces that Americans might have access to inshore fisheries and the right to navigate the St. Lawrence River and Canadian canals in return for admitting freely a considerable list of natural products to the American market. Elgin did his work well and did not give the Americans reason to suspect that "the British Government was prepared to make sacrifices for the sake of averting a dissension with the U.S., while engaged in an arduous warfare with the European Powers."[108]

The perilous excitements of the Crimean War did not fail to rouse the British provinces. The Legislatures of New Brunswick and Nova Scotia sent addresses of loyalty to Queen Victoria, and the respective Lieutenant-Governors were led to believe that local militia might be embodied for garrison duty should the British Army consider further withdrawal of regular troops.[109] Governor James Douglas of the far western Crown colony of Vancouver Island offered to raise an irregular force of white men and Indians for possible employment against Russian fur traders, but he was advised that the Royal Navy would provide any measure of protection that might be necessary.[110]

More positive action was taken in Canada. The provincial government employed 150 of the enrolled pensioners sent out earlier from Great Britain under the aegis of Lord Grey for garrison duty at forts vacated by the British regulars.[111] On October 13, 1854, the Canadian Government appointed a Commission to investigate and report on the best means of reorganizing the militia and providing an "efficient and economical system of Public defence."[112] It was also directed to plan for a more efficient police in the cities and larger towns since regular troops would no longer be as available as an "aid to the civil power." Included in the Commission's membership was Colonel George de Rottenburg, then Quartermaster General of the British Army in Canada.

[107]D. C. Masters, *The Reciprocity Treaty of 1854: Its History, Its Relation to British Colonial and Foreign Policy and to the Development of Canadian Fiscal Autonomy* (London, 1936), 48–90.
[108]C.O. 537/96, Hammond to Merivale, May 9, 1854; Clarendon to Elgin, May 4, 1854.
[109]Documents are on W.O. 1/551.
[110]W.O. 1/551, Douglas to Newcastle, May 16, 1854; Newcastle to Douglas, Aug. 5. 1854.
[111]C.O. 42/603, Head to Labouchere, Jan. 12, 1856.
[112]E/State Book O, Memorandum by MacNab, Oct. 13, 1854.

"The defence of the Province, from the nature of the Country, must at all times be mainly dependent upon Artillery and Infantry," the report submitted by the Commission on February 19, 1855, emphasized, "the services of Cavalry being principally confined to keeping up communications, and to patrol and outpost duties."[113] The "most efficient, economical and popular system of public defence" would be the formation of a volunteer force of 4,047 all ranks. The Commission recommended that the force be organized into 16 troops of cavalry, 7 field batteries and 5 foot companies of artillery, and 50 companies of rifles. The resulting Militia Bill was opposed in the Legislative Assembly on general principle and because Canadians were reluctant to assume any real responsibility for the cost of defence, but it passed its third reading by a vote of 58 to 34 on April 11, 1855.[114]

Naturally the British Government was pleased. Yet the Colonial Secretary's letter of April 13, which the new Governor General, Sir Edmund Head, sent to the Legislature, emphasized that there would be no change in British military policy. It would, he wrote, continue to regard defence against a threat as an obligation:

. . . remain charged as before with the supply and maintenance of Military force for the defence of *Canada*, as of any other part of Her Majesty's dominions, in the event of it being menaced by foreign arms. They propose, also, to continue to maintain the force now existing in *Canada*, or whatever force may be strictly required, for the military occupation of the few posts of first-class importance, so as to form a nucleus for the defence of the Province.[115]

The Militia Act, which came into effect on July 1, 1855, was to continue for three years only unless "there should happen to be War between Her Majesty and the United States of America."[116] The appointment of Adjutant General of Militia was accepted by Colonel de Rottenburg on the understanding that he could continue to draw half-pay as a British Army officer as well as 750 pounds sterling annually from the Province of Canada.[117] A militia officer held the appointment of Deputy Adjutant General for each of Upper and Lower Canada (these names continued in military use, whereas the political terms now were

---

[113]*Report of the Commission appointed to investigate and report upon the best means of re-organizing the Militia of Canada, and upon an improved system of Police* (Quebec, 1855), 3.
[114]Stacey, *Canada and the British Army, 1846–1871*, 94.
[115]*Journals of the Legislative Assembly of the Province of Canada*, 1854–1855, 1104.
[116]18 Vict., c. 77.
[117]C.O. 42/598, Head to Russell, June 21, 1855.

Canada West and Canada East). The Canadian Government left supervision of militia matters to the Receiver-General, Dr. E. P. Taché, who was a veteran of both the War of 1812 and the Rebellion of 1837 in Lower Canada. In wartime the sedentary militia would be required to undertake its familiar roles of transporting supplies, building roads and fortifications, and guarding prisoners, but no training for these tasks was necessary in peace time, and there was still to be only the traditional annual muster. The new volunteer force, on the other hand, copied the practice of several American states where gaily uniformed units of horse artillery, lancers, hussars, and rifles had sprung up as the traditional militia fell more and more into disrepute during the years following the War of 1812.[118]

The first Canadian units were authorized in a Militia General Order of August 31, 1855; others were promulgated every succeeding week. There was nothing to prevent them drilling more than the number of days for which pay was authorized; as in Massachusetts and New York, the early units tended to double as social clubs and exercise the right to exclude socially undesirable citizens of the community from membership. Colonel de Rottenburg's first annual report was encouraging:

> The persons who have joined this Force are not the dissolute and the idle, but they are, on the contrary, the respectable Mechanics of the several Towns and Villages where the Companies of this Force are located. The idle or the dissolute would never devote the time nor the money which are required to qualify the Men of the Active Force to gain a knowledge of their duties and to provide their Uniforms—and so respectably is this Force constituted, that the By-Laws of the several Companies generally contain clauses providing for the expulsion of any Member whose conduct in any way may bring discredit on the Corps they belong to.
>
> . . . it is of course natural that Gentlemen of the same national origin and the same sentiments, whether Scotch or French, Irish or English, become members of the same Company, Troop or Field Battery. Thus, we have a French Field Battery at Quebec, a French Troop of Cavalry at Montreal, and some French Rifle Companies in Montreal, Quebec and Ottawa, five Highland Companies of Rifles at different places, and some others who are principally if not entirely Irish.[119]

The Canadian Government initially purchased enough arms and equipment in England for half the authorized number of volunteers. An arrangement was soon made whereby it could purchase warlike stores from the British Army's own depots in Canada, at cost price in England

---

[118]*Journals of the Legislative Assembly of the Province of Canada*, 1857, appendix 3.
[119]*Ibid.*

plus 15 per cent to cover departmental expenses.[120] As an initial gesture of goodwill the British Government donated twenty-nine field guns and sufficient stores for the field batteries, on condition that they be inspected annually by the senior Royal Artillery officer in Canada.[121] Units had to purchase their own uniforms, which were patterned on those worn by the British regulars with whom they would be serving and for whom it was hoped the enemy would mistake them.[122]

Indiscreet efforts by British consular officials and agents in the United States to recruit a foreign legion for service in the Crimean War, and the American Government's demand for their recall in the spring of 1856, caused a diplomatic furore and occasioned some alarm in Canada.[123] When the Crimean War ended, the fiery Lord Palmerston, Britain's Prime Minister, decided on forthright measures. Lieutenant-General Sir William Eyre was ordered to North America in the revived appointment of Commander of the Forces, and the British army then in the Crimea was ordered to provide three infantry regiments and an artillery company for Canada and two infantry regiments for Nova Scotia. Ill-informed newspapers, however, magnified this into 10,000 troops who were to be convoyed across the Atlantic by the Royal Navy which was then concentrated at Spithead. This report caused alarm in Washington, but it also brought Lord Elgin to his feet in the House of Lords on April 18, 1856. Elgin believed that there was no serious anti-British feeling in the United States to worry about, and he was perturbed that the British Army in North America was to be increased after all the effort he had expended to have it reduced in size. However, the Secretary of State for War merely answered him that the Government intended "to send back to British North America a certain number of regiments, which were taken from the garrisons of those provinces at the commencement of the war . . . the report that these troops are being sent out for the purpose of aggression is entirely without foundation."[124]

Undoubtedly the 50,000 British troops who spent the winter of 1855–56 in the Crimea were much better equipped, trained, and led than those who had landed with Lord Raglan during September, 1854, and

[120]*Report on the State of the Militia of the Dominion of Canada for the year 1870* (Ottawa, 1871), 147.

[121]*Journals of the Legislative Assembly of the Province of Canada*, 1857, appendix 3.

[122]Militia General Order, Canada, Aug. 16, 1855.

[123]J. B. Brebner, "Joseph Howe and the Crimean War Enlistment Controversy between Great Britain and the United States," *Canadian Historical Review*, XI (December, 1930).

[124]Great Britain, House of Commons, *Debates*, 1856, CXLI, 1142–3.

had subsequently been decimated by battle or disease. Whereas Raglan continually asked himself "what would the Duke [of Wellington] have done," his successor followed the example of Napoleon and, for the first time in British military history, had a Chief of Staff to co-ordinate the work done by his staff officers. Other changes followed.

The long overdue reforms of the military organization in London were drastic. During December, 1854, the Commissariat was transferred from Treasury control to that of the Secretary of State for War, Lord Panmure. Early in February, 1855, he became both Secretary of State for War and Secretary at War, to merge these two offices at long last. On May 25 the Board of Ordnance was abolished and the appointment of Master General of the Ordnance allowed to lapse. All civilian administrative functions now became centred in the War Department under the Secretary of State. (During 1857 it became known officially as the "War Office.") All military functions were now handled by the Commander-in-Chief's staff at the Horse Guards. Because the royal prerogative remained very real to Queen Victoria, the functions of command and discipline continued to be handled by her cousin, H.R.H. George Duke of Cambridge, as General Commanding-in-Chief, even though the Secretary of State for War answered in Parliament for the British Army. (Not until 1887 was the Duke of Cambridge actually titled Commander-in-Chief.) The Adjutant General was his principal staff officer and was responsible for much of what was handled by a general staff in the best European armies, but the Duke of Cambridge might on occasion consult anyone he chose, such as the Inspector General of Fortifications who was the very knowledgeable, but elderly, General Sir John Fox Burgoyne.[125]

On May 2, 1856, the Colonial Secretary wrote to Sir Edmund Head that there had been no departure from the policy for British North America enunciated by Lord Grey in 1851. The British Government still desired "to place their main dependence on the well-proved loyalty and courage of Her Majesty's Canadian subjects to repel any hostile aggression should the occasion ever unfortunately occur, although in that event Her Majesty's Government would not fail to give to the Province the full support of the whole power of the British Empire."[126] When Elgin asked a further question in the House of Lords on May 27, the Secretary of

[125]An illegitimate son of "Gentleman Johnny," who surrendered his army at Saratoga in 1777, Burgoyne had been commissioned in the Royal Engineers in 1798. He served in the Peninsular War, 1808–14, yet managed to get to the Crimea "in a sort of nondescript capacity" in 1854. The *Dictionary of National Biography* also makes it clear that Burgoyne's "opinion was eagerly sought on every sort of question, and he sat on innumerable commissions, from one on the penny post to one on the proposed site of Waterloo Bridge."
[126]C.O. 42/604, Labouchere to Head, May 2, 1856.

State for War replied briefly to the effect that no change in policy was intended, but that peace time stations had to be found for the units concerned.[127] Nor is there any indication in the private papers of Sir William Eyre that he attempted to alter the existing defence plans for British North America. When visiting Fredericton on September 3, 1856, he merely instructed the Commanding Royal Engineer to report on the "strategic or decisive points" that it would be desirable to occupy with militia or volunteers if there should be an American threat of invasion of northwestern New Brunswick.[128] After visiting the line of the vital overland route between New Brunswick and Canada, the Commanding Royal Engineer recommended that field works of logs and earth should be built at Little Falls, Grand Falls, and Woodstock, but only if and when danger seemed imminent.[129]

Another alarm by the Hudson's Bay Company, because a detachment of American cavalry briefly visited Pembina during the summer of 1856, resulted in 120 officers and men of the Royal Canadian Rifles being sent to Fort Garry in 1857.[130] This company also travelled via Hudson Bay, but by ship from Montreal. Its commander, Major George Seaton, could see no need for regular troops, particularly infantry, at this lonely, isolated post where the inhabitants were peaceful and the nearest U.S. Army post was Fort Riley, some 400 miles distant and garrisoned by only about 130 officers and enlisted men. Seaton refused to be influenced by the Hudson's Bay Company's efforts to ensure that the troops got as much physical enjoyment as possible at Fort Garry, and he remained convinced that their presence was desired only to scare away the free traders who were again challenging the ancient monopoly.[131] Nevertheless the detachment remained at Fort Garry until 1861.

During the spring of 1858 the discovery of gold in the Fraser valley of unsettled British Columbia had attracted fortune-hunters from all over the world. Late in May Governor Douglas of Vancouver Island took advantage of the presence of H.M.S. *Satellite* at Esquimalt, where a stores depot for the Pacific Station of the Royal Navy had been built in 1855, to visit the gold diggings on the Fraser River with a naval detachment.[132] On July 1 the Colonial Secretary wrote expressing the hope that

[127]Great Britain, House of Commons, *Debates*, 1856, CXLII, 691–4.
[128]Eyre Papers, Box 17, Eyre to Ford, Sept. 3, 1856.
[129]*Ibid.*, Ford to Eyre, Nov. 8, 1856.
[130]C/364, Shepherd to Clarendon, Nov. 4, 1856; Shepherd to Labouchere, March 23, 1857.
[131]C/364, Seaton to Officer Commanding, Royal Canadian Rifles, March 14, 1858; see also Gluek, *Minnesota and the Manifest Destiny of the Canadian Northwest*, 127–128.
[132]C.O. 60/1, Douglas to Stanley, June 10, 1858.

Douglas would be able to get the more reliable American miners to co-operate with the civil government of what was now to become a separate mainland Crown colony of British Columbia. Douglas was, for the time being, to be governor of both colonies. British sailors and marines could be employed in aid of the civil power if absolutely necessary, but they might be tempted to desert if sent inland.[133] On July 31 the Colonial Secretary wrote that Colonel R. C. Moody and a company of Royal Engineers (4 officers and 150 other ranks) were being sent from Britain to assist him. However, this was a temporary measure:

> This force is to be maintained at an Imperial cost for only a limited period, and that, if required, afterwards, the Colony will have to defray the expenses thereof.
> This force is sent for scientific and practical purposes, and not solely for military objects. As little display as possible should therefore be made of it. Its mere appearance if prominently obtruded might serve to irritate rather than appease the miscellaneous population which will be collected in British Columbia. It should be remembered that the real strength lies in the conviction of the emigrants that their interests are identical with those of the Government which should be carried on in a harmony with, and by means of the people of the country.[134]

Travelling by ship, via Cape Horn, Colonel Moody's company reached Vancouver Island in December of that year. Moody's orders directed him to survey the new settlements, supervise the construction of roads and bridges, and lay out a proper seaport and capital.[135]

Defence against external aggressors remained the responsibility of Rear-Admiral R. L. Baynes, Commander-in-Chief of the Pacific Station. He intervened during the summer of 1859 when a detachment of American troops occupied the disputed San Juan Island while the Anglo-American Boundary Commission was still at work. San Juan was strategically placed alongside the best channel for navigation between Vancouver Island and the mainland of southern British Columbia; heavy guns mounted there could deny passage to local shipping. Baynes had four warships on the scene when Lieutenant-General Winfield Scott appeared, once again in the role of peace-maker. Scott's suggestion of October 25 that token forces of both American infantry and Royal Marines should occupy the island pending a settlement was accepted.[136]

[133]C.O. 398/1, Lytton to Douglas, July 1, 1858.
[134]*Ibid.*, July 31, 1858.
[135]Frederick W. Howay, *The Work of the Royal Engineers in British Columbia, 1858–1863* (Victoria, 1910).
[136]Admiralty Pacific Station Records, vols. 37–9 contain naval correspondence on San Juan dispute. There is a detailed treatment of this particular incident in James O. McCabe, *The San Juan Water Boundary Question* (Toronto, 1964), 36–59.

In Great Britain there was growing concern over the aggressive policies of the Emperor Napoleon III of France. Fear that the French were planning to invade across the English Channel, something that the much greater Napoleon I had not been able to do, prompted nearly 160,000 members of the British artisan and middle classes to join a new volunteer movement in 1859.[137] Lord Palmerston declared that "steam has bridged the Channel," and his Government spent 10 million pounds sterling building fortifications, mostly martello towers, for the seaports on the south coast of England.[138] The immediate cause for alarm in 1859 was the launching of the world's first armoured battleship, *La Gloire*, by the French navy and the British realization that the wooden warships of the Royal Navy could not stand up to her in battle. Britain countered by launching the more powerful ironclad H.M.S. *Warrior*,[139] but it would take years to replace the Royal Navy's wooden warships, so there were valid grounds for the invasion scare and for the appointment of a Royal Commission to study the defence of Great Britain.

An early summer visit in 1859 to the defenceless Prince Edward Island by Sir William Fenwick Williams, Lieutenant-General Commanding British troops in North America, prompted that province's Lieutenant-Governor to seek authority to form volunteer companies.[140] As early as January 30 the Lieutenant-Governor of Nova Scotia had proposed the creation of a volunteer force, and a number of companies were functioning there before the end of 1859.[141] Similar action appears to have been taken in New Brunswick because the scheduled visit of the Prince of Wales to North America in 1860 would provide a wonderful opportunity for parades and *fêtes*.[142]

The visit of the Prince of Wales in 1860 may be taken as a gala occasion which seemed to symbolize the end of a period of suspicion and uneasiness. He visited each of the provinces of British North America and inspected both British troops and local volunteers wherever they were to be found; he made an equally good impression in the American cities which were included in his itinerary. "Anglo-American relations proper had never seemed so auspicious," writes H. C. Allen: "With the main

---

[137]Brian Bond, "Prelude to the Cardwell Reforms. 1858–68," *Journal of the Royal United Service Institution*, CVI (May, 1961).
[138]Captain S. W. Roskill, *The Strategy of Sea Power* (London, 1962), 94.
[139]M. Lewis, *The History of the British Navy* (London, 1959), 226–227.
[140]C.O. 226/91, Dundas to Newcastle, July 25, 1859.
[141]*Journal and Proceedings of the Legislative Council of the Province of Nova Scotia, 1862*, Appendix 1.
[142]New Brunswick Letter Book. I (1861–1864), Gordon to Newcastle, Dec. 23, 1861.

traditional causes of disagreement for the most part settled, and with a greater mutual tolerance and respect than had hitherto been possible, it seemed, despite much residual ill-feeling in the United States, as if Anglo-American friendship might, henceforth, go broadening steadily down from precedent to precedent."[143]

[143]H. C. Allen, *Great Britain and the United States: A History of Anglo-American Relations (1783–1952)* (London, 1954), 451.

(8)

THREAT OF WAR

The outbreak of the American Civil War on April 12, 1861, was viewed as an ill-omen by Sir Edmund Head, still Governor General of British North America. "The aspect of affairs is most serious," he wrote twelve days later, "whenever their own fighting is over I do not think it will be a pleasant thing to have 100,000 or 200,000 men kicking their heels with arms in their hands on our frontier & all the habits acquired in a Southern Civil War."[1]

The British Government, however, was soon to be faced with an immediate dilemma: could Great Britain remain neutral without permanently alienating either the new Confederate States of the South, which might win independence and become a great nation, or the continuing United States of the North, which already was one? Southern sympathizers and many newspapers in Britain were demanding that help be extended to the Confederates and that the United States Navy be prevented from blockading the seaports from which raw cotton was normally shipped to British mills. Northern sympathizers, on the other hand, did not know what to say or think because of President Lincoln's reiterations that the issue was one of states' rights, not slavery. The Proclamation of Neutrality issued by Queen Victoria on May 13, recognizing the existence of a *Justum Bellum*, was popular on neither side of the Atlantic. Some Americans even hoped that the North and South could be reunited if the United States should pick a fight with Great Britain.[2]

Before the month of May was out the British Government ordered three infantry regiments of the line and a battery of field artillery to Canada[3]

---

[1]D. G. G. Kerr, with the assistance of J. A. Gibson, *Sir Edmund Head: A Scholarly Governor* (Toronto, 1954), 217.

[2]H. C. Allen, *Great Britain and the United States: A History of Anglo-American Relations, 1783–1952* (London, 1954), 452–63.

[3]C.O. 42/630, Newcastle to Head, May 31, 1861.

to increase its modest garrison to 5,100 regular troops.[4] The War Office agreed to provide guns for a battery to protect the important coal mines at Sydney, Nova Scotia, and additional rifles for the volunteer militia in Prince Edward Island.[5] As for the sea, the First Lord of the Admiralty, the Duke of Somerset, felt that Rear-Admiral of the Red Sir Alexander Milne's naval force on the North America and West Indies Station was sufficient. He pointed out to the Prime Minister, Lord Palmerston, in August that there were two sound reasons why it would be preferable to keep additional warships in British ports, ready to sail if needed. One was the avoidance of the cost of shipping additional stores across the Atlantic and of commissioning more ships. The other was desertion. One warship at Halifax had already lost 70 men, lured into the United States Navy by the prospect of high wages and the chance of prize money.[6]

The War Office sent 500 stand of arms to Vancouver Island for use by volunteers to be recruited there.[7] The American token garrison was withdrawn from San Juan Island,[8] but a detachment of Royal Marines remained there until the dispute was finally settled in 1872.[9] Rear-Admiral of the White Sir Thomas Maitland was at Vancouver with the flagship of his Pacific Squadron, a frigate, a sloop, and two gunboats. As early as July 15 the First Lord of the Admiralty had suggested to Palmerston that the situation on the west coast of North America was satisfactory:

> The amount of naval force on the station is considerable, and I have not heard any reasons which induce me to think a large reinforcement necessary. If there should be some privateering, a naval force would be more useful than a regiment [transferred from China]. Any addition to our naval force will, I fear, cause an excess in our estimates.[10]

To aid in its decisions about the St. Lawrence River and the Great Lakes the Admiralty possessed little recent knowledge. Except for 1860, when Rear-Admiral Milne had escorted the Prince of Wales to Quebec and Montreal, only troopships had used the St. Lawrence River in recent years.[11] Captain Richard Collinson, R.N., one of the most efficient officers

[4]W.O. 17/1565, Monthly Strength Return, Canada, Nov. 1, 1861.
[5]C.O. 43/126, Rogers to Cunard, Aug. 16, 1861; Rogers to Under Secretary of State, War Office, Aug. 16, 1861.
[6]Palmerston Papers, Somerset to Palmerston, June 25 and Aug. 19, 1861.
[7]C.O. 43/126, Elliott to Colonial Agent, Aug. 5, 1861.
[8]C.O. 43/126, Rogers to Hammond, Aug. 26, 1861.
[9]Admiralty Pacific Station Records/39, Hall to Hillegar, Nov. 16, 1872.
[10]Palmerston Papers, Somerset to Palmerston, July 15, 1861.
[11]Adm. 128/114, Report by Vice-Admiral Sir Alexander Milne, March, 1864.

at the Admiralty and soon to be promoted to flag rank, had once spent a short holiday in Canada, so he was directed in 1861 to prepare a study. To supplement his own recollections he had only the reports submitted nearly twenty years earlier by Captain Edward Boxer. Collinson's memorandum, presented on September 2, suggested that the presence of British warships at Quebec would make it possible to entrust the citadel to volunteer defenders; the garrison of British regulars could then join the principal field force in the vicinity of Montreal. His proposed distribution of the Royal Navy's assistance is interesting:

Off Quebec, two line of battle ships, one-half of the crews to be detailed for service in such vessels as are capable of carrying guns on the Lakes; their crews to be filled up from the fishermen, boat and raft men; and some of their boats to be detached to assist the squadron between Montreal and Quebec in their operations on the rivers St. Francis, Yamaska and Richelieu.

Between Montreal and Quebec two corvettes of not more than 18 feet draft of water; two dispatch vessels; six gunboats of 7 feet draft.

At the head of the Lachine Canal two large-size gun-boats to annoy the enemy in the event of their attempting to cross from La Prairie.

In the event of the canals not being destroyed, the more vessels that can be passed up to the lakes the better, and the smaller sized floating batteries, 44¾ feet beam will be extremely serviceable. With three of these vessels, one of which should be stationed at Port Dalhousie, a second at Toronto, and a third at Kingston, no enemy dare attempt a landing, as his communication would be certain to be cut off.[12]

Obviously Collinson considered that it would not be possible to undertake naval operations on Lakes Erie and Huron for he emphasized the importance of preventing the Americans from seizing the Welland Canal and then transferring their own naval vessels to Lake Ontario.

Collinson's memorandum reached the First Lord of the Admiralty while members of Palmerston's Cabinet were worrying about the Prime Minister's latest proposal. His letter of August 26 to Sir George Cornewall Lewis, Secretary of State for War, had expressed the opinion that there would not be "any Blowup this year in Europe," but suggested that British relations with Washington were in a ticklish condition and might well call for additional British strength in the colonies:

No reliance can be placed on Seward & Lincoln from week to week. The only Security we can have against wrong Insult and aggression on their Part must consist in our being strong in our Provinces, and in our squadron off their Coast.

---

[12]Adm. 7/624, Memorandum on the assistance that can be rendered to the Province of Canada by Her Majesty's Navy in the event of War with the United States, Sept. 2, 1861.

Our Naval Force is nearly sufficient, but will be added to; our Land Force of Regulars in our Provinces is far from sufficient. We ought not to have less than Ten Thousand Regulars there during the winter, when all communication with Europe is cut off except with Halifax, between which and Quebec owing to our economical mood there is no Railway Communication except through the States, and to march round at that time of year would be next to impossible.[13]

Palmerston felt that the large steamship *Great Eastern* should be engaged to transport three infantry regiments to Quebec before navigation of the St. Lawrence came to an end for the winter. Arms and stores for use by the Canadian militia should also be shipped at once. The Prime Minister sent similar letters to both the Colonial and the Foreign Secretaries.

The Secretary of State for War admitted in his reply that an American attack on Canada was possible, but he did not think that the Government in Washington was "insane" enough to "make an enemy of the principal maritime power in the world" while it still had a civil war on its hands.[14] Moreover, he believed that there was no barrack accommodation in Canada for three more regiments. The Duke of Cambridge, Commanding-in-Chief at the Horse Guards, was disturbed by the thought of having to find three regiments at short notice for despatch to Canada.[15]

The Duke of Newcastle replied to Palmerston along the same line but went much further. Although Colonial Secretary and a civilian, his letter gave quite forceful military reasons against the Prime Minister's proposal:

. . . such an ill-appointed Army as theirs could never invade Canada in the winter. All the horrors of Moscow would be repeated.

But I have an objection as regards our own Troops, unless necessity overrules that and every other. We have no Barrack accommodation for more troops and to billet them in frontier towns (and all the towns except Quebec are close to the frontier) would be fatal. The temptations to desertion will be greater and the possibilities more frequent in the winter and I fear a general demoralization will be too probable.

If in the Spring matters look threatening, the Great Eastern will soon carry out as many Regiments as we want, and those Regiments will be in high order and fit for anything.[16]

Somehow or other the story of Palmerston's scheme got into the London newspapers and annoyed Queen Victoria and the Prince Consort, who had had no idea what was being suggested.[17] Their disapproval may have

---

[13]Palmerston Papers, Palmerston to Lewis, Aug. 26, 1861.
[14]Palmerston Papers, Lewis to Palmerston, Sept. 3, 1861.
[15]Colonel Willoughby Verner, assisted by captain E. D. Parker, *The Military Life of H.R.H. George, Duke of Cambridge* (London, 1905), I, 312.
[16]Palmerston Papers, Newcastle to Palmerston, Aug. 30, 1861.
[17]Palmerston Papers, Lewis to Palmerston, Sept. 10, 1861.

been a convenient excuse for Palmerston to let his generally unpopular proposal die quietly in mid-September.

Shortly thereafter the Colonial Secretary received a reply to his letter to Sir Edmund Head of August 21 inquiring whether Canada might be willing to share the additional expense of a larger British garrison. According to Sir Edmund Head's letter dated September 9, any outbreak of hostilities would be caused by purely Anglo-American differences, and he anticipated that Canada would feel no enthusiasm about expenses which these differences might create:

The Colony would have no voice in determining this question and there exist no causes of difference with the Government of the United States arising out of the affairs or interests of Canada. The Colony would be involved in such a war only as part and an exposed part of the Empire. . . .

The feeling of the Colony and its representatives in the Provincial Parliament would I believe be adverse to any contribution in money out of Colonial Funds towards the cost of such increased armament.

That our long exposed frontier is inaccessible by sea and not easily reinforced in winter, is a line of weakness through which an enemy might wound England is the misfortune of Canada as well as the Mother Country, but I doubt whether the people of Canada would see in this fact a sufficient reason for charging them with a large portion of the burden of defence in a war caused by interests in no degree of a local or colonial character.[18]

By this time Major-General C. Hastings Doyle had become depressed by conditions in the subordinate Nova Scotia command he had recently assumed. There were but 2,235 British regulars at his disposal, and the only troops in the whole of New Brunswick were 25 artillerymen and 128 infantrymen at Fredericton.[19] Following an inspection trip to New Brunswick he sent a very forthright letter to the Secretary of State for War in November:

With so few troops at my disposal, I must naturally in case of sudden invasion, look to the Militia of these Provinces for assistance, but we should do so in vain, for altho' it would be numerous, & those composing it loyally disposed, it exists alone on paper, & altho' nominally officered, they are generally speaking too old for service (in some instances from 60 to 90 years of age) entirely unacquainted with their duty, totally ignorant of Drill, & without Adjutants or Staff, so that a considerable period must elapse, with the small means of instruction available, before this mass of men could be formed into working order or properly disciplined, nor can this state of affairs be remedied, as the local legislatures of the provinces have repeatedly refused to provide money for the purpose of Defence *generally*, altho' in Nova Scotia £2000 was granted to establish Volunteers.[20]

[18]C.O. 42/630, Head to Newcastle, Sept. 9, 1861.
[19]W.O. 17/2408, Monthly Strength Return, Nova Scotia, Nov. 1, 1861.
[20]C/1671, Doyle to Secretary of State for War, Nov. 28, 1861.

The Lieutenant-Governor of New Brunswick had managed to raise 3,000 volunteers who were partially trained. In neither New Brunswick nor Nova Scotia, however, would the Legislature provide money to organize the militia before there was an actual outbreak of hostilities. Beyond organizing a corps of lumbermen to render roads impassable to an invading enemy, Doyle could attempt nothing in the St. John valley. Elsewhere in the Atlantic provinces successful defence would have to depend largely on the efforts of the Royal Navy's North America and West Indies Squadron. Rear Admiral Milne had six line of battle ships, three frigates, eight sloops, and eight smaller war vessels.[21] His squadron had considerably more fire power than the eight frigates, nine corvettes, and twenty-four sloops which the Admiralty believed the United States Navy had on duty in the Gulf of Mexico and off the Atlantic coast.[22]

During the early autumn there were complaints that Americans were trying to recruit soldiers in British North America (with one officer in uniform going so far as to use a hotel room in Hamilton as a recruiting office); British regular soldiers received tempting offers from American units in need of experienced personnel; and occasional parties of American soldiers violated Canadian soil in their search for deserters.[23] Yet the situation remained quiet until news reached Quebec that U.S.S. *San Jacinto* had stopped the British mail steamship *Trent* on the high seas on November 8, 1861, and had forcibly removed two Confederate diplomatic agents on their way to Europe. The Governor General, now Lord Monck, ordered the Lieutenant-General Commanding in North America, Sir William Fenwick Williams, to place his regular troops on a war footing and arrange makeshift accommodation for the reinforcements certain to be sent from Great Britain. The Canadian Government agreed to the Governor General's request that the number of its volunteers be increased. Applications to form new companies were pouring in, and existing volunteer units found all their members once again drilling with enthusiasm. Large numbers of the sedentary militia also turned out to drill at this time of crisis, and the Canadian Government agreed to embody 38,000 if it should be necessary. At long last a Minister of Militia was designated, the appointment going to John A. Macdonald who already was Attorney General for Canada West and joint leader of the Government.[24]

Lieutenant-General Williams paid a whirlwind visit to the most vulner-

[21]Palmerston Papers, Somerset to Palmerston, Sept. 26, 1861.
[22]*Ibid.*, Aug. 31, 1861.
[23]Correspondence in C/696–699; see also Robin W. Winks, *Canada and the United States: The Civil War Years* (Baltimore, 1960).
[24]C.O. 42/628, Monck to Newcastle, Dec. 19 and 27, 1861.

able points in Upper Canada. Additional guns were mounted at Kingston and Toronto, where a Canadian engineer, Mr. H. H. Killaly, joined his party. Killaly, a former Public Works official and now Inspector of Railways for the Province of Canada, knew the whole country well and was considered to have a "strong, clear practical head."[25] The provincial authorities agreed to build batteries at Port Dalhousie and Port Colborne and to erect twelve blockhouses at locks along the Welland Canal. Fort Wellington at Prescott was reoccupied and strengthened as a connecting link between Kingston and Montreal because the American town of Ogdensburg on the opposite shore of the St. Lawrence River was now the terminus of two railway lines which could be used to assemble an invading force. Plans were made to stop any American advance on Montreal along the Lake Champlain–Richelieu River route, and even to secure the initiative by capturing the American fort at Rouse's Point. Finally, the whole province was divided into five military districts for the British Army, with headquarters at London, Toronto, Kingston, Montreal, and Quebec. Captain F. W. de Winton, R.A., who accompanied Williams, subsequently wrote privately to Captain Collinson that he hoped the Admiralty would provide war vessels for service on the Great Lakes: "You know the impossibility of defending the frontier without some command of that Kind and could we obtain possession of Lake Erie by establishing a post on its southern shore, you might cut off the [American] north and west by communicating with the Southern Army, whose posts are not more than 100 miles from it."[26]

The Admiralty did not bother to tell the Commander-in-Chief of the North America and West Indies Squadron what action should be taken on the inland waters of Canada following the reopening of navigation in the spring of 1862, or even what action he should take in the North Atlantic if hostilities began. Rear-Admiral Milne, however, had his own ideas respecting the latter. Milne later wrote that, after ensuring the safety of his own bases at Halifax and Bermuda, he would have raised the United States Navy's blockade of the Confederate coastline using his own squadron and that of Commodore Hugh Dunlop, R.N., who was watching the course of a revolution in Mexico in case French or Spanish forces might try to intervene when the United States was not in a position to invoke the Monroe Doctrine. Then Milne would have blockaded the coast of the northern United States to the best of his ability and co-operated in Chesapeake Bay with the Confederate land forces "who

[25]Adm. 7/624, De Winton to Collinson, Jan. 1, 1862.
[26]*Ibid.*

would practically, if not in terms, have been our allies, and where our aid would have been invaluable."[27]

Through late November and early December the staffs of both the Horse Guards and the War Office were very busy preparing the despatch of 11,175 regular troops to North America: two battalions of foot guards, six infantry battalions of the line, twelve batteries of artillery, three companies of engineers, two battalions of the military train, and sizable detachments of commissariat and medical personnel. Envisaged disposition of the augmented garrisons was:[28]

	Officers	Other Ranks
Canada	611	12,341
New Brunswick	154	2,282
Nova Scotia	147	2,738
Newfoundland	12	297
	924	17,658

A delegation of Canadian ministers was then in London to press for British financial aid in the construction of an Intercolonial Railway, and it expressed some doubt in the command ability of Lieutenant-General Sir William Fenwick Williams, although it did concede that the "hero of Kars" was immensely popular in the province.[29] One of the additional staff officers being posted to Canada later described Williams as "a very handsome old gentleman, with charming manners."[30] What senior officer was available to supersede him, however, was a decision the youthful Duke of Cambridge decided to postpone until later. The military planners proceeded to gather advice and make appointments. Lieutenant-General Sir George Wetherall, a good twelve years older than Williams, was called to the Horse Guards for consultation because of his long and varied service in Canada. Colonel Patrick L. MacDougall, Commandant of the recently established Staff College at Camberley, was seconded to an *ad hoc* planning staff, which also received advice from Lord Seaton (the former Sir John Colborne) and General Sir John Fox Burgoyne. Colonel E. R. Wetherall, who had served in his father's regiment during the Rebellion of 1837 in Lower Canada and who had been Chief of Staff of the Central India Force during the recent Great Mutiny, was selected to be Chief of Staff to Williams. Colonel K. D. Mackenzie was appointed

[27]Adm. 128/114, Report by Vice-Admiral Sir Alexander Milne, March, 1864.
[28]C/1671, Strength States published by War Office, Jan. 3, 1862.
[29]Verner, *Military Life of H.R.H. George, Duke of Cambridge*, I, 314.
[30]Field-Marshal Viscount Wolseley, *The Story of a Soldier's Life* (London, 1903), II, 111.

Deputy Quartermaster General, succeeding Colonel I. F. Napier who was given the local rank of major-general and command of troops. Major-General D. Russell was ordered from Aldershot to command another field formation. Major-General Lord Paulet was selected to command the 1st Battalion, Grenadier Guards and the 2nd Battalion, Scots Fusilier Guards which were brigaded separately. Mr. W. J. T. Power, one of the Deputy Commissary Generals, was ordered to Canada to perform the duties of a Commissary General.

Considerable quantities of arms, ammunition, and accoutrements were shipped from Woolwich Arsenal for possible issue to the Canadian militia, and particularly to its volunteer units of cavalry, artillery, and rifles. Colonel Daniel Lysons, who had served in Canada during the Rebellions and in the Crimea, and who had been intimately involved with the volunteer movement which swept Great Britain in 1859, was despatched to advise the Canadian Government which had done without an Adjutant General of Militia for reasons of economy since Colonel de Rottenburg's resignation in 1858.[31] Colonel Lysons was accompanied by 12 field officers and 46 sergeants to instruct the Canadian volunteers. Smaller instructional cadres were sent to train the volunteers of New Brunswick and Nova Scotia, but not those of Prince Edward Island.[32]

During the third week of December the first troopships were able to attempt the St. Lawrence River, because it had been a mild and open season for navigation. Only S. S. *Persia* was able to proceed very far. It reached Bic and landed its troops, who were transported in sleighs by the local inhabitants to the eastern terminus of the Grand Trunk Railway at Rivière-du-Loup. Since the only railway linking Montreal with the Atlantic coast had its terminus at Portland, Maine, preparations were put in hand to land the remaining troops in New Brunswick and move them by sleigh over the previously used winter route to Rivière-du-Loup. Responsibility for this movement rested with Major-General Doyle at Halifax. Captain William Fitzroy of the 63rd Regiment, who had been sent from Halifax in civilian clothes via Portland and that branch of the Grand Trunk Railway, to headquarters at Montreal with despatches for Williams, made a detailed reconnaissance on his return trip overland. Major-General R. Rumley was sent to New Brunswick with an *ad hoc* staff to arrange overnight accommodation and supervise the actual troop movement. Serious thought was given to the erection of stockaded blockhouses at intervals along the Madawaska-Temiscouata portion of the

---

[31]C.O. 42/630, Newcastle to Monck, Dec. 4, 1861.
[32]C/696, Forster to Williams, Dec. 12, 16, and 26, 1861; C/1037, Scarlett to Williams, Dec. 17, 1861.

route which ran close to the border with Maine (an action which had been recommended in 1856). Such strong points would be occupied by detachments of troops during the passage of the rest of the force. The most likely points from which attack might come were Fort Fairfield on the Aroostook River and Houlton, which was opposite the New Brunswick town of Woodstock. Major-General Rumley was also responsible for opening up an alternative and militarily safer route from Shediac to Métis. This partially built road, passing through the Matapedia valley, was much the same route as would be followed later by the Intercolonial Railway.[33]

By the time troopships began straggling into Halifax on December 25, however, the crisis was passing. Queen Victoria's dying Prince Consort had managed to tone down Palmerston's ultimatum to the United States following the *Trent* affair, and the British Government then authorized its Minister in Washington to delay official delivery so that President Lincoln's administration would not be called on to make a hasty decision. At an American cabinet meeting on December 26, Secretary of State William H. Seward persuaded the President to release the Confederate diplomatic agents to a British ship at Baltimore. The British Government then conveniently overlooked American failure to apologize for stopping *Trent* on the high seas.

Britain decided to proceed with the overland troop movement to Canada anyway, since another crisis might develop. Plans to build block-houses along the way were abandoned, however, as was the opening of the alternate route from Shediac to Métis. On December 30, 1861, the 62nd Regiment of Foot, which had been stationed in Nova Scotia for some time, was sent forward by shallow draft steamer to St. Andrew's, New Brunswick. Two days later the first party of 3 officers and 150 other ranks travelled to the end of the rail at Canterbury where hired sleighs were waiting to take them to Woodstock. Lieutenant-Colonel James Daubeny made an excuse to visit Houlton and found little to fear:

. . . which place the 62nd Regt. were to have taken in case of war with America. The Town consists of scattered houses extended over more than a mile in length & lying at the bottom of a hill. The only garrison in the place were 60 Volunteers, whom I saw marching in the Town without arms to the inspiriting air of Yankee Doodle played on a solitary fife accompanied by a big drum, so that the 62nd would not have had a hard task to perform.[34]

---

[33]J. Mackay Hitsman, "Winter Troop Movement to Canada, 1862," *Canadian Historical Review*, XLIII (June, 1962), 127.
[34]C.O. 42/632, Journal of Lieut. Col. Daubeny, C.B., 62 Regt. from 20th December 1861 to 18th January 1862.

The larger steamships docked at Saint John, whence 160 soldiers went forward daily, riding 8 to a sleigh. Four days travelling took them to Woodstock where they merged with the smaller parties that had travelled part way by rail. Another six days travelling took everyone to Rivière-du-Loup where accommodation was available until a train should leave for Montreal. A few staff officers had travelled from Halifax in civilian clothes via ship to Boston and then by an American railway in order to get to Montreal before the troops. The final return submitted by Major-General Doyle on March 17, 1862, showed that 6,823 all ranks actually went forward by sleigh to Canada. Only nine men succeeded in deserting from halting places close to the Maine boundary. They were lured by offers of a substantial bounty for trained soldiers who would serve in the American army and managed to circumvent the precautions taken to prevent desertion. The remaining troops, together with the military stores, were held at Halifax until spring when ships could again navigate the St. Lawrence River.[35]

The regular troops assigned to Upper Canada were concentrated at Kingston, Toronto, Hamilton, Guelph, and London, whence they might launch counter-attacks against any attempted invasion. Williams resisted all pleas for regular garrisons from Lake Erie and Lake Ontario towns, whose worried mayors were afraid of attack.[36] The greatest number of the troops in Canada, as always, was in the Montreal area. A number of officers subsequently obtained leave to visit, as military observers, the American armies opposing each other.

The Canadian volunteers had increased to 829 officers and 13,390 other ranks and were organized in 34 troops of cavalry, 27 batteries of artillery, 182 companies of rifles, and 5 companies of engineers.[37] On March 15, 1862, a Canadian Parliamentary Commission, appointed by the Governor General to plan a more effective militia, submitted its report. It recommended the establishment of an Active Force of 50,000 and a Reserve Force of the same size. The former, consisting of all the existing volunteers and the balance of 50,000 men selected by ballot from the sedentary militia, should be liable for anywhere from fourteen to twenty-eight days annual drill: "A reference to the map of Canada will clearly point out that even this number of men would be insufficient, without the co-operation of a strong body of regular troops and a powerful fleet of gunboats on the lakes."[38]

[35]Hitsman, "Winter Troop Movement to Canada," 127 ff.
[36]J. Mackay Hitsman, "Please send us a Garrison," *Ontario History*, L (Autumn, 1958) and correspondence on C/696.
[37]*Sessional Paper No. 17, Province of Canada*, 1862, 3.
[38]*Ibid.*, 8.

By this time, however, most Canadians had again lost interest in military matters. "Make the militia efficient," the Toronto *Globe* had urged three days earlier. "Drill and arm the volunteers, and let the business of the country go on. We are not afraid of the Americans provoking a war; we are not afraid of them if they do provoke it." Since the United States was making no headway in its war with the Confederate States of America, it would have been pointless to argue on the score of danger. A Militia Bill which reflected the Commission's recommendations and the Government which introduced it seemed doomed. The Government, headed by John A. Macdonald and George E. Cartier, had grown corrupt during its tenure of office, and there was a widespread feeling that a change was needed. While opposition mounted on a variety of counts, Macdonald absented himself from the debate to engage in one of his drinking bouts. When he resumed his seat on May 20, in time for the Bill's second reading, it was defeated by a vote of 61 to 54. Next day the Government resigned.[39] The incoming Ministry, headed by John Sandfield Macdonald and Louis V. Sicotte, managed to secure passage of a Militia Act which merely doubled the number of days of paid annual drill for volunteers from six to twelve for a maximum of 10,000 volunteers and permitted the Governor General to raise volunteer regiments independently of the militia in wartime.[40]

British newspapers were very outspoken in their criticism of the Canadian Legislature. *The Times* declared on June 6 that, "if Canada will not fight to protect its independence from foreign invasion, neither will England." This, of course, brought a typically Canadian retort from the Toronto *Globe* in its issue of June 18:

The Times has done more than its share in creating bad feeling between England and the United States and would have liked to see the Canadians take up the quarrel which it has raised. . . . There would be no talk of war but for the mischief-making of newspapers in England and America. . . . We cannot agree to the dogma that Canada should provide entirely for her defence when she is not the author of the quarrels against the consequences of which she is called to stand upon her guard.

The British Government was much more circumspect. Permanent officials of both the Colonial Office and the War Office were well aware how small was public expenditure for all purposes in any of the self-governing colonies. Only a few weeks before a request for preferential

---

[39]C. P. Stacey, *Canada and the British Army, 1846–1871: A Study of the Practice of Responsible Government* (rev. ed.; Toronto, 1963), 132–5.
[40]25 Vict., c. 1.

treatment for the volunteers of Prince Edward Island, made by its Lieutenant-Governor who considered that most corps were too poor to supply the extras not provided through public funds, had evoked the following minute:

The burthen of this song is the same that reaches us from so many quarters in North America. The Inhabitants say that they are willing to give their personal services, but not to spend local funds either private or public. The Governor therefore hopes that arms and accoutrements may be furnished free, and Even a small quantity of ammunition.

This is an embarrassing subject. A genuine volunteer movement is valuable, but if the greater share of the pecuniary part is to be borne by Great Britain, it can no longer be viewed as a local effort or as a proof of local public spirit. On the other hand a decline of the volunteers will be a loss.[41]

These worries continued. The Colonial Secretary sent a lengthy despatch on August 21 to Lord Monck expressing the British Government's concern over Canada's lack of defensive measures when the United States had a large army for the first time in its history. Newcastle suggested that 50,000 partially trained militia were a necessary adjunct to the British regulars and Canadian volunteers. Monck was directed to investigate the possibility of creating a uniform militia system which might be entered into willingly by all the colonies:

The political union of the North American Colonies has often been discussed. The merits of that measure and the difficulties in the way of its accomplishment have been well considered, but none of the objections which oppose it seem to impede a union for defence. This matter is one which all the Colonies have interests common with each other and identical with the policy of England.[42]

By this time a commission of experts had completed a survey of the Canadian border from Lake Superior to New Brunswick and was completing its report, which was submitted to Lord Monck on September 2. Monck had appointed this commission on February 6, instructing Colonel J. W. Gordon, R.E., Lieutenant-Colonel H. L. Gardiner, R.A., Mr. H. H. Killaly, and Captain W. Crossman, R.E., to report on a system of fortification and defence for Canada. On March 31 Colonel E. R. Wetherall and Captain John Bythesea, V.C., R.N., Naval Attaché in Washington, were added to the commission because of detailed instructions received from the Secretary of State for War. These had been written by the Inspector

---

[41]C.O. 226/96, Minute on Dundas to Newcastle, April 24, 1862.
[42]Newcastle to Monck, Aug. 21, 1862, in *Sessional Paper no. 15, Province of Canada*, 1863.

General of Fortifications, General Sir John Fox Burgoyne. He virtually
ruled out an attack on Quebec at any time of the year as being too difficult for Americans to attempt with their resources. Burgoyne admitted
that he lacked any practical first-hand knowledge of the Canadian border,
but he felt that "some favourable battlefields could be selected on that
line; these, previously thoroughly well studied, could no doubt be rapidly
entrenched, and made very formidable."[43]

The lengthy report submitted by the commissioners was based on the
premise that the United States was now a "military power." It had
demonstrated its ability to raise and equip large armies in a short space of
time, and to bring them to bear on "any part of their enemy's frontier
that may be necessary."[44] Recent operations in the Mississippi valley had
shown that the Americans "also possess the power of rapidly extem-
porizing a formidable fleet, adapted for Lake warfare." The report
envisaged American attack:

> By a naval descent on the shores of Lake Huron, at Goderich or Collingwood.
> By the passage of a force across the Detroit River into the London District.
> By the passage of a force across the Niagara frontier.
> By the passage of troops across the St. Lawrence from Ogdensburgh.
> By several columns acting in concert between Derby Line and Huntingdon, with
> a view of converging on Montreal and cutting the communication with Kingston,
> as well as with Quebec.

By threatening each of these five areas, an enemy could force a dispersal
of the defending troops along the whole frontier for fear that feints might
be turned into real attacks. Undoubtedly, however, the main offensive
would be directed against Montreal, and this would be facilitated by the
enemy being able to turn the line of the Richelieu River from his
fortified base at Rouse's Point.

The commissioners conceded that defending troops would have to be
distributed to a certain extent but argued that they should be concentrated on specific strategical points. From these centres they could be
thrown in masses upon the enemy or await the development of his plans.
Permanent fortifications existed only at Quebec and Kingston; as the
temporary works elsewhere had been allowed to decay, new strong points
would have to be constructed. Financial considerations limited the commissioners to the suggestion that only those fortifications that were
"absolutely required" be built but these were considerable and of varying

[43]W.O. 33/11, Report of the Commissioners appointed to consider the Defences
of Canada, 1862.
[44]*Ibid.*

strength. Permanent works were recommended for Sarnia, Amherstburg, Guelph, Fort Erie, Port Colborne, Port Dalhousie, Fort Mississauga, Short Hills, Hamilton, Toronto, Bay of Quinte, Fort Prescott, Montreal, St. Johns, Isle aux Noix, and Lévis, at an estimated cost of 1,611,000 pounds sterling. The construction of many more entrenched positions, in which troops could offer battle, was also recommended. Otherwise the numerically smaller defending forces would not stand a chance of success.

Success would also, however, depend upon naval supremacy on the Great Lakes being acquired immediately on the outbreak of war. The commissioners then became very frank about what this entailed, including enlargement of the canals to facilitate the passage of armoured vessels:

> They are aware that by existing treaties no fleets can be maintained on the lakes in time of peace, but they recommend, as soon as the canal communications shall have been improved, as hereafter proposed, that iron-plated vessels with all the armament and stores necessary, should be kept in readiness at Ottawa, or other convenient places not affected by the stipulations of the treaty, whence they could be taken into Lakes Ontario and Erie.
>
> During the progress of any negotiations likely to end in war, these vessels without any breach of treaty or faith, could assemble at Gananoqui, below Kingston, for the purpose of passing into the lakes immediately war was proclaimed.
>
> A portion of the St. Lawrence canals not being available after the actual commencement of hostilities, the enlargement of the Ottawa, Rideau and Welland Canals, to an extent that will enable armoured vessels to pass through them, becomes an essential requirement in the defence of Canada.

However, the Admiralty had not yet decided upon the dimensions for the iron-plated vessels the commissioners had in mind, so there was no knowing how wide the canals would have to be. Shore headquarters for a naval force of 2 line of battle ships, 2 corvettes, 9 floating batteries, 6 dispatch vessels, and 53 gunboats should be established at Montreal. The naval base for Lake Ontario should be in the Bay of Quinte, rather than in the more exposed harbour of Kingston. Dunnville on the Grand River was the most suitable location for a naval base on Lake Erie. Unless and until a canal should be constructed to make it unnecessary to use the narrow Detroit River to get to Lake Huron, there would be no point re-establishing the base at Penetanguishene.

Manpower requirements were placed even higher than the 100,000 mentioned earlier by the provincial Parliament's commission: 65,000 effectives of whom only a large nucleus should be British regulars, another 65,000 in reserve, and 20,000 to replace casualties. Disposition of the effectives was envisaged as being 15,000 in the London district, 17,000 at Toronto and Niagara, 10,000 at Kingston, 5,000 at Prescott, 15,000 in

the Montreal area, and 3,000 at Quebec. Naval requirements were estimated as 9,350 officers and ratings. "The necessity of having a secure
base of operations in communication with the Mother Country," it was
emphasized, "renders the maintenance of the fortress of Quebec indispensable." The commissioners also recommended the construction of an Intercolonial Railway, along the "North Shore" route (much as eventually
built), to ensure communication with the fortress of Halifax during the
months when the St. Lawrence River was filled with ice.

The Canadian Government had conveniently put off consideration of
Lord Newcastle's despatch of August 21, 1862. Finally, on October 28
and after prodding by the Governor General, it decided against establishing compulsory military training for the militia. The Government felt
that the Volunteer Movement was the outlet through which "the military
spirit of the people must find vent in a period of peace."[45] The country-
side was too sparsely populated for farmers to be forced to abandon their
labour in order to drill at a distance from their farms. In the event of
war able-bodied men everywhere could be depended on, but it was "not
desirable to excite discontent amongst them, by any premature attempts
to exact compulsory service." Canadians would never do anything to
provoke war with the United States. Furthermore, any attempt at defence
would be pointless:

No probable combination of regular troops and militia would preserve our soil
from invading armies; and no fortune which the most sanguine dare hope for
would prevent our most flourishing districts from becoming the battlefield of the
war. Our trade would be brought to a standstill; our villages destroyed, homes,
happy in peace, would be rendered miserable by war, and all as a result of events
for the production of which Canada would be in no way accountable.

Union of all the provinces, even for defence, was not feasible until there
should be an Intercolonial Railway, an opinion that was subsequently
confirmed by the Lieutenant-Governors of New Brunswick and Nova
Scotia and by the Governor General.[46]

On December 17 Monck tried again, urging the necessity of creating
the substantial part-time force that had been recommended.[47] Again the
Canadian Government's answer was in the negative. It was equally imper-
vious to a further appeal by the Colonial Secretary, which attempted to
refute the stand taken by the Canadian Government on October 28 and

[45]Executive Council Minute, Oct. 28, 1862, in *Sessional Paper no. 15, Province
of Canada*, 1863.
[46]Monck to Newcastle, Oct. 30, 1862, *ibid*.
[47]Monck to Macdonald, Dec. 17, 1862, *ibid*.

argued that "the main security against aggression which Canada enjoys as a portion of the British Empire is the fact known to all the world that war with Canada means war with England; not in Canada only, but upon every sea and upon the shores, where situated, of the aggressive power itself."[48]

In January 1863 yet another report on defence was submitted. As a follow-up to the Royal Commission which had reported on the defences of Great Britain on February 7, 1860, the Secretary of State for War had appointed a committee to report on colonial defences generally. This Defence Committee was instructed to recommend which existing fortifications should be placed in an efficient state, and which should be either dismantled or turned over to local authorities. The committee's report was based largely on views submitted by Royal Engineer officers employed in the several colonies rather than on its own observations throughout the British Empire. Part of it is worth quoting here, the description of the fortresses considered essential, with Quebec leading off as usual:

Since Quebec is the place through which all succours from Great Britain to Canada must pass, it is obviously necessary that this fortress should be maintained in the most efficient and secure condition. If it fell into the hands of an enemy, the military communication between the province and the mother country would be cut off. The Committee are therefore of opinion that Quebec should be kept up as a first class fortress, but with such modification of the old line of works around the town as may be found necessary. . . .

Halifax, in Nova Scotia, is an important naval and military station, the maintenance of which is required for national objects. The Citadel appears to be in a fair state of repair, but the works on George's Island require to be remodelled and re-armed, to meet the modern improvements in gunnery. The works called Grand Battery, Fort Charlotte [on George's Island], Fort Clarence and Point Pleasant should, owing to their position, be retained; but require to be remodelled. York Redoubt and Sherbrooke Tower appear to be useless as they now stand; they should either be remodelled, or else abandoned and replaced by floating harbour defences. Fort Needham may be dismantled.

The works at Windsor and at Annapolis, in Nova Scotia, may be abandoned.

The harbour of St. John's, in New Brunswick, is a position of importance, both on account of the direct access it affords to Quebec and Canada, through the province of New Brunswick, and also on account of its commanding the Bay of Fundy—of which the possession by an enemy would threaten the province of Nova Scotia, and one main line of communication with Canada. Some of the existing works require to be remodelled and and re-armed; while Partridge Island calls for special attention as a point essential to the defence of the harbour.

The works at St. Andrew's, in New Brunswick, are reported to be in a very delapidated state. Considering their immediate proximity to the frontier, the

---

[48]Newcastle to Monck, Dec. 20, 1862, *ibid.*

Committee do not think it necessary that they should be renewed, but recommend their abandonment.

At Sydney, Cape Breton, the works are in a ruinous state; but considering the value of the coal mines in time of war to the operations of the navy, it is desirable that they should have some suitable defence.

At Newfoundland it is considered unnecessary to have any permanent works beyond a few coast batteries for the defence of St. John's Harbour.[49]

A considerably more critical view of these works was expressed in a letter which Major-General Hastings Doyle penned a mere three weeks later. Doyle considered that in its present state Halifax would be "defenceless" in the face of a powerful fleet and wrote that Saint John was "absolutely defenceless in every way, either against organized attack or predatory incursions."[50] No one bothered to mention Prince Edward Island because it no longer had either fortifications or a British garrison.

The situation on the Pacific coast was considered so satisfactory that Colonel Moody's company of Royal Engineers was scheduled for withdrawal from British Columbia at the end of 1863. Since the colonists had refused to contribute to the financial support of its primarily civilian work, they would have to form a volunteer militia if they were worried unduly about local defence.[51] The British Government permitted 130 of the Royal Engineers to take their discharge in British Columbia and gave them land grants as promised—but not in the goldfields as requested—to provide the colony with masons, carpenters, blacksmiths, tanners, surveyors, and the like. Several of these men joined the volunteer company of New Westminster Rifles formed during November of the same year.[52]

Another request for a British garrison for Red River, this time from the Roman Catholic Bishop and settlers who were worried about the danger of attack by Sioux Indians who had wandered across the international border from the Minnesota Territory, was rejected by the Colonial Office on March 12, 1863. The Duke of Newcastle considered the Hudson's Bay Company to be responsible for defence, since they "claim to be the sole and absolute proprietors."[53] He suggested that the inhabitants form their own volunteer militia. Assuming that the traders of the Hudson's Bay Company had dealt fairly with the Indians, what reason could the latter have for being hostile?

[49]Cardwell Papers 6/40, contains a copy of Report of Defence Committee, Jan. 8, 1863.
[50]W.O. 55/1558(8), Doyle to Military Secretary, Jan. 22, 1863.
[51]C.O. 43/129, Elliott to Under-Secretary of State, War Office, March 28, 1863.
[52]F. W. Howay, *The Work of the Royal Engineers in British Columbia* (Victoria, 1910).
[53]C.O. 43/129, Fortescue to Berens, March 12, 1863; see also *A. Gluek, Minnesota and the Manifest Destiny of the Canadian Northwest* (Toronto, 1965), 172ff.

The British Government became convinced following the Confederate loss of Vicksburg and defeat at Gettysburg, both of which occurred in July, 1863, that the United States would win the Civil War. It would then have armies available to attack British North America. A new state of alarm arose. The commission headed by Colonel Gordon in 1862 had certainly been thorough in its report, but its recommendations for military and naval expenditure in Canada had been so large that the British Government hesitated about implementing any part of it.[54] Therefore Lieutenant-Colonel W. F. D. Jervois, R.E., was directed to make a new study. Jervois had served as secretary of the Royal Commission on the Defences of Great Britain; now Deputy-Director of Fortifications, he was the right-hand man of the elderly Burgoyne. On September 13, 1863, Jervois landed at Halifax, where he spent a week. He was in Saint John for four days, in Canada for almost four weeks, in the northeastern United States for three weeks, and in Bermuda for a week. His opinion substantiated the British Government's worst fears about the new American armies. "Even if they were disbanded, or much reduced," Jervois reported to the Secretary of State for War on March 24, 1864, "the knowledge and experience of military operations obtained both by officers and men during the civil war would still remain as elements greatly contributing to the warlike power of the American people."[55] At least some of the defeated Confederates would be willing to serve against a foreign foe, and there were many Northerners who thought that a foreign war would be the best way to smooth over the problems of reconstruction.

Jervois' report was based on the premise that "no distinct system of defence" had ever been proposed to the Canadian people for adoption and that they would do their share if the right approach were made.[56] Militia legislation recently enacted by the Canadian Parliament had increased the authorized number of volunteers to 35,000 all ranks and provided for a careful enrolment of the sedentary militia in 1864. Battalions of sedentary militia might be embodied by ballot for six days annual drill; their officers would be qualified at military schools to be operated by British regiments in garrison at Quebec and Toronto. There were then 11,130 British troops actually serving in Canada: 1,857 at Quebec, 4,118 at Montreal, 1,081 at Kingston, 1,153 at Toronto, 946 at Hamilton, 1,292 at London, and 683 elsewhere in small detachments. There were 23,580 volunteers in Upper Canada and 12,540 in Lower

[54]Palmerston Papers, Lewis to Palmerston, Dec. 30, 1862.
[55]*Report on the Defence of Canada and of the British Naval Stations in the Atlantic*, Part I, *Canada* (London, War Office, 1864).
[56]*Ibid.*

Canada. These defenders were too weak to meet the Americans in the open field on the outbreak of war, but Jervois considered they should be able to hold a few vital strong points until help could arrive from overseas. However, there would be no point trying to defend as many fortresses and field works as the Defence Commission had recommended in 1862, since vastly superior enemy armies would merely leave forces to invest each and move on.

There was no doubt that any main American effort would be directed against Montreal, and Jervois foresaw up to 100,000 Americans advancing from Rouse's Point across the imaginary boundary of the 45th parallel. An American army corps might cross the St. Lawrence from Ogdensburg to Prescott and proceed downriver towards Montreal, and there might be diversionary attacks along the Niagara and Detroit frontiers for the purpose of drawing British forces inland. The ultimate American objective would be the capture of Quebec City, but Jervois felt that this would be difficult to achieve:

Owing . . . to its distance from the enemy's resources, and to the nature of the country through which an advance upon it must be conducted, an operation against Quebec is one of infinitely greater difficulty than against Montreal. One plan that has been discussed by the Americans is to collect their forces on the head waters of the Kennebec and Penobscot rivers, and then advance upon Quebec through the valley of the Chaudière, a distance of some 250 miles, along a route but little travelled, and passing through an almost uninhabited wilderness. It does not appear likely that this plan would be adopted. The most probable line of operations upon Quebec, if the attack were made simultaneously with that upon Montreal, is by the Grand Trunk Railway from Portland. In this case the plan of the enemy would be to seize Richmond, to which he might also communicate from Lake Champlain, and from whence, the railway diverges both to Montreal and Quebec. From Richmond he would therefore equally menace both these places.

Jervois thought that Quebec could be defended until help arrived from overseas even if the existing fortifications were obsolescent, or possibly obsolete. Although the masonry fortifications of Sevastopol had been crumbled with comparative ease by projectiles from rifled muzzle-loading guns, the Crimean War had been so badly mismanaged that officers were chary of drawing lessons from it. On the other hand, the conduct of even the opening phase of the American Civil War had demonstrated beyond any shadow of a doubt that masonry fortresses were vulnerable to rifled gunfire and that something different was needed. There seemed to be an answer in the method of certain of the German states where old fortresses were being rehabilitated by the construction on their perimeters of detached forts made largely of earth. These detached forts would keep an enemy beyond artillery range of the principal target. Jervois therefore recommended that the Quebec citadel and other existing fortifications should be strengthened and that a line of earthworks should be constructed to the south of Lévis to keep an enemy well beyond artillery range of Quebec City.

Jervois did not believe, however, that anything could be done to prevent the Americans achieving naval supremacy on the upper Great Lakes and recommended damaging the Welland Canal so they could not use it. Only by enlarging the canals on the Ottawa River and Rideau waterway would it be possible to maintain a force of armour-plated war vessels on Lake Ontario. These would have to operate as far down the St. Lawrence River as Prescott in order to prevent an American invasion from Ogdensburg. The Grand Trunk Railway, which stretched from Montreal to Sarnia, ran too close to the border for troops and stores to be moved along it safely. In short, it would not be possible to defend the western part of the Province of Canada, and Jervois recommended that the outbreak of hostilities would have to mean concentration of efforts and men in the lower province:

. . . before the actual commencement of hostilities, the whole of the Queen's troops should be brought into Lower Canada . . . excepting perhaps 1,000 men for garrison and other duties, they should in the first instance be concentrated at or near Montreal. In like manner, as regards the volunteers, the best course would be for the Governor General to exercise the power vested in him by the Volunteer Militia Act, and to bring the whole of this force to join the main body near Montreal.

Objections would, of course, be raised to the Western districts being thus left in the possession of the enemy, but we should gain strength by this system of concentration; whereas the enemy, if he thought it worth while to make an attack upon this part of the country, would be expending considerable resources upon operations which would not lead to the attainment of his object. He would gain no real military advantage by the occupation of the western peninsula, and it would be bad policy on his part to overrun the country if no such advantage could be obtained. If the Americans, as no doubt they do, desire the conquest of Canada, they would wish to conciliate the country, and if the Canadians are loyal now, the presence of hostile armies amongst them would make them more attached to the mother country than before. The great object of an American invasion would be the expulsion of the British power from the country.

But even by concentrating the whole of the Queen's troops and the volunteers in the eastern districts, we could scarcely calculate in the first instance on more than about 10,000 regulars, and from 25,000 to 30,000 volunteers, for the defence of Lower Canada; that is, unless reinforcements were supplied from England before the actual outbreak of hostilities.

The enemy, on the other hand, would probably make his attack with some

100,000 men, and whatever might be the amount of our reinforcements from home, the disparity would be so great that we could not oppose him in the field with any prospect of success, and in the absence of any defensive works to enable our small force to resist one so superior in numbers, we could not prevent his occupying Montreal; the only alternative would be for our force to fall back upon Quebec.

If Quebec, then, were put into a state of siege, we might hold out there; with this view it has been proposed on previous occasions, when the question of the defence of Canada has been under consideration, to strengthen the fortifications of Quebec only, without doing anything of a similar nature for the protection of Montreal.

Though Jervois thought Quebec was the key it would be unwise to abandon Montreal at the outset; fighting could take place only during the summer months when British ironclads could prevent the enemy crossing the St. Lawrence River and could harass their movement along the south shore. Why needlessly discourage the local volunteers and sedentary militia and necessitate the recapture of Montreal later by the expeditionary force sent from Great Britain? Instead he recommended construction of a line of defensive works well south of Montreal. The increased defences he recommended for Quebec and Montreal, together with their armament, would cost 750,000 pounds sterling, but this was less than the cost of maintaining the existing British troops in Canada for a single year.

The British Government which studied the Jervois Report during the spring of 1864 was faced with a nasty situation in Europe. After Prussia and Austria wantonly attacked tiny Denmark over the question of Schleswig-Holstein on February 1, Lord Palmerston announced that aggressors would find that "it will not be Denmark alone with whom they will have to contend."[57] However, only one-third of the British Army's infantry battalions were serving at home and these were under strength. Britain was thus unable to back Palmerston's threat of intervention to prevent the balance of power being upset in Europe.

Over-all reform of the British Army's organization would take time, but something could be achieved immediately in this crisis by reducing the size of the commitment in Canada and concentrating the bulk of the continuing regular troops in Lower Canada as Jervois had suggested. The two battalions of Foot Guards and the Military Train were ordered back to Britain, and Williams was advised in a letter dated May 25, 1864, that it was "highly desirable to retain the Troops in Canada in two

[57]C. P. Stacey, "Britain's Withdrawal from British North America, 1846–1871," *Canadian Historical Review*, XXXVI (September, 1955), 187.

principal masses at Quebec & Montreal, & to diminish as far as possible the number of scattered stations in that Colony, other than the small posts occupied by the R. C. Rifles for the purpose of checking desertion."[58]

Not knowing of this letter, Charles Adderley, a long-time critic of British expenditures on colonial defence, introduced a motion into the House of Commons to the effect that the continuing 9,000 British troops in Canada should not be scattered in detachments along an indefensible border. His motion was debated on June 27 while the House of Lords was discussing the Austro-Prussian defeat of tiny Denmark. Adderley admitted that it "might be desirable" to have a few British troops stationed in Canada as a nucleus for its defence, but asserted that these should be concentrated at Quebec.[59] Unfortunately, he added, Quebec was virtually defenceless. Lord Robert Cecil (afterwards Lord Salisbury and Prime Minister of Great Britain) suggested that it would be a national disgrace if a body of British troops stationed farther inland was cut off and forced to surrender. *The Times* seized on this point and editorialized that 9,000 British troops might serve only as a lure to large American armies interested in another victorious campaign once they had disposed of the Confederate States of America.[60] The debate was settled by the newly appointed Secretary of State for the Colonies, Edward Cardwell, who quoted the orders that had been sent to the Lieutenant-General Commanding in North America.[61]

Williams had successfully opposed such a policy earlier, but he now raised no objection beyond suggesting that Fort Henry at Kingston should be either retained or dismantled. His letter of June 13 to the Secretary of State for War indicated personal disillusionment that Canadians had put forth no real effort in their own defence. In his opinion they had learned to rely too much on the Mother Country:

. . . they seem to look on their coming dangers with the eye of a child, under the protection of a Parent who is bound to fight, whilst they pursue their ordinary business, or agitate themselves by fruitless party politics and parliamentary conflicts. Yet Upper Canada will witness the withdrawal of the Queen's Troops with regret and mortification, mingled with a bitter reflection that they have made so little effort towards self defence, or in responding to the urgent, earnest, and unceasing calls of their Governor General! I only trust it may lead them to reflect and seriously to set about the organization of a *Militia*, for certes, a few *Volunteers* never can or will defend Canada.[62]

---

[58]G. 20/11316, Lugard to Williams, May 25, 1864.
[59]Great Britain, House of Commons, *Debates*, 1864, CLXXVI, 374–377.
[61]Great Britain, House of Commons, *Debates*, 1864, CLXXVI, 378–381.
[62]G. 20/11316, Williams to Secretary of State for War, June 13, 1864.

The Governor General, however, expressed his opposition to the new policy in no uncertain terms. His confidential letter of June 16 to the Colonial Secretary argued that, by means of the provincial railway and telegraph systems, concentration of regular troops could be effected in a week, and there would be at least that much warning before war erupted. The infantry battalion at Toronto was providing a military school for militia officers, and its withdrawal would put an untimely end to this recently introduced and popular instruction. Monck was then busily engaged with the formation of a coalition government pledged to seek a union of the provinces of British North America that would make impossible any repetition of the recent political deadlock in Canada. Upper Canadians might now be disposed to contribute to fortification schemes unless "they saw the whole of H.M. troops quartered in the eastern section of the Province and the demand were made upon them for contribution towards the expense of fortifications to be erected solely with a view to the security of Quebec and Montreal."[63]

The War Office agreed to let the 16th Regiment of Foot remain temporarily at Toronto; but otherwise preparations continued for the British troops to be concentrated in Lower Canada. On August 26 the Canadian Coalition Government resolved that British persistence in such a policy would cause alarm and discouragement in Upper Canada. There was no basis, of course, for its contention that Canada could be defended as efficiently as during the War of 1812. It wished to see the British regulars left where they were, "nothing being more effective in stimulating Military Spirit, and noble emulation in the hearts of youth than the presence of troops, with whose past career so numerous and such glorious recollections are connected."[64] A memorial signed by seventy leading citizens of the Toronto district and received by the Governor General on August 17 had further suggested that Canadians would regard the military abandonment of Upper Canada as the prelude to a complete separation from the Mother Country.[65]

The Duke of Cambridge seems to have been favourably impressed by the arguments received from Canada and could see no great danger in British troops being scattered about that province in time of peace. His letter of September 9 to the Secretary of State for War suggested that orders be sent to Williams, "leaving it to him, in conjunction with the Governor-General, to distribute the troops in Canada as he may think

[63]G. 20/11316, Monck to Cardwell, June 16, 1864.
[64]E/State Book A.A., Executive Council Minute, Aug. 26, 1864.
[65]Copy in G. 20/11392.

most prudent and best, throwing upon him the responsibility of their security and easy means of concentration by means of railroads. . . ."[66] These orders were sent, and everyone became happy for the moment.

Only for the moment, though, because the American Civil War was still being bitterly contested. The North would probably win and then anything could happen. But signs of war weariness were everywhere, and there was a possibility that President Lincoln might not be re-elected. The prospect of peace was likely to be much more enticing to American soldiers and civilians alike than the waging of a brand new war to annex British North America.

[66]Verner, *The Military Life of H.R.H. George, Duke of Cambridge*, I, 360.

(9)

FEDERATION AND FENIANISM

A memorandum on Canadian defence was circulated among members
of the British Government on 12 July, 1864, by the Chancellor of the
Exchequer, William Ewart Gladstone. It aroused considerable controversy.
Gladstone had concluded that the United States would pursue a policy
aimed at the peaceful annexation of the provinces of British North
America instead of invading them as military men were then suggesting.
As a counter, he suggested that the centre of responsibility for British
North America should be shifted from London to a single colonial capital.
According to Gladstone's line of reasoning, which implied union of the
several provinces, a British presence in the colonies of any strength did
not increase security:

The United States can scarcely have a quarrel with Canada for its own sake.
The more Canada and the British Colonies are detached, as to their defensive
not less than their administrative responsibilities, from England, the more likely
the Union will be to study friendly relations with them; but, on the other hand,
the more we make ourselves the prominent personages in defending North America,
the more the Americans will feel that through the Colonies they wound us in
honour and in power; the more an invasion, otherwise almost inhuman, will be
justified in the eyes of the world.[1]

That great imperialist Lord Palmerston was still Prime Minister, however, and he settled the matter in the following minute to the Colonial
Secretary, dated July 29:

It is a question for consideration or division whether our North American
Provinces are to be fought for or abandoned. There may be much to be said for
the theory put forward by some, that our Colonies are an encumbrance and an

---

[1]Paul Knaplund, *Gladstone and Britain's Imperial Policy* (London, 1927), 238.

expense, and that we should be better without them, but that is not the opinion of England, and it is not mine.[2]

Therefore Edward Cardwell, the Colonial Secretary, wrote Lord Monck on August 6 suggesting that the time had now come for Britain and Canada to discuss the problems of North American defence in all its aspects. Cardwell indicated that whatever help Great Britain might provide in an emergency, the defence of Canada would "ever principally depend upon the spirit, the energy and the courage of her own people."[3] He enclosed a copy of the report made by Lieutenant-Colonel Jervois for the attention of the Canadian Government and for comparison with the report submitted by the Defence Commission of 1862. Cardwell's letter continued:

> In any assistance towards a system of defence which Her Majesty's Government could recommend to Parliament, the two primary objects must be—first, an adequate protection for British Troops in Canada; and, secondly, a secure communication with the Naval Forces of Great Britain.
> It is obvious that Quebec is the Position which best fulfills these conditions. But Her Majesty's Government have no wish to confine your attention and that of your Advisers to any one point, however important. It is their desire that the whole subject of the defence of Canada should be considered in a comprehensive spirit.

As soon as the British Government learned how much money Canada was prepared to spend on defence, it would decide how much assistance might be sought from the Parliament at Westminster.

The members of the Canadian Government were, however, preoccupied with preparations to attend the conference which was being convened at Charlottetown on September 1 to discuss a union of the maritime provinces, and to which they had literally invited themselves. The knowledge that Jervois was being sent back to advise them was an additional reason for postponing an answer to Cardwell's letter.

Jervois arrived at Halifax on September 3 and travelled overland, arriving at Quebec on September 23. Following interviews with Monck, Williams, and individual Canadian ministers, Jervois had a formal meeting with the whole Executive Council on October 14, four days after the Quebec Conference met to continue discussion of a confederation for British North America. To answer the questions sent him on October 18, he made a further reconnaissance before submitting a report to the Canadian Government on November 10. This differed from his previous report

[2]Quoted in Donald Creighton, *John A. Macdonald. I. The Young Politician* (Toronto, 1952), 361.
[3]G. 1/160, Cardwell to Monck, Aug. 6, 1864.

because he now understood that the Canadian Government was planning
to create a naval base at Kingston, a step which would make it possible
to maintain war vessels on the Great Lakes for their defence. Jervois
explained the vital importance of certain key points:

. . . that although, owing to the length and nature of the frontier of Canada, it
was impossible to protect it throughout its whole extent, an enemy must nevertheless acquire possession of certain vital points before he could obtain any decided
military advantage; that there are only a few such points,—and that if proper
arrangements were made for the defence of those places by the construction of
fortifications, the provision of gun-boats, and the improvement of communications;
—the militia and volunteer forces of the country, if properly organized, and
aided by British troops, would be enabled to hold them during the period (only
about six months in the year), when military operations on a large scale could
be carried on against them, and thus those forces could resist an attack with the
best chance of success.[4]

With the key points of Quebec and Montreal placed in a proper condition
for defence and the St. Lawrence River commanded by iron-plated warships, a "successful resistance could be made to any attempt to subjugate
the country so long as Great Britain had the command of the sea." From
the purely military point of view, the defence of Lower Canada was the
principal consideration, but it was quite possible to devise a scheme for
the defence of Upper Canada. Jervois outlined the necessary conditions:

. . . that efficient communication should be established with the Western districts;
that the country between Lake St. Louis and Lake Ontario should be protected
by naval, in combination with military means; that a naval depot should be provided at Kingston, which place should be fortified so as to form a secure harbour
for the gun-boats on Lake Ontario. With the naval command on that lake, troops
acting for the defence of the Western Peninsula might, if overpowered, fall back
upon its shore at Toronto, where, if proper works were constructed, they might
act in conjunction with the naval force for the defence of that position, either
until reinforcements arrived from other parts of the country, or until the winter
season obliged the enemy to withdraw.

Fortifications at Quebec and Montreal would cost 643,000 pounds
sterling, plus 100,000 pounds for armament. Fortifications for Kingston
and the Toronto-Hamilton area would cost a further 500,000 pounds,
plus 100,000 pounds for armament. He estimated the cost of gunboats as
being another 300,000 pounds sterling. Jervois had been impressed by

[4]*Report on the Defence of Canada, (Made to the Provincial Government on
10th November, 1864,) and of the British Naval Stations in the Atlantic; together
with observations on The Defence of New Brunswick* (London, War Office, 1865).

what he had seen of the Canadian volunteers; they should do well against an invader if they had fortifications upon which to fall back.

Jervois subsequently reported to the Secretary of State for War that there were a further 1,764 volunteers in New Brunswick and 1,300 in Prince Edward Island. During the previous summer 34,873 militia had attended summer camp for a week in Nova Scotia, while 2,364 volunteers had trained for a longer period. "With the exception of the western frontier of New Brunswick, the maritime provinces of British North America are bounded by the sea," he wrote, "consequently their defence must be provided for by naval forces; and hence, amongst other reasons, the importance of Halifax as a centre of refuge and action for our fleet. . . ."[5] With regard to the land frontier of New Brunswick with Maine, he wrote almost as optimistically:

. . . it is considered that, unless with a view of advancing against the town of St. John, desultory attacks from the state of Maine, for the purpose of cutting off the land communication to Quebec, would alone have to be guarded against. Considering the present wild and unsettled state of the country, and the almost entire absence of communication from any point in the United States which would serve as a base for an enemy to act upon those parts where the eastern road from Nova Scotia to Canada is nearest the frontier, it does not appear likely that any expedition in force would be employed for the latter object, unless the enemy first obtained possession of St. John as a base of operations. Any desultory attacks upon the western frontier of New Brunswick might therefore be met by a militia force in the field, aided by such temporary defences as might be deemed necessary in time of war, by the general officer in command. Gun boats on the St. John River might play a part in the defence.

Jervois could not, however, resist posing the most important question of all: "Whether the British force now in Canada shall be withdrawn, in order to avoid the risk of its defeat, or whether the necessary measures shall be taken to enable that force to be of use for the defence of the province."

Even before Jervois reported to the Canadian Government on November 10, however, there had been a drastic change in the local situation as a result of Confederate activities emanating from Canadian bases. As a climax, a small band of Confederate soldiers in uniform had raided St. Albans, Vermont, on October 19, robbed the town's banks, wounded two citizens, and set fire to some buildings before escaping across the international border to Canadian territory. Five days later Secretary of State Seward in Washington instructed the American Ambassador in London to give the six months' notice required for abrogation of the

5*Ibid.*

Rush-Bagot Agreement of 1817. With the American elections only a few days away, Seward suggested to the British Minister in Washington that it would be difficult to resist widespread pressure to abrogate the Reciprocity Treaty of 1854.[6] As a result, the members of the Canadian Government agreed on November 15 to ask Parliament to spend $1 million on the militia and to pay for the construction in the Montreal area of the fortifications recommended by Jervois, provided that the British Government undertook to erect the additional fortifications recommended for Quebec and to furnish the armament necessary for both places. However, the Canadians were not willing to accept any financial responsibility for the fortifications Jervois had recommended for Kingston and the Toronto-Hamilton area for fear the other colonies might decide that the price of the proposed Confederation was too high to pay.[7]

Since the Canadian offer, forwarded in Monck's despatch of November 16 to the Colonial Secretary, hinged on there being a British guarantee of the Canadian loan that would have to be floated to pay for the proposed fortifications at Montreal, members of the British Government were not impressed. They were far more impressed by the text of the Quebec Resolutions proposing a federal union of the several provinces of British North America.[8] This was a realistic attitude for Englishmen who believed that colonies were a useless and unnecessary expense and who secretly hoped that federation would be one more step on the road to complete independence from Britain; but it was unfair to Canadians, who were not really to blame for the poor state of Anglo-American relations. It was Canada's credit rating that had been damaged in the financial markets of the world by the potential danger of her situation, and she could float a loan herself only at a very disadvantageous interest rate. Canada, who had never defaulted on a bond issue, was spending most of the money collected in taxes on the development of the province, which still showed vestiges of the pioneer era, and it was only natural that she should attempt to save interest money by getting the British Government to guarantee the loan.

The month of December brought further complications. On December 13 a misguided Montreal magistrate discharged the apprehended Confederates who had raided St. Albans. Although the Canadian Government had repaid the money stolen from the St. Albans banks and managed to rearrest a number of the raiders, an enraged United States

[6]Donald Creighton, *The Road to Confederation: The Emergence of Canada, 1863–1867* (Toronto, 1964), 194–5.
[7]E/State Book A.A., Executive Council Minute, Nov. 16, 1864.
[8]G. 21/26, Cardwell to Monck, Dec. 3, 1864.

Congress voted to abrogate the Reciprocity Treaty, and a Presidential
Order was issued which required passports from all inhabitants of the
British colonies wishing to visit the United States.[9] The Canadian government then decided on December 16 to call out thirty companies of volunteer militia for duty at border points and to create a detective and
preventive police force to watch and patrol the whole frontier. The
volunteer companies assembled on December 26 and were organized into
western, central, and eastern administrative battalions, with headquarters
at Windsor, Niagara Falls, and Laprairie, respectively.[10]

The British Government was more worried by the news that Major-
General William T. Sherman had split the Confederacy by marching
through Georgia and had captured Savannah in South Carolina on
Christmas Eve. Would these battle-experienced troops and the other
federal armies directly under the command of Lieutenant-General U. S.
Grant be ordered to attack British North America after the Confederacy
was forced to yield? The re-election of Abraham Lincoln as President
of the United States indicated that the North would adopt a stern attitude
towards a number of incidents. For instance, Napoleon III had ignored
the Monroe Doctrine and placed the Archduke Maximilian of Austria
on the throne of Mexico in 1864, and as well permitted French shipyards
to build commerce-raiding ships for the Confederate States of America.
The British Government had allowed several raiders to be built for the
Confederacy, *Alabama* and *Florida* being merely the best known and most
successful. Confederate raiders had destroyed 275 American ships and
provoked shipowners to transfer another 700 merchant ships to foreign
registry before the United States Navy was able to capture or destroy
them.

What occurred at the British Cabinet meetings held on January 19 and
20, 1865, to discuss the plan for fortifying Quebec and the Army and
Navy estimates for the coming financial year, was summarized by Lord
Palmerston for Queen Victoria:

Mr. Gladstone has been as troublesome and wrong-headed as he often is upon
subjects discussed in Cabinet. He objected strongly to fortifying Quebec, and
insisted upon a considerable reduction in the number of men for the Navy. The
whole Cabinet, however, was against him, with the exception of Mr. Milner
Gibson, who feebly supported him, and the Duke of Argyll, who put in a word
or two in his favour. It has been, however, pretty well decided that a sum of fifty

---

[9]Creighton, *The Road to Confederation*, 212–13.
[10]*Correspondence relating to the Fenian Invasion, and the Rebellion of the
Southern States* (Ottawa, 1869), 25–8.

thousand pounds shall be put into the Army estimates, for the purpose of making a beginning of the fortification of Quebec. The estimate for the whole work is two hundred thousand pounds, but fifty thousand will cover the expense of all that can be accomplished in the ensuing summer. The Canadians are disposed to spend four hundred and fifty thousand pounds in fortifying Montreal, and according to Colonel Jervois those two points made safe will constitute the best foundation for the defence of Canada.

Mr. Gladstone at great length urged a reduction of five thousand men in the Navy, but the great majority of the Cabinet were against such a measure, considering the very hostile spirit towards England which pervades all classes in the Federal States; and looking to the probability that, whenever, the Civil war in America shall be ended, the Northern States will make demands upon England which cannot be complied with, and will either make war against England or make inroads into your Majesty's North American possessions which would lead to war; and it is felt by the majority of the Cabinet that the best security against a conflict with the United States will be found in an adequate defensive force. Mr. Gladstone seems disposed to yield to the strong opinions of his colleagues. . . .[11]

The Colonial Secretary's letter of January 21 advised Monck that the Parliament at Westminster would be asked to vote money for improving the defences of Quebec, because it would be a matter of "just reproach against the British Government if those Troops were suffered to remain in a position which, on the outbreak of war, they might not be able to hold until the military and naval resources of the Country [Britain] could be made available for their support."[12] Parliament would not, however, be asked to guarantee the suggested Canadian loan. The British Government did not want to have any more discussion of colonial defence expenditure in the House of Commons than was absolutely necessary. Cardwell's letter blithely suggested that the "proposed defences at Montreal are so important to the general safety of the Province, and to the maintenance of the communication between the District West of Montreal, and the naval and military power of the Mother country, that Her Majesty's Government trust they may look with confidence to the Government of Canada for the immediate construction of these Works." The British Government would supply the armament required at Montreal as well as at Quebec. As the Canadian Government had suggested, a decision on the question of fortifications for Kingston and the Toronto–Hamilton area might be postponed until after Confederation was achieved.

[11]George Earle Buckle, ed., *Letters of Queen Victoria*, Second Series (London, 1926), I, 248–9.
[12]*Papers relating to the Conferences which have taken place between Her Majesty's Government and a Deputation from the Executive Council of Canada, appointed to confer with Her Majesty's Government on the subject of the Defence of the Province*, 4th Session, 8th Parliament of Canada, 1865, 1.

At the same time that the Army Estimates were submitted to the British Parliament, calling for 50,000 pounds to be spent at Quebec during the coming fiscal year, the latest Jervois report was tabled. The result was stormy debate in both the House of Lords and the House of Commons, the opponents arguing that it would be impossible to defend Canada against the United States and urging that all British troops should be withdrawn to avoid the possible ignominy of their being captured by invading American armies. The appropriation was approved by the House of Commons on March 23, by a vote of 275 to 40, but the stipulation was accepted that the defence of Canada "must rest partly on the mother country, but mainly and principally on Canada herself."[13]

On the following day, March 24, the Canadian Government appointed a delegation to visit London to confer with the British Government on confederation, defence, negotiation of another reciprocity treaty with the United States, and the settlement of the Hudson's Bay Company's claims in the Northwest.[14] New Brunswick had definitely rejected confederation and it seemed unlikely that any of the other maritime provinces would follow Canada's example and approve the Quebec Resolutions. Worried by the fact that the British Government was going to spend only 50 thousand pounds on the defence of Quebec during 1865, the Canadian Government subsequently instructed its delegation of John A. Macdonald, George E. Cartier, George Brown, and Alexander T. Galt to state that, if Britain would defend Canada in the event of war, Canada would "bear its rightful share of the burden of military defence."[15] No indication was given, however, as to how this might be calculated.

On April 6 the Canadian Government filled the long vacant post of Adjutant General of Militia with a highly recommended British officer, Colonel Patrick L. MacDougall.[16] Commissioned in 1836, he had obtained his captaincy in the Royal Canadian Rifles in 1844. Following employment as a staff officer during the Crimean War, MacDougall had written a textbook entitled the *Theory of War*. As has already been mentioned, he had also served as first Commandant of the Staff College at Camberley and had helped plan the troop movements to Canada occasioned by the *Trent* affair.

On April 9, 1865, General Robert E. Lee surrendered the remnants of his Army of Northern Virginia at Appomattox Court House. Although Confederate resistance would continue elsewhere until May 26, the time

[13]C. P. Stacey, *Canada and the British Army, 1846–1871* (Toronto, 1964), 171–3.
[14]*Papers relating to the Conferences which have taken place between Her Majesty's Government and a Deputation from Executive Council of Canada*, 2.
[15]C.O. 42/648, Monck to Cardwell, March 28, 1865.
[16]RG 9, IC 8/14, Minutes of Executive Council, April 6, 1865.

of possible Anglo-American crisis was at hand. Macdonald wrote to Brown on April 11 that decisions were imperative:

Either the United States, flushed with success, with their armies full of fight and their fleet in prime condition, will at once put the pistol to England's head and demand satisfaction for the *Alabama* and *Florida* affairs, or, we may look for peace for a series of years. Should the first contingency arise, it will be sudden and speedy and no time is to be lost in putting on our armour of defence. Should peaceful counsels prevail, we should settle now the gradual and systematic growth of a defensive system, to be carried on steadily until we find ourselves strong enough.[17]

Cartier and Galt, who arrived in London first, had an informal conversation with the Colonial Secretary on April 26. That evening Cartier spoke at a banquet of the Worshipful Company of Fishmongers about the benefits the British Empire would derive from a confederation:

We wish to bring about the adoption of the scheme, not only that we may be stronger and more prosperous ourselves, but also that we may be in a better position to take our share in the defence of the British Empire. . . . Singly we, in Canada, cannot defend ourselves; but if we united with the maritime provinces a perfect system can be devised in connexion with the mother country.[18]

The Colonial Secretary, however, was unimpressed by Galt's proposals to further the defence of North America. The Canadian Parliament had recently voted $1 million for training its militia to a standard acceptable to the Secretary of State for War, but Britain was expected to spend between 8 and 10 million pounds sterling to assuage the current Canadian alarm.[19]

Following the arrival of Macdonald and Brown in London on May 1, serious discussion began. The British Government had already instructed its Minister in Washington to negotiate for a renewal of the Reciprocity Treaty. The Cabinet now readily agreed to support Canadian negotiations with the Hudson's Bay Company for the acquisition of the Northwest. In a memorandum dated May 17, the Defence Committee of Great Britain, whose august membership included the Duke of Cambridge, General Burgoyne, and Admiral Sir Frederick W. Grey, confirmed that the latest Jervois report was based upon sound principles. The main base for defence was "clearly Quebec, which may be considered as the

[17]Brown Papers/6, Macdonald to Brown, April 11, 1865.
[18]*The Times*, London, April 27, 1865.
[19]Macdonald Papers/161, Unofficial and Confidential, Memorandum of an Interview with Mr. Cardwell, April 27, 1865.

Torres Vedras of Canada."[20] It was an apt simile, for the Duke of
Wellington had had the three lines of Torres Vedras constructed across
the Lisbon Peninsula during 1809–10 so that he could retire from the
French, when necessary, into a secure position where his army could be
replenished by the Royal Navy. The Defence Committee having approved
Jervois' recommended fortifications for Kingston, Toronto, and Hamilton,
the Canadian delegates now demanded a one-package deal. They agreed
to ask the Canadian Parliament to undertake the recommended fortifications at Kingston, Toronto, and Hamilton, as well as those at Montreal,
provided the British Parliament would immediately agree to guarantee
the necessary Canadian loan and provided they were assured that the
Royal Navy would earmark an adequate naval force for employment on
Lake Ontario in any emergency.[21]

Once again, however, Gladstone led the opposition to expenditure on
Canadian defence. He now conceded that, "if Canada desires to be
British, and to fight for British connection as men fight for their country,
I do not think we can shrink from the duty of helping her," but he argued
that it would be sufficient to "prosecute the works at Quebec with all
dispatch."[22] Gladstone thought the United States would be too busy
pacifying the South to attack Canada in the immediate future, and that
the period of danger would have passed before the proposed fortifications
could be completed, "for no country can afford to keep going these vast
armies on speculation and for what may happen or may not a year or two
or three years hence."[23] Gladstone was in agreement with his Cabinet
colleagues and with the Canadian delegates that priority should be given
to the confederation of the several provinces. Otherwise the British ministers merely agreed that, if the Canadian Parliament actually undertook
primary liability for the proposed fortifications, the British Government
would apply for a guarantee of the amount required and would furnish
the necessary armament. The British ministers very conveniently argued
that the existence of the Rush-Bagot Agreement made it impossible for
the Royal Navy to take any action prior to an outbreak of war; subsequent
action would have to depend upon the exigencies of the situation.[24]

[20]Memorandum by the Defence Committee on the Report of Lieutenant-Colonel
Jervois on the Defence of Canada is available in both the Palmerston and Macdonald Papers.
[21]Macdonald Papers/161, Canadian Memorandum, June 2, 1865.
[22]Knaplund, *Gladstone and Britain's Imperial Policy*, 243–4.
[23]*Ibid.*, 244.
[24]*British Parliamentary Papers*, 1865, XXXVII, no. 3535; Papers relating to the
Conferences which have taken place between Her Majesty's Government and a
Deputation from the Executive Council of Canada appointed to confer with Her
Majesty's Government on Subjects of Importance to the Province, 2–3.

Nevertheless the Canadians regarded the penultimate paragraph of Card-well's letter to the Governor General dated June 17, detailing the decisions of the conference, as a permanent commitment by Great Britain to defend Canada:

> . . . it seemed sufficient that Her Majesty's Government should accept the assurances given by the Canadian Ministers on the part of Canada, that that Province is ready to devote all her resources both in men and money to the maintenance of her connexion with the Mother Country, and should assure them in return that the Imperial Government fully acknowledged the reciprocal obligation of defending every portion of the Empire with all the resources at its command.[25]

The British Government adopted "every proper means" to secure the early assent of the maritime provinces to a federal union calculated to simplify the system of defence.[26] Lieutenant-Governor Arthur Gordon of New Brunswick did as he was instructed and pushed the cause of confederation; but the Lieutenant-Governor of Nova Scotia proved intractable and had to be replaced by Sir William Fenwick Williams who had been born in that province.[27] Sir John Michel assumed the appointment of Lieutenant-General Commanding in North America.

Contrary to Canadian fears, the war-weary veterans of the Grand Army of the Republic quickly melted away; 640,000 of the more than 1,000,000 officers and enlisted men were demobilized by the end of the first week in August, 1865.[28] This prompted Lieutenant-General Sir John Michel to advise the Governor General during September that the United States Government had "no desire to annex Canada."[29] But, he continued, "it stands to reason that the extreme weakness at present of our military position in this country must embolden that large party in America who are hostile to England." Since Canadians were loyal, and Britain would not desert them, it was necessary to render the country defensible against filibustering expeditions.

These were already being planned by the Irish-American secret society commonly known as the Fenian Brotherhood. This organization was attracting the support of Irish veterans, many of whom had not held steady employment prior to enlistment and who now expressed interest in striking a blow against the hated English who were considered to be

[25]*Ibid.*, 3.

[26]*Ibid.*, 2.

[27]James A. Gibson, "The Colonial Office View of Canadian Federation, 1856–1868," *Canadian Historical Review*, XXXV (December, 1954).

[28]Information from Chief Historian, Office of the Chief of Military History, Headquarters, Department of the Army, Washington, U.S.A., Feb. 28, 1964.

[29]Macdonald Papers/100, Michel to Macdonald, Aug. 14, 1867 and enclosure.

oppressing their relatives still living in Ireland. The dissemination of Fenian propaganda was greatly helped by the American politicians who had managed to keep alive old grudges by fiery anti-British speeches aimed at winning votes and distracting attention from the slum conditions in which most of the Irish lived in Boston, New York, and other large cities.

Agents in the pay of the British and Canadian Governments found it comparatively easy to infiltrate the inner circles of the Fenian Brotherhood, and its plans therefore became known. After a warning from the British Consul at New York the Canadian Government acted on November 9, 1865. Nine companies of volunteer militia were called out for border duty at Prescott, Brockville, Niagara, Windsor, and Sarnia, and placed at the disposal of Lieutenant-General Michel.[30] He did not anticipate any Fenian action that he could not easily crush. Should anything serious develop, Michel wrote the Colonial Secretary on November 13, he would "at once call out the remainder of the volunteer militia, and act as respects H. M.'s troops as circumstances may appear to demand."[31] By this time the Canadian volunteers were reasonably proficient because of the instruction received from British drill sergeants. Four additional military schools had been opened during 1865—by British units at Montreal, Kingston, Hamilton, and London—to qualify militia officers, and a three-week camp had been held at Laprairie during September for 1,050 of the graduates.[32] For several weeks the unmobilized volunteer militia units at Montreal, Kingston, Toronto, and London maintained a nightly guard on their armouries. Along the land frontier of the 45th parallel, from St. Regis to Rouse's Point, a system of squad alarm posts was established at two-mile intervals.[33]

Contrary to normal practice, a few warships had remained at Halifax when the balance of the North America and West Indies Squadron left to spend the winter at Bermuda.[34] The defences of Halifax were being improved in accordance with recent recommendations. Most of the work would be completed by 1870, and the individual forts armed with the latest pattern of rifled muzzle-loading guns; but even then the landward defences would not be strong enough to hold off an army that might be landed from a powerful enemy fleet which had achieved local naval

[30]*Report on the State of the Militia of the Province of Canada* (Ottawa, 1866), 65–6.
[31]C.O. 42/650, Michel to Cardwell, Nov. 13, 1865.
[32]*Report on the State of the Militia of the Province of Canada*, 1866, 15–21.
[33]*Ibid.*, 5.
[34]Adm. 128/114, Memorandum by Admiral Sir Rodney Mundy, Aug. 31, 1869.

superiority. Vice-Admiral Sir Alexander Milne had written to this effect
earlier:

I imagine in the event of a War that the Military would still look to the Navy to
assist in protecting that Port; and that it will be in vain to point out, as I have
often had occasion to do, that a Naval Port should serve as a place of refuge,
where a fleet may be protected while refitting and the dismantled fleet should not
be relied on for the Protection of the Port.[35]

Secret service reports that the Fenians were planning an invasion on
St. Patrick's Day, 1866, led the Canadian Government to call out 10,000
volunteer militia on Thursday, March 7. By Saturday afternoon nearly
14,000 officers and men were on duty. Whole companies had turned out
instead of merely the designated quotas, and other patriotic citizens had
just turned up, including a number of men who had hurriedly abandoned
jobs in the United States and rushed home. The excitement and expec-
tancy were heightened by widespread requests for arms and ammunition
to equip groups calling themselves "Home Guards." As nothing happened,
all but the companies which had been on full-time duty all winter were
dismissed before the end of the month.[36]

During the same month Fenians began to collect at Calais and Freeport
in Maine. The Lieutenant-Governor of New Brunswick had, however,
been kept fully aware by secret agents and informers of the invasion being
contemplated there. As a precaution British war vessels were patrolling
Passamaquoddy Bay, the number of British regulars in the province was
increased, local volunteers and home guards were on duty, and arrangements were in hand to summon help from Nova Scotia. American politicians did not want to alienate the large Irish vote with a mid-term
election in the offing, but news that consignments of rifles had reached
Calais finally forced the United States Government to act. On April 18
Major-General George C. Meade, the victor of Gettysburg, reached Calais
with a small force of regular troops. He seized the store of arms and
warned the Fenian leaders that any breach of neutrality would be followed by their arrest. This put an end to the planned invasion, but the
British regulars and local volunteers now deployed along the border as
far north as Woodstock remained there for several weeks until the last
of the Fenians had drifted back to Boston or New York.[37]

[35]Adm. 128/114, Memorandum by Vice-Admiral Sir Alexander Milne, March,
1864.
[36]*Report on the State of the Militia of the Province of Canada*, 1866, 6–8.
[37]Harold A. Davis, "The Fenian Raid on New Brunswick" *Canadian Historical
Review*, XXXVI (December, 1955).

In the face of reports that the Fenians planned a three-pronged invasion of Canada, 14,000 volunteer militia were called for service on May 31. The remainder were called out on June 2, putting more than 20,000 amateur soldiers at the disposal of Sir John Michel. There was, however, no administrative organization to provide them with blankets, tents, or rations, so they had to depend upon the local population for sustenance unless they were lucky enough to be attached to a column of British regulars.[38] The Canadian Government had already chartered thirteen steam vessels for service as gunboats on the St. Lawrence River and Great Lakes.[39] Nucleus crews were provided by H.M.S. *Aurora* and H.M.S. *Pylades* which had been ordered to Quebec and Montreal, respectively, by the Commander-in-Chief of the North America and West Indies Station. The gunboats' crews were completed from the naval companies of volunteer militia.[40] Since Major-General George Napier, commanding British troops in the western part of the province from his headquarters at Toronto, was widely considered "quite useless at all times as a commander," Michel sent his Assistant Quartermaster General, Colonel Garnet Wolseley, to advise him.[41]

By the time Wolseley reached Toronto, however, the campaign was over. The 600 Fenians who had actually crossed from Buffalo into the Niagara Peninsula on the night of May 31 had managed to defeat about 850 volunteers at Ridgeway on the morning of June 2. Yet the Fenians, who were no longer the disciplined soldiers who had fought in the Civil War and were no longer interested in running any real risk of being killed, promptly retired on Fort Erie. Here they dispersed a small force of Canadian volunteers, who had disembarked from the requisitioned tugboat *W. T. Robb* instead of continuing to patrol the Niagara River as ordered. By the following day, when Lieutenant-Colonel George Peacocke's column of regulars and volunteers got to Fort Erie, the Fenians were all back in Buffalo and temporarily in the custody of American federal authorities. Fenian concentrations at Ogdensburg and Malone were deterred from crossing the St. Lawrence by the presence of gunboats in the river and of volunteers on the Canadian shore. On June 7 a strong party of Fenians did cross from Vermont into Missisquoi County and occupied Pigeon Hill after driving off the nearest volunteer companies on duty, but they were not reinforced and American authorities seized their supply of stores at

---

[38]*Report on the State of the Militia of the Province of Canada*, 1866, 22–24.
[39]K. R. Macpherson, "List of vessels employed on British Naval Service on the Great Lakes, 1755–1875," *Ontario History*, LV (September, 1963).
[40]Adm. 128/114, Report by Vice-Admiral Sir James Hope, May, 1867.
[41]Wolseley, *The Story of a Soldier's Life*, II, 160.

St. Albans. They retreated back to Vermont when British regulars from
Montreal appeared two days later. With danger seemingly at an end,
the Canadian Government dismissed all but 2,500 volunteers on June 18;
a busy summer season was approaching, and the Adjutant General of
Militia had advised that he would "have great difficulty in getting even
that number who would desire to remain."[42]

A Volunteer Camp of Exercise was opened at Thorold on August 22,
1866, amid reports of renewed Fenian activities along the Niagara
frontier. Its commandant, Colonel Wolseley, was given a wing of the 16th
Regiment of Foot and a demi-battery of Royal Artillery as a permanent
brigade nucleus for the volunteer units which were limited to a single
week of camp. In practice, of course, there were only five days of instruction in each of the seven periods of camp, during which 472 officers and
6,157 other ranks received training intended to prevent a repetition of
the reverses suffered at Ridgeway and Fort Erie. Wolseley subsequently
reported that the efficiency of volunteer units varied in direct proportion
to the number of retired British officers and graduates of the military
schools present in camp. Range practice disclosed that a "large proportion
of the arms would not go off, for although clean outside, the nipples of
many were clogged with dirt."[43] The Adjutant General of Militia,
Colonel MacDougall, explained in his annual report the importance
of the volunteers' weapons:

. . . take a pride in turning out on parade smart and clean and soldierlike as
regards the outward appearance; but it is too often the case . . . that their rifles
are so foul that they cannot be fired. Yet it is upon the serviceable condition of
his weapon at any moment that the value of a volunteer depends. Unless it is kept
constantly in a state for immediate use the volunteer is only a sham soldier, and
his external trappings are but a useless expense to the country.[44]

Plans to hold a similar camp at St. Johns in October for the rural
volunteers of Lower Canada were ruined by continued inclement
weather.[45]

The Governor General's request for the transfer of an additional
infantry battalion of British regulars from Halifax had been approved,
and he was allowed to retain temporarily the two battalions due to leave
Canada that summer.[46] Also at his request, the Admiralty sent three of

[42]E/State Book A.C., Minute of Executive Council, June 18, 1866.
[43]*Report of the State of the Militia of the Province of Canada for the year
1867* (Ottawa, 1868), 3–4, 105 and 112.
[44]*Ibid.*, 2.
[45]*Ibid.*, 4.
[46]C.O. 42/655, Monck to Cardwell, June 6 and 21, 1866.

its "Crimean Gunboats," *Heron, Britomart*, and *Cherub*, to serve on the Great Lakes.[47] One of these gunboats, with a crew of 6 officers and 35 ratings, was positioned on each of Lake Ontario, Lake Erie, and Lake Huron. Control of all inland naval operations was exercised by Captain Algernon F. R. Horsey, R.N., of H.M.S. *Aurora*.[48] That autumn the 13th Hussars, two infantry battalions and a reinforcement draft of 500 rank and file joined the British Army in Canada. By the end of the year there were 11,741 British other ranks in Canada and 4,976 in Nova Scotia command.[49] Arrangements now existed to facilitate the employment of volunteers with the regular forces. Three mixed brigades were organized "on paper" in Upper Canada and four in Lower Canada for employment in a mobile role. Each brigade was to comprise of one infantry battalion of regulars and three of volunteers, a field battery of regulars or volunteers, and a cavalry troop of volunteers. The commander and his principal staff officers were to be British regulars.[50]

These British reinforcements had been reluctantly approved by the Conservative Government that Lord Derby had formed during the summer of 1866. His Chancellor of the Exchequer, Benjamin Disraeli, was still as much of an anti-imperialist as the previous incumbent of that office, W. E. Gladstone, and in a letter of September 30 to the Prime Minister he expressed a widely held view:

We must seriously consider our Canadian position, which is most illegitimate. An army maintained in a country which does not permit us even to govern it! What an anomaly!

It can never be our pretence, or our policy to defend the Canadian frontier against the U.S. If the colonists can't, as a general rule defend themselves against the Fenians they can do nothing. They ought to be, and must be, strong enough for that. Power and influence we should exercise in Asia; consequently in Eastern Europe, consequently also in Western Europe; but what is the use of these colonial deadweights which *we do not govern*?

I don't regret what we did the other day about Canada, because the circumstances were very peculiar. A successful raid of the Fenians was not off the cards, which would have upset your untried Ministry, and have produced an insurrection in Ireland; and it was not fair to the Canadians, when, at the last, they were making some attempts at self-defence, to allow them to be crushed in the bud of their patriotism. But the moment the American elections are over, we should withdraw the great body of our troops, and foster a complete development of self-government.

---

[47]*Ibid.*, June 22, 1866.
[48]Adm. 128/114, Report by Vice-Admiral Sir James Hope, May, 1867.
[49]W.O. 73/8, Other Rank Strength, Canada and Nova Scotia, Jan. 1, 1867.
[50]*Report on the State of the Militia of the Province of Canada for the year 1867*, 12.

Leave the Canadians to defend themselves; recall the African squadron; give up the settlements on the west coast of Africa; and we shall make a saving which will, at the same time enable us to build ships and have a good Budget.

What is more, we shall have accomplished something definite, tangible, for the good of the country. In these days, more than ever, the people look to results. What we have done about Canada is perfectly defensible, if it is not looked upon as a permanent increase of our Canadian establishments.[51]

It was only natural therefore, with opinion set towards disengagement, that Lord Derby's Government should throw its wholehearted support behind the proposals for a federal union of British North America and that its Secretary of State for the Colonies, Lord Carnarvon, should bring provincial delegations into conference at Westminster in December, 1866. The Westminster Resolutions then agreed upon became the basis of the British North America Act. Introduced into the British House of Lords on February 12, 1867, the Bill attracted little attention. The accompanying Canada Railway Loan Bill, which would provide a British guarantee that an Intercolonial Railway would actually be constructed, attracted as little comment. Both measures were designed to lessen the colonial defence burden borne by the British people. The Intercolonial Railway would not be completed until 1876, but the Dominion of Canada became a reality on July 1, 1867.

The summer of 1867 passed quietly, without a single Fenian scare. The augmented British military garrison of the year before remained, and Royal Naval personnel patrolled the Great Lakes, despite suggestions that their strengths might be reduced. The United States Navy was further reduced as a post-war measure to 56 ships and vessels on squadron service and was "almost exclusively employed on foreign stations."[52] Its North Atlantic Squadron of 10 units, mounting a total of 79 guns, was obviously no match for the Royal Navy's strength on the North America and West Indies Station.[53] By September 30 the United States regular army was reduced to 56,815 officers and enlisted men, of whom only 1,323 were stationed in 18 infantry and artillery companies along the Canadian border from Eastport, Maine, to Lake Superior.[54] In anticipation of relinquishing his appointment of Lieutenant-General Commanding in North America in September, Michel had sent his political-military

[51]Quoted in Stacey, *Canada and the British Army, 1846–1871*, 193–4.
[52]*Report of the Secretary of the Navy, with an Appendix, containing Bureau Reports*, etc., December, 1867 (Washington, 1867,) 1.
[53]*Ibid.*, 10.
[54]Information from the Chief Historian, Office of the Chief of Military History, Headquarters, Department of the Army, Washington, D.C., U.S.A., Feb. 28, 1964.

views to the Dominion of Canada's first Prime Minister, Sir John A. Macdonald, on August 14. Although current Anglo-American matters in dispute might lead to war, making it necessary for Canada to look to her defences and prepare to put up such a good fight that the United States would be deterred from aggression, Michel was anything but pessimistic in his memorandum:

In reviewing this subject, it is evident that the United States of to-day is far different in point of strength to what it may become a few years hence. I think we may assume that for some years the United States Government will (if possible) avoid external political complications. She has work enough on her hands in repairing the state of her finances and in bringing the late Confederate States into hearty Union, and it is hardly to be conceived that she would think of endeavouring to annex Canada until these matters are satisfactorily adjusted.

A war between England and the United States would be so totally opposed to the best interests of each, that nothing but the temptation held out of an early conquest of Canada would induce the Government of the United States to enter upon so suicidal a course.

As each year rolls by, so the vast inter-commercial trade between England and the United States increases. There is a growing tendency towards a better understanding on the head of International Law, whilst the policy of England and the United States as respects external trade, and the general freedom of the human race, is daily becoming more and more alike.

Thus distant complications are less to be feared, and war between England and the United States will become more and more improbable.[55]

At the moment the citadel at Quebec was being modernized, and three earthen forts were being built across the St. Lawrence River beyond Lévis, to ensure Quebec's continuance in British hands as the key base for a successful defence of Canada against the United States. Active defence would be facilitated by the large-scale maps, known as "Fortification Surveys," which had been compiled by the Royal Engineers for all the strong points in Canada. These and map sheets of the vulnerable land frontier of Canada East were based on engineer surveys made in 1839 and the early 1860s. For, despite continued British efforts to reduce colonial military expenditure, each crisis had found Great Britain ready to make a display of strength on behalf of people who wanted to remain within the British Empire. If she did not, how could she claim to be a first-class power in the world?

[55]Macdonald Papers/100, Michel to Macdonald, Aug. 14, 1867.

(10)

BRITISH WITHDRAWAL

As 1868 began for the new Dominion the Fenians were reliably reported to be still too disorganized as a result of the fiascos of 1866 to attempt more raids, and there seemed to be every reason to believe that the Canadian-American border would be as quiet as it had been during the year of Confederation. The Governments in London and Ottawa could therefore turn once again to long-range planning.

On February 5, 1868, on the advice of the Defence Committee of Great Britain, the Secretary of State for War pointed out that although great progress was being made by the British Government with the fortifications at Quebec, nothing had yet been done by the Canadian Government at Montreal, Kingston, Toronto, or Hamilton. The Defence Committee was also worried about the defenceless state of Saint John.[1] On February 22 therefore the Colonial Secretary wrote to ask the Governor General, Lord Monck, to find out what the Canadian Government proposed to do about the commitment made in 1865 to construct permanent defences once Confederation had been achieved. This same letter also announced that the British Government intended to withdraw three regular battalions of infantry from garrison duty in what were now the provinces of Ontario and Quebec.[2]

Individually and collectively the members of the Canadian Government were opposed to the withdrawal of any of their British defenders, but they received no sympathy from the Governor General. On March 20 he pointed out to them the absurdity of having a large British force in Canada "when they did not find it necessary to call out for duty any

[1]Bright Papers, "Memorandum respecting Fortifications in Canada, in connection with the recent Act passed by the Canadian Legislature for raising a Loan of £1,000,0000 under the Imperial Guarantee for certain Works of Fortifications," May 6, 1869.
[2]G. 1/169, Buckingham to Monck, Feb. 22, 1868.

of the troops which are under their own control."[3] Thereupon the Canadian Government attempted to stave off British action by quickly agreeing to provide money for the suggested permanent defences. On May 27 Monck was able to send to London an act for raising a loan for fortifications not to exceed 1,100,000 pounds sterling, charged upon the revenue of Canada, with priority for payment immediately after that of the loan floated for the construction of the Intercolonial Railway, provided such loan should be guaranteed by the British Treasury.[4] The Canadian Parliament also passed its first Militia Act at this time. Based on the militia legislation of the former Province of Canada, this Act continued the traditional sedentary militia but placed emphasis on an active militia which was to consist of a volunteer militia, a regular militia of men aged 18 to 40 who were to be balloted or volunteer when called upon, and a marine militia composed of men who were sailors by profession. The Militia Act provided for annual drill by a maximum of 40,000 all ranks, who might be entirely volunteers or might, if desired, be completed with men selected by ballot.[5]

Instead of going ahead and introducing a bill into the British Parliament to guarantee the Canadian loan required for the intended fortifications, the British Government ordered the withdrawal of two further battalions of regulars from Canada in late October. This brought the total strength reduction for the year 1868 to 3,592 all ranks.[6] Orders were also issued to withdraw the three Crimean gunboats from service on the Great Lakes and the Royal Navy personnel who were manning the Canadian Government's two remaining gunboats, *Prince Alfred* and *Rescue*.[7] A further cause for worry for the Canadian Government was the rapid spread of American settlement in Minnesota and the resultant clamour for the United States to annex the whole Northwest. The Canadian Government decided that its best course was to send two of its members, Sir George E. Cartier and William McDougall, to London. There they were to hasten negotiations with the proprietory Hudson's Bay Company for adding Rupert's Land and the far Northwest Territories to Canada and attempt a reconciliation of views with the British Government

[3]G. 10/3, Memorandum for the Privy Council, March 20, 1868.
[4]Bright Papers, "Memorandum respecting Fortifications in Canada, in connection with the recent Act passed by the Canadian Legislature for raising a loan of £1,100,000 under the Imperial Guarantee for certain Works of Fortifications," May 6, 1869.
[5]31 Vict., c. 40.
[6]G. 1/172, Buckingham to Officer Administering Government, Dec. 8, 1868, encloses copy of Lugard to Rogers, Nov. 17, 1868.
[7]Adm. 128/114, Memorandum by Admiral Sir Rodney Mundy, Aug. 31, 1869.

on military matters.[8] Cartier, it should be noted, was Minister of Militia and Defence in the Government headed by Sir John A. Macdonald.

Cartier and McDougall soon discovered that the British political climate of December, 1868, was far different from what it had been two years earlier when the Westminster Resolutions had been accepted as the basis for Confederation. A general election had brought into office on December 3 a Liberal Government headed by William Ewart Gladstone. It will be remembered that as early as July 12, 1864, Gladstone had expressed the belief that the "more Canada and the British Colonies are detached, as to their defensive not less than their administrative responsibilities, from England, the more likely the Union will be to study friendly relations with them."[9] Off and on since June 29, 1864, *The Times* had argued that British garrisons in the interior of Canada served only as a lure to American armies interested in waging another victorious campaign. Now that he was Prime Minister, Gladstone was in a position to implement his views, particularly since his Cabinet included such distinguished Little Englanders as Robert Lowe and John Bright, who had clearly stated their belief that the separation of self-governing colonies from Britain would be for the good of both. The new Colonial Secretary, Lord Granville, subsequently took it upon himself to write the Governor General of Canada that the British Government had no desire to maintain the imperial connection "a single year" after it became "injurious or distasteful" to Canada.[10]

Gladstone was faced with two immediate problems: he wanted to effect the reductions in national expenditure promised during his election campaign, and he had to improve Britain's military position in Europe. The British people were becoming increasingly impressed by the efficiency of the Prussian army, which had humbled Austria in the six weeks' war of 1866, and more and more disturbed by the unreformed state of the small British Army, which was too scattered about the Empire to provide a field force for intervention in Europe the next time the balance of power might be threatened there. Gladstone and his Cabinet colleagues were also convinced that the next crisis in Europe would be the occasion for trouble in North America.[11] The Foreign Secretary, Lord Clarendon, explained this danger to Queen Victoria:

It is the unfriendly state of our relations with America that to a great extent paralyzes our action in Europe. There is not the slightest doubt that if we were

[8]Canadian Sessional Papers, 1869, no. 60.
[9]Paul Knaplund, *Gladstone and Britain's Imperial Policy* (London, 1927), 238.
[10]C.O. 43/156, Granville to Young, June 16, 1869.
[11]C. P. Stacey, "Britain's Withdrawal from North America, 1864–1871," *Canadian Historical Review*, XXXVI (September, 1955), 187.

engaged in a Continental quarrel we should immediately find ourselves at war with the United States.[12]

Gladstone now instructed the new Secretary of State for War, Edward Cardwell, to undertake reform of the British Army and to create an army reserve which would keep units up to strength during the early stages of a general war. Reduction of colonial military garrisons would assist recruiting, by ensuring that soldiers spent more of their service in Great Britain; and it would result in a reduction of government expenditure sufficient to please the voters. Lord Clarendon, for his part, managed to negotiate with the United States Minister in London, Reverdy Johnson, on 14 January, 1869, a possible settlement of the Anglo-American differences, subject, of course, to ratification by the Senate.

Granville proved most willing to help Cartier and McDougall reach a satisfactory settlement with the Hudson's Bay Company for Canadian acquisition of the Northwest, but he took them completely by surprise with the suggestion that all British troops might be withdrawn from Canada. According to a memorandum Granville sent Cardwell on December 27, 1868, Cartier and McDougall argued that withdrawal of British troops would encourage the Fenians to try again, and they refused to accept the reasoning that "a small Imperial force was a red flag, which enticed the Fenians and gave increased zest to any possibility of a victory."[13] Undoubtedly the British reasoning was sound, but would the Fenians act in a logical manner? Secret Service reports reaching the Canadian Government indicated that General John O'Neill had become president of the Canadian wing of the Fenian Brotherhood and that he was anxious to try again if the necessary men and munitions could be collected. Even though O'Neill's invasion of the Niagara Peninsula in 1866 had failed, it must be remembered that, both at Ridgeway and Fort Erie, the Fenians had defeated a considerable strength of partially trained Canadian volunteers in action for the first time without the steadying influence of British regulars.

On January 9, 1869, Cardwell suggested to Gladstone that the number of British troops stationed in the colonies around the world could be reduced from 56,000 to 12,000 all ranks.[14] Gladstone agreed at once,[15] and Cardwell proceeded to work out the details. On January 25 Cardwell wrote Granville that he proposed to withdraw one cavalry regiment, three batteries of field and three batteries of garrison artillery, and three

[12]George Earle Buckle, ed., *The Letters of Queen Victoria*, Second Series (London, 1926), I, 594.
[13]Cardwell Papers, Box 5/28, Granville to Cardwell, Dec. 27, 1868.
[14]Cardwell Papers, Box 2/6, Cardwell to Gladstone, Jan. 9, 1869.
[15]*Ibid.*, Gladstone to Cardwell, Jan. 11, 1869.

battalions of infantry from Ontario and Quebec, and one field battery of artillery and two battalions of infantry from New Brunswick and Nova Scotia. This would leave about 2,000 all ranks in Nova Scotia for the defence of Halifax, which was an "imperial station," and another 4,000 British troops for the whole of Ontario, Quebec, and New Brunswick. There was nothing new about this proposal, which had been attempted by Lord Grey in 1851 and the Duke of Newcastle in 1853, but the following paragraphs about minimum establishment warrant close scrutiny:

> The Government of the new Dominion has displayed an anxiety to improve the organization of its own defences, which is deserving of encouragement on our part; and, in doing so, has availed itself of the assistance of some of Her Majesty's regiments in training the Officers and men of its own volunteers and militia. The reductions which I now propose to your Lordship will not interfere with these arrangements.
>
> I shall be glad, therefore, to be favoured with your Lordship's opinion, whether it is necessary that any portion of Her Majesty's troops should be left in the Dominion of Canada, beyond such as it may be deemed expedient to retain with a view to the training of the militia and the volunteers, and the maintenance of the Schools of Instruction.
>
> This number would be sufficient, in any case of emergency, to furnish the garrison of Quebec.[16]

Granville decided to get the opinion of the Governor General, now Sir John Young, who replied on February 18 that Cardwell's figure of 6,000 British troops was close enough to his own estimate that 6,400 regulars was the minimum force required to protect Canada and Newfoundland. Young assumed that both Quebec and Halifax would continue to be imperial stations but that Canada would soon be asked to pay for any garrison maintained elsewhere.[17] The fact that the Canadian Government was opposed to any reduction at this, or any other, time was ignored by both Young and Cardwell.

When introducing his army estimates in the House on March 11, Cardwell emphasized that the "true defence of our colonies is that they live under the aegis of the name of England and that war with them is war with England."[18] Cardwell also drew a clear distinction between colonies and mere "stations for our fleet," which required imperial fortresses for

---

[16]*Returns to Addresses of the Senate and House of Commons, relative to the Withdrawal of the Troops from the Dominion; and of the Defence of the Country; and Honorable Mr. Campbell's Report* (Ottawa, 1871), 5–6 [subsequently cited as *Withdrawal Correspondence*].

[17]G. 10/3, Young to Granville, Feb. 18, 1869.

[18]Great Britain, House of Commons, *Debates*, 1869, CXCIV, 1139.

their defence, and he mentioned Halifax specifically. His boast that there would be a total net saving of just under 1.2 million pounds over the previous fiscal year disarmed most opposition and made it possible for the Colonial Secretary to write the Governor General on April 14, explaining how the new army programme would affect Canada. Except for the following quotation, it was virtually a rewrite of the letter Cardwell had sent Granville on January 25, an extract of which was appended:

. . . I am disposed to agree with Mr. Cardwell in the opinion that it will soon become unnecessary to maintain any British force in those Provinces [Ontario, Quebec, and New Brunswick], beyond what may be required for the training of the Militia and Volunteers and the maintenance of Schools of Instruction. The terms on which any of H.M.'s Regiments can be retained in the colony, for this or any other purpose, will be a matter for future consideration. Meantime the Secretary of State for War informs me that Colonial Governments will receive all possible assistance in obtaining, at their own charge, the services of such commissioned and non-commissioned officers as they may desire to employ for the organization or instruction of any local force, for the construction, inspection or maintenance of fortifications, or for any other matter connected with Military defence. The War Department will also be ready, when practicable, to furnish them at cost price with such arms, ammunition and military stores as they may need. . . .

I have further to point out to you that, in the opinion of the Secretary of State for War, any body of men, who are to be a charge upon the Imperial Exchequer, ought to be a body raised for the general service of Her Majesty, and not limited either by the conditions of enlistment or by necessity to a particular Colony. The [Royal] Canadian Rifles do not, as you are aware, satisfy this condition, and Mr. Cardwell is accordingly about to reduce four companies of that corps, and to take measures to relieve the Imperial Treasury from the cost of supporting it. It becomes matter for the consideration of the local Government, whether that corps or any part of it, useful as I believe it to be for local purposes, should be maintained at the expense of the Colony.[19]

Granville also suggested that it would be wise to cease violating the arrangement made by the Rush-Bagot Agreement of 1817 as soon as the Fenian menace should become less acute, even though the Colonial Naval Defence Act of 1865 did empower Canada to commission warships of its own.

Although on this same April 14 Granville sought an answer from Cardwell to the "practical question" of "whether Quebec is to be considered an 'Imperial or a Colonial Fortress,' "[20] there can really be no doubt that the Secretary of State for War had decided in his own mind

[19]*Withdrawal Correspondence*, 3.
[20]Cardwell Papers, Box 5/28, Granville to Cardwell, April 14, 1869.

that it must become a Canadian responsibility. The Citadel had recently been strengthened at British expense, and work was still continuing on the three new forts beyond Lévis, so that it should be capable of continuing to serve as the "Torres Vedras of Canada." Surely the small body of regular troops, which Cardwell proposed to leave in Canada for the instruction of the volunteer militia, or the colonial regiment which he was suggesting might be formed in place of the Royal Canadian Rifles, would be able to make a fighting withdrawal on Quebec and, with the assistance of the Canadian levies, hold off American invaders until British help arrived, as it had in the spring of 1776. Cardwell had reiterated the pledge of assistance given in his despatch of June 17, 1865, when he stated in the House of Commons on March 11, 1869, that the "true defence of our colonies" was the realization by foreigners that "war with them is war with England."[21] Admittedly Cardwell was prepared to take a "calculated risk." Only time could tell whether it would prove to be a well-calculated risk or whether, as his critics argued, it would lead to disaster.

Cardwell had already expressed concern over the disposition of the regular troops remaining in central Canada during 1869. The letter sent on February 20 to Sir Charles Windham, the Lieutenant-General Commanding in North America, wanted garrisons withdrawn from such small posts as St. Johns and London and from Toronto which was "an expensive and isolated position."[22] Concentration of troops would permit reductions in the military staff and other economies. However, Windham was not to take any action if the Governor General and his Canadian ministers should strenuously object. They did object, and for many of the same reasons put forth in 1864. This time, the Lieutenant-General Commanding agreed. He pointed out that Toronto was not an isolated position: it had excellent railway connections which would permit the rapid transfer of troops elsewhere in the event of an emergency. Removal of the British infantry regiment would make it necessary to close the military school and would be resented by the people of Ontario. Additional barracks would have to be found, at considerable expense, if the Toronto garrison was relocated at Montreal and Quebec.[23]

The calculations of Cardwell and Granville were soon upset by the news that the United States Senate had, on April 13, rejected the Johnson-Clarendon Convention by a vote of 54 to 1, following a speech

[21]Great Britain, House of Commons, *Debates*, 1869, CXCIV, 1139.
[22]C/37, Lugard to Lieutenant-General Commanding, Feb. 20, 1869.
[23]C/37, Windham to Secretary of State for War, March 12, 1869.

by Senator Charles Sumner which hinted that the only way Britain could provide sufficient compensation for the damage done by the Confederate raider *Alabama* would be to permit the annexation of Canada by the United States. The situation was fraught with danger because Sumner's demands for compensation for the damage caused by all the Confederate commerce raiders totalled $2.125 billion, an astronomical figure even today. Clarendon was afraid that the ugly tempers raised on both sides might precipitate a war in North America, something that Britain could not afford. The Gladstone Ministry could not muzzle public opinion in Britain, but it could prevent debate in the House of Commons. This it did, as its contribution to keeping the peace.[24]

Cardwell once again expressed concern about the safety of British troops in Ontario and Quebec, but he still did not want to disregard the wishes of the Governor General and the Canadian Government. On April 29 a letter went out from the War Office trusting to Windham's discretion "not to permit the force under your command to incur the risk of remaining unsupported in any such situations" as might occur.[25]

On May 28 Colonel Jervois prepared a military appreciation which was circulated among the members of the British Cabinet. Respecting the possibility of an American invasion of Canada, Jervois now expressed more concern than was evident in his earlier reports. He began by covering familiar ground, particularly the folly of calculating on successful defence of all of a long frontier:

> In considering the amount of force that the Americans would be likely to bring to bear upon this object, it must be observed that a war with England would not arouse that spirit of enthusiasm with them that existed during the Civil War with the Southern States. Moreover, they would be obliged, when at war with England, to keep a large force for the defence of their towns, shipping, and government establishments at the several harbours along their coasts from the State of Maine to that of Texas. In addition to this they would also have to keep a force for the maintenance of order in the Southern States, and if at a time when war occurred, the Southern States had sufficiently recovered from their recent defeat to entertain again the idea of separation, we should, of course, take advantage of the circumstance.
>
> But making every deduction on these accounts, it is apparent that in estimating the power of the Canadians to protect themselves against attacks of an American Army, it must be out of the question for a country with a frontier of about a 1,000 miles in extent, without any prepared basis of defence, with a population not exceeding four millions, and with very limited means, to defend itself against

---

[24]Allan Nevins, *Hamilton Fish: The Inner History of the Grant Administration* (New York, 1936), 170–171.

[25]C/37, Lugard to Windham, April 29, 1869.

a country possessing a population of more than thirty millions, and with the vast resources of the United States. It is only by the aid of fortifications, combined with an efficient organization of local forces, properly disciplined, and supported by military and naval forces from this country, that the capture of Canada could be prevented.

And even with the best preparations within, and with all the support Great Britain could afford, it is not at all probable that the whole frontier of Canada could be efficiently defended.[26]

Jervois then reverted to the recommendations made by the Defence Commission in 1862 and to his own reports of 1864 and 1865. None of the fortifications west of Quebec then recommended had been constructed; naval vessels required for service on Lake Ontario could not negotiate the canals and would have to be either sent out in frame from England and assembled on the spot or completely built there. Jervois now stated quite definitely that "from a purely military point of view it would be desirable to restrict our operations as much as possible to the defence of the Lower Province [Quebec]." He followed this with a statement which must have attracted the most attention:

It is certain that the main attack of the Americans upon Canada would be directed against Montreal and Quebec, and the first condition of the defence of Canada (pre-supposing we are superior at sea) is the construction of the permanent entrenched camps to southward and westward of Montreal, and to southward of Quebec. That to southward of Quebec is far advanced towards completion, but its use will be in a great measure neutralized if the proposed works of defence at Montreal are not carried out.

The Royal Navy could destroy American commerce on the high seas, establish a blockade of American seaports on the Atlantic coast and Gulf of Mexico, and combine with the British Army in amphibious operations against any of these ports. In the long run such activities would seriously cripple an American war effort, but Jervois practically conceded that Montreal would fall in short order to a large American army and that even Quebec might not be able to hold out for the time required to reinforce its garrison against enemy troops advancing along the northern bank of the St. Lawrence River from Montreal.

The only really bright spot in the Memorandum was in respect of Halifax:

. . . when the fortifications now in course of construction are completed, and a small work, not yet provided for, has been established on the southern end of

---

[26]Bright Papers, "Considerations on the Military position of Great Britain with respect to the United States," May 28, 1869.

McNab's Island, there can be no doubt that, with proper armaments and the application of torpedos, the harbour may be defended against any naval attack likely to be made upon it.

With the citadel adapted for a modern armanent, the place will, moreover, be secure against *capture* by a force landed for the purpose of attacking Halifax.

If, however, an enemy had landed in force to the eastward of the place, and had succeeded in pushing his way through the forests and intricate country which intervenes between Halifax and Ship Harbour (the nearest harbour to the eastward which he could use as a base), which is 45 miles distant, he would be able to burn the shipping, town and naval establishment from the eastern side of the harbour. Considering our probable superiority at sea, it is, however, hardly to be expected that he would undertake this operation, and with the Militia of Nova Scotia properly organized, and supported by about 2,200 British troops, Halifax may, when the defensive arrangements above referred to are completed, be considered sufficiently secure to meet any attack to which it is likely to be subjected.

On June 4 Windham replied to the War Office letter of April 29 that he agreed about withdrawal of British troops on purely military grounds, but that there were local political conditions mitigating against the removal of British garrisons from their existing stations and that he was averse to assuming the heavy responsibility being thrust upon him.[27] Only on August 4 was War Office sanction given to Windham's troop dispositions. For the "present at least," the Secretary of State for War was willing to let existing dispositions continue.[28]

By this time Cardwell must have been aware of what had transpired when the Canadian Minister of Finance, Sir John Rose, had visited Secretary of State Hamilton Fish in Washington, on July 8, in an effort to promote another Reciprocity Treaty. Fish and Rose had then agreed that a British diplomat, as good as Lord Ashburton or Lord Elgin had been, might be able to secure a combined settlement of all American-British-Canadian problems after present tempers had cooled in both Washington and London.[29]

In London Cardwell was engaged in a behind-the-scenes struggle with the Duke of Cambridge who, as Queen Victoria's cousin and Commanding-in-Chief, was determined not to take direction in certain purely military matters from the Secretary of State for War. The immediate and ostensible issue was the Duke's refusal to move his own headquarters from the Horse Guards to the War Office, where Cardwell was supreme. In retaliation Cardwell refused to read Cambridge's memorandum of August 3 which urged the retention of British troops in Canada. The Duke had

[27]G. 3/4, Windham to Under-Secretary of State for War, June 4, 1869.
[28]C/37, Storks to Lieutenant-General Commanding, Aug. 4, 1869.
[29]Allan Nevins, *Hamilton Fish: The Inner History of the Grant Administration* (New York, 1956), I, 212–13.

little that was constructive to contribute to the question and certainly
nothing that the Gladstone Ministry wanted to hear. As an ardent
imperialist, the Duke of Cambridge thought Britain had a duty to protect
the Canadians, who wanted only to live at peace with the world and
have no part of the Anglo-American disputes. He thought that "a small
and compact permanent force ought always to be maintained by the
Mother Country, to furnish the ordinary Garrisons absolutely necessary to
occupy the fortified works, and to be a nucleus upon which the Local
Forces can form, such permanent force being paid by the Mother Country
and not by the Colony."[30] Cardwell did condescend to read Cambridge's
letter of December 14 which suggested that Quebec should be continued
as an "imperial fortress" in order to persuade the Canadians actually to
fortify Montreal. This letter also argued that no local permanent force
would be as good as British regulars.[31] Cardwell paid no attention to the
Duke's arguments.

What may have helped persuade the Gladstone Ministry to go ahead
and withdraw all British troops from the interior of Canada was intelligence received from Sir Edward Thornton, the British Minister in
Washington. Thornton had been unable to make any progress reopening
the *Alabama* case, but he reported Hamilton Fish's suggestion that, if
the British withdrew from Canada, the controversy over the amount of
the American claims could be settled quite easily.[32] This suggestion,
implying that Canadian independence would be only the prelude to
peaceful annexation by the United States, had naturally been rejected
by the British Minister, but there was cause for further thought: Were
self-governing colonies worth keeping in the British Empire? Even Thornton had replied to Fish that the "Canadians find great fault with me for
saying as openly as I do that we are ready to let them go whenever they
wish. . . ."[33]

In any event, the bad news was transmitted to Canada in Lord Granville's despatch to the Governor General dated 12 February 1870. The
city of Halifax would continue to be garrisoned by about 1,500 British
regulars as an imperial station. For the balance of the current year a
battery of artillery and a battalion of infantry would remain at Quebec,
but the rest of the British troops in Canada would be withdrawn. On the
other hand, the British Government was desirous of affording the Canadian Government "all possible assistance in organizing such a Military

[30]Cardwell Papers, Box 3/12, Cambridge to Cardwell, Aug. 3, 1869.
[31]*Ibid.*, Dec. 14, 1869.
[32]Nevins, *Hamilton Fish*, I 300.
[33]*Ibid.*

and Naval power as they may consider befitting for a country which has an increasing population of three and a half millions."[34] The British Parliament would be asked to guarantee the Canadian Government loan of 1.1 million pounds sterling for fortifications if it "is still in favor of the plan heretofore accepted." Following the earlier suggestion that a small body of British regular troops might be left in Canada to instruct the active militia, the Secretary of State for War was now ready "to facilitate the formation of a Colonial Regiment out of Her Majesty's army, by enabling officers and men, now in the Dominion, to accept any offer made to them by the Government for the transfer of their services, and this even though an entire battalion were to volunteer as a Colonial Regiment for service in Canada, [only] the Head quarters and a small nucleus returning to this country [Great Britain] on which the Regiment could be reformed." The barracks and fortifications to be vacated by the British Army would be turned over to Canada on the understanding that the Canadian Government would house British troops that might be returned for any local or imperial reason. This was most important because the despatch emphasized in its concluding paragraph that "the arrangements contemplated . . . and which are based on principles applicable not exclusively to the Dominion, but to the other self-governing British Colonies, are contingent upon a time of peace, and are in no way intended to alter or diminish the obligations which exist on both sides in case of foreign war."[35]

Henceforth the headquarters of the Lieutenant-General Commanding in North America would be located at Halifax. Sir Charles Windham had died on February 2, 1870, at Jacksonville, Florida, where he had gone on holiday in an attempt to recoup his ailing health. This appointment was given to Sir Charles Hastings Doyle, the long-time commander of the Nova Scotia district who was now serving as Lieutenant-Governor of that province. Lieutenant-General the Hon. James Lindsay was detailed to supervise the rundown of the British Army in Central Canada. Lindsay generally referred to himself as "Lieutenant-General Commanding Ontario and Quebec."

Lindsay was soon nonplussed to find that the Canadian Government was not interested in forming a colonial regiment, as suggested, or any permanent force.[36] The reason was simple. The Canadian Government, as the Minister of Militia and Defence eventually wrote on May 19, still

[34]*Withdrawal Correspondence*, 8.
[35]*Ibid.*, 9.
[36]*Ibid.*, 52–7.

hoped to persuade the British Government to modify its declared policy
and continue to garrison Quebec as an imperial fortress. "It must not be
lost sight of," Cartier's letter continued, "that Quebec is the principal
fortified place in the Dominion, and forms, as it were, the gate of entrance
to the River St. Lawrence, and holds towards that river and the great
lakes, about the same position that Gibraltar does towards the Mediter-
ranean."[37] Cartier was a politician, not a soldier, and may be excused for
likening Quebec to Gibraltar instead of to Torres Vedras; at least he
recognized how important Quebec was in existing British strategy. In a
letter dated June 3, his Deputy Minister explained that Canadian garrisons required elsewhere could be formed from volunteers belonging to
the active militia and that these would serve, under Section 20 of the
Militia Act, "for any service whatever, and under such regulations as
may, from time to time, be made."[38] Should experience indicate that such
garrisons were not satisfactory, the Canadian Parliament could amend the
Militia Act. The Government was not interested in raising any naval force
because of its conviction that, in case of war, it would be the "duty" of
Great Britain to undertake the naval defence of Canada.

During the summer of 1870 the Canadian Government's position was
ably argued in London by its Postmaster General, Hon. Alexander Campbell, but to no avail. Lord Kimberley, who had succeeded Granville as
Colonial Secretary on July 6, listened very courteously and replied that
the British Government would again consider the matter. Kimberley noted,
however, that the matter had been repeatedly and very fully considered,
and that the decision that had been arrived at was not likely to be
departed from.[39] As something of an anti-climax, the bill placed before
the British Parliament to guarantee the cost of Canadian construction of
fortifications at Montreal, Kingston, Toronto, Hamilton, and Saint John
became law while Campbell was in London.[40]

What Kimberley did want the British Cabinet to discuss was the fact
that a new Commanding Royal Engineer in Canada had reported the
fortifications at Quebec were "quite ineffective and unfit to receive the
armaments requisite for their defence."[41] If this were true, so soon after
the expenditure of 300,000 pounds of the British taxpayers' money, the
fortress of Quebec was not going to be much of a gift to the Canadians.
Cardwell had already admitted as much, pointing out that it had been
considered impossible in 1865 that an American army might be able to

[37]*Ibid.*, 67.   [38]*Ibid.*, 75.
[39]*Ibid.*, 26.   [40]*Ibid.*, 28.
[41]Cardwell Papers, Box 5/31, Kimberley to Gladstone, Dec. 9, 1870.

capture Montreal and approach Quebec along the north bank of the St. Lawrence where there were no outer defences to emulate the three redoubts still under construction in the area just south of Lévis.[42] (Their final cost to the British Government would be 249,456 pounds sterling.) Even as Cardwell wrote, the rifled siege guns of the German armies invading France were battering into submission with comparative ease those French masonry fortresses not sufficiently protected by an outer ring of detached forts. A year earlier, General of the Army W. T. Sherman had urged the United States Congress to replace stone forts along the American sea coast by "barbette batteries of earth, with deep parapet, and a liberal number of bombproof and magazine traverses."[43]

Final British withdrawal from Quebec and New Brunswick was delayed until 1871. A Fenian scare during May, 1870, led to the mobilization of 13,489 officers and men of the volunteer militia for frontier duty, even though parties of Fenians made only two brief incursions into the province of Quebec.[44] The local Missisquoi volunteers, reinforced by volunteer units from Montreal, had no trouble beating off O'Neill's long-expected invasion at Eccles' Hill. A mixed force of British regulars and Canadian volunteers routed the Fenian attempt at Trout River. The British component of the Anglo-Canadian expedition, despatched during the same month under the command of Colonel Garnet Wolseley to establish law and order in the newly created province of Manitoba, did not return to Eastern Canada until late autumn. (The Ontario and Quebec Battalions of Rifles, organized under Section 20 of the Militia Act from volunteers, remained in Manitoba as garrison troops.)[45] U.S. Secretary of State Hamilton Fish's suggestion that all Anglo-American questions in dispute might be settled together soon led to the establishment of the International Commission[46] which met in Washington during the winter and spring of 1871. In order that the bargaining position of the Canadian member, Sir John A. Macdonald, should not be unduly weakened, the British Government had earlier decided that a regular battalion of rifles and a battery of artillery should remain at Quebec as a visible sign of continued Anglo-Canadian solidarity until after a treaty was concluded.[47]

The many-sided Treaty of Washington was signed on May 8, and

[42]*Ibid.*, Cardwell to Kimberley, Sept. 18, 1870.

[43]Russell R. Weigley, *Towards an American Army: Military Thought from Washington to Marshall* (New York, 1962), 140.

[44]*Report on the State of the Militia of the Dominion of Canada for the year 1870*, 6–7.

[45]*British Parliamentary Papers*, 1871, XLVIII, c. 298.

[46]Nevins, *Hamilton Fish*, 443ff.

[47]Cardwell Papers, Box 5/31, Kimberley to Cardwell, Dec. 2, 1870.

ratified by the United States Senate on May 24, but the British Army did not finally vacate the Citadel at Quebec until November 11, 1871. By that time the United States Army was reduced to 31,108 officers and enlisted men; by far the greatest number was stationed west of the Mississippi River, and only 867 were in the region of the Great Lakes.[48]

Canadians did realize that an epoch had been completed by the withdrawal of the green-clad battalion of the 60th (The King's Royal Rifle Corps), which had been raised during the course of the Seven Year's War for service in North America and which had also fought on the Plains of Abraham in 1759, and the blue-uniformed Royal Artillerymen from Quebec, but they had no way of knowing that the Treaty of Washington would usher in an era of good relations that would never seriously be endangered. Much was being left to chance, and in view of the ill feeling that had been so prevalent during the previous decade there were bound to be many dubious people in Canada, Great Britain, and the United States for many years to come.

[48]Information from Chief Historian, Office of the Chief of Military History, Department of the Army, Washington, U.S.A., Feb. 28, 1964.

(11)

EPILOGUE

As long as war with the United States remained a possibility, British officers continued to make plans involving the return of regular troops to Quebec, either by troopship up the St. Lawrence River or overland across New Brunswick. The much-discussed Intercolonial Railway was finally completed in 1876, providing an all-weather, all-Canadian transportation route between Halifax and Quebec. Despite the smallness of the British garrison remaining at Halifax, command was exercised by a lieutenant-general who would be expected to direct the defence of Canada in the event of war. The Royal Navy retained considerable strength on its North America and West Indies Station.

Members of the Canadian Government headed by Sir John A. Macdonald had convinced themselves early on that Canada would never do anything to provoke an Anglo-American conflict; naturally then there was no hurry to spend Canadian money on defence measures. The Canadians waited until October 20, 1871, to authorize the creation of two small batteries of garrison artillery to look after the forts, armament, and warlike stores turned over by the British Army in Ontario and Quebec and to provide gunnery schools for the active militia. Command was exercised by two Royal Artillery officers made available by the British Government. Officers and other ranks of the active militia volunteered to serve with "A" Battery at Kingston or "B" Battery at Quebec City on either continuous duty under Section 20 of the Militia Act rather than on a permanent and pensionable basis, or while attending courses of instruction. British non-commissioned officers pensioned from the Royal Artillery provided a skilled nucleus for each battery. Anglo-Canadian agreement was obtained in 1873 that the British guarantee of a Canadian loan for the construction of the costly fortifications earlier approved for Montreal, Kingston, Toronto, Hamilton, and Saint John could be utilized to help build the transcontinental railway promised the people of British Columbia for accepting Confederation in 1871.[1] Guns were mounted to defend the Esquimalt naval base during the Russian "scare" of 1878, and permanent defences were eventually constructed at joint Anglo-Canadian expense. The first military use of the Canadian Pacific Railway occurred during March-April 1885, while it was still incomplete: 3,323 officers and other ranks of the active militia were transported from eastern Canada to suppress the Northwest Rebellion that had erupted in Saskatchewan. Included were personnel of "A" and "B" Batteries and the Cavalry and Infantry School Corps authorized in 1883, all units which were now regarded as permanent in nature.[2]

The brief Anglo-American war scare caused by President Cleveland's special message to Congress on December 17, 1895, condemning Britain's attitude towards the long-standing boundary dispute between Venezuela and British Guiana, prompted the dying Conservative Government in Ottawa, headed by Sir Mackenzie Bowell, to purchase modern rifles for the active militia. The British Government reiterated its pledge to defend Canada from aggression, but the Admiralty and War Office planners were not agreed as to what assistance could actually be given. The Admiralty was becoming increasingly pessimistic about the ability of the Royal Navy to challenge a rapidly growing United States Navy in North American waters and was convinced of the impossibility of gaining control of Lake Ontario during the early stages of any Anglo-American conflict. Plans produced at the War Office showed the influence of Wellington, Carmichael-Smyth, and Jervois, and obviously required updating.

Not until early 1898, however, did the Canadian Government, now a Liberal ministry headed by Sir Wilfrid Laurier, finally agree that two of its Cabinet Ministers should join a British committee headed by Major-General E. P. Leach, V.C., for the purpose of producing an up-to-date defence plan for Canada.[3] Reports were submitted, but most Canadians discounted the possibility of another war with the United States, and the Governor General had to find an excuse for the Colonial Office in a letter dated April 18, 1903, that "pressure of work" had made it impossible for his Government to consider the plans officially.[4] In the previous July, Laurier had spoken very frankly to the newly arrived Major-General

---

[1]*British Parliamentary Papers*, 1873, I, Bill 159.
[2]Various annual *Reports on the State of the Militia of the Dominion of Canada*.
[3]Richard A. Preston, *Canada and "Imperial Defense": A Study of the Origins of the British Commonwealth's Defense Organization, 1867–1919* (Durham, N.C., 1967), 234–237 and 244–249.
[4]C.O. 42/892, Minto to Colonial Secretary, April 18, 1903.

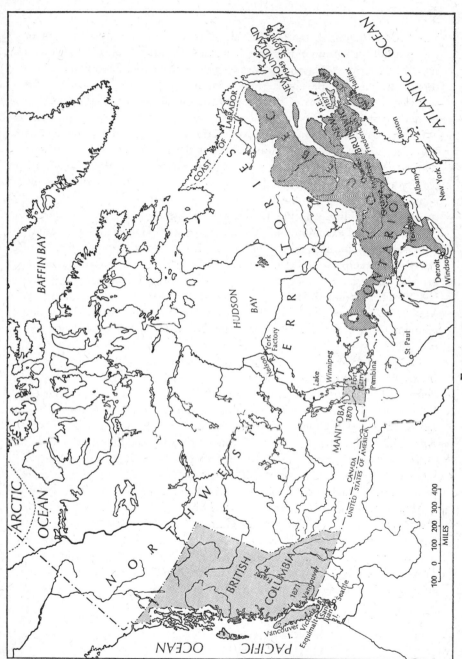

From sea to sea.

The Lord Dundonald, the last British officer to hold the appointment of General Officer Commanding the Canadian Militia. "You must not take the Militia seriously," Laurier is reported to have told Dundonald, "for though it is useful in suppressing internal disturbances, it will not be required for the defence of the country, as the Monroe Doctrine protects us against aggression."[5]

During the autumn of 1903, Canadians were angered by the Alaska Boundary Commission's decision to accept the American claim, but they realized that Lord Alverstone had sided with the three American arbitrators against his two Canadian colleagues so that there could be no rupture of good Anglo-American relations. What Canadians were not supposed to realize was the fact that the British Government was no longer interested in maintaining the naval bases at Halifax and Esquimalt; Admiral Sir John Fisher was planning the concentration of the Royal Navy's battleship strength in home waters, where it could combat the growing imperial German navy should there be a European war.[6] The last British troops left Halifax on January 18, 1906, and Esquimalt on May 22 of the same year. Canada did not, however, take formal possession of the naval dockyards until after a tiny Royal Canadian Navy had been created in 1910.

The Great War, 1914-18, provided the occasion for the United States finally to come to the aid of Great Britain and her Allies to secure the defeat of Germany. Thereafter it became unreasonable to believe that the United States, Great Britain, and France could ever fight among themselves. In 1931 the Chief of the General Staff in Ottawa, Major-General A. G. L. McNaughton, observed that "the direct defence of Canada against invasion by the United States is a problem which in the last ten years has become increasingly susceptible to political solution but quite incapable of being satisfactorily answered by Empire military action."[7]

Most readers of this volume will probably agree that the above statement by the most able soldier that Canada has yet produced could have been made much sooner. How much sooner is the real question, however, and one that can never be answered to everyone's complete satisfaction. War is an art rather than an exact science, and the generally accepted principles of war are not scientific laws that have a known result when

[5]Lieutenant-General The Earl of Dundonald, *My Army Life* (London, 1926), 191.
[6]The story of how the British Government induced the Canadian Government to assume responsibility for Halifax and Esquimalt is told succinctly in R. Preston, *Canada and "Imperial Defense,"* 336-343.
[7]Colonel C. P. Stacey, *Six Years of War: The Army in Canada, Britain and the Pacific, Official History of the Canadian Army in the Second World War* (Ottawa, 1955), 30.

correctly applied. American invaders were driven out of Canada in 1776 and prevented from obtaining any substantial foothold on Canadian soil during 1812–14. Yet the Duke of Wellington later admitted that he had been "astonished that the [British] officers of the army and navy employed in that country were able to defend those provinces during the last war; and I can attribute their having been able to defend them as they did only to the inexperience of the officers of the United States in the operations of war, and possibly likewise to the difficulty which they must have found in stationing their forces as they ought to have done, upon the right bank of the St. Lawrence."[8] However, as long as the United States regular army remained small and was kept busy protecting settlers streaming westward from the Indians, and the various state militias were as untrained as the provincial militias in British North America, successive Commanders of the Forces in Canada believed that they could conduct what would today be referred to as a "limited war" with a reasonable hope of success.

Whether the British Army and Canadian militia could have held off large American armies composed of veterans of the Civil War is an entirely different matter. The fortifications considered necessary by Colonel Jervois to support a successful delaying action until large numbers of British troops could be rushed to Quebec were never constructed; not even the Citadel and environs of that city were made defensible against a determined enemy. Furthermore, settlement now met on both sides of the land international border for the most part, instead of being separated by miles of wilderness guaranteed to slow down any invading army. There were better roads and miles of railroad track. Ships plying the inland waters no longer had to depend on sail. As the age of steam brought more and more of the Industrial Revolution to North America, both strategy and tactics had to be revised, and mere physical geography became much less important as a factor in any successful defence of territory.

Yet there is no tangible evidence to suggest that the United States ever seriously contemplated an offensive campaign against Canada during the years between the conclusion of the War of 1812 and the negotiation of the Treaty of Washington. Americans had more important things on their minds, such as the settlement and exploitation of their own western territory, and the political issue of "state's rights" which has never been really resolved. Politicians might make fiery anti-British speeches at election time in order to attract support from Irish-American voters, but these attempts at "twisting the lion's tail" were not supposed to be taken

[8]*Despatches, Correspondence and Memoranda of Field Marshal Arthur Duke of Wellington.* IV, 394.

seriously. The true believers in "manifest destiny" were convinced that annexation of Canada by the United States was inevitable and could be achieved peacefully and without bloodshed.[9] Surviving veterans of the Grand Army of the Republic paraded locally whenever the occasion seemed to warrant it, but generally speaking they were in agreement with General Sherman that "war is hell" and would not have been interested in risking death in a Canadian campaign. When not busy fighting Indians, American officers in the regular army worked for the creation of a relatively small but highly skilled professional army that would obviate any need for large citizen armies such as those which had defeated the Confederacy. These officers also took advantage of civilian fears that foreign navies might attack American seaports to secure large appropriations from Congress for coast defence forts and guns.[10]

Surviving war plans now held in the National Archives in Washington, apart from documents prepared during the Venezuelan Crisis, may be categorized as staff studies designed to test an officer's professional capabilities.[11] They were just as unrealistic as any study attempted in London or Ottawa. The idea of preparing plans for such an unlikely possibility as an Anglo-American war would seem never to have died but merely to have faded away like the old soldiers who drafted them.

[9]Donald F. Warner, *The Idea of Continental Union: Agitation for the Annexation of Canada to the United States, 1849–1893* (University of Kentucky Press, 1960).
[10]Russell R. Weigley, *Towards an American Army: Military Thought from Washington to Marshall* (New York, 1962), 136 and 140 ff.
[11]The conclusion reached by Lieutenant (now Professor) J. L. Granatstein as the result of an official visit to Washington, during the period July 22–August 10, 1964, to make a survey of the surviving material dealing with Canadian-American defence, 1867–1914.

APPENDIX

BRITISH ARMY IN CANADIAN THEATRE OF OPERATIONS

WAR OF 1812: When war broke out in 1812 the British Army in Canada had an effective combatant strength of about 5,600 all ranks. There were four companies of Royal Artillery, the 1/8th, 1/41st, 49th, and 100th Regiments of Foot, the 10th Royal Veteran Battalion, the Royal Newfoundland Regiment of Fencible Infantry, and the Canadian Fencibles. In addition the newly authorized Glengarry Light Infantry Fencibles was being organized at Trois-Rivières. The Canadian Voltigeurs being organized at Chambly was a provincial corps, but it would be included in the British Army's monthly strength returns for the period of the war.

The 103rd Regiment reached Quebec in July, 1812. It was in August followed by the 1/1st Royal Scots from the West Indies.

The 104th Regiment travelled overland from New Brunswick during the winter of 1813. A company of Royal Artillery and the 98th Regiment of Foot travelled by ship from Halifax to Quebec later in 1813. The 13th Regiment arrived from Martinique and the 2/41st Regiment from Bermuda. The 19th Light Dragoons—the only cavalry regiment to come to Canada—arrived from Ireland, as did the 70th Regiment of Foot. A detachment of Royal Artillery Drivers, a company of Royal Sappers and Miners, and the 1/89th and 101st Regiments of Foot arrived from Great Britain. De Meuron's foreign regiment came from Italy; De Watteville's foreign regiment had been in Spain and Portugal. The 1st and 2nd Battalions of Royal Marines were sent from Halifax to Quebec during the autumn of 1813; a company of Royal Marine Artillery was attached to each and there was a detachment of rocket artillery.

With the war in Europe concluded in April, 1814, three companies of Royal Artillery and battalions of the 3rd, 5th, 6th, 9th, 27th (both), 37th, 39th, 57th, 58th, 76th, 81st, 82nd and 88th Regiments of Foot were sent from France to Quebec during the summer of 1814. Somewhat earlier the 2/8th Regiment had reached Quebec from New Brunswick, the 4/1st Royal Scots and the 97th Regiments had arrived from Ireland, and the Nova Scotia Fencibles from Newfoundland. The 90th Regiment, from Grenada, was in Montreal briefly during the summer of 1814. The 2/89th Regiment reached Quebec in August. Total effective strength at the end of that month was better than 30,000 officers and other ranks.

DISCIPLINE OF BRITISH TROOPS IN UPPER CANADA, 1838–1840*

Courts-Martial	1838	1839	1840
Mutiny	1	1	—
Desertion	30	56	46
Violence to superiors and insubordination	11	34	26
Disobedience	4	10	16
Quitting post or sleeping on duty	4	18	10
Drunk on duty under arms	54	90	36
Disgraceful conduct	25	58	45
Absence without leave	25	61	44
Making away with necessaries	23	78	60
Habitual drunkenness	112	280	280
Miscellaneous	69	163	119
Deserters			
Attempted	166	247	174
Apprehended and court-martialed	30	56	46
Successful	136	191	128

*Based on Army Strength Returns.

BRITISH EXPENDITURE IN NORTH AMERICA OUT OF ARMY FUNDS*
(pounds sterling)

Fiscal year	Canadian Command†			Nova Scotia Command			Total
	Fortifications and Military Defences	Barracks	Other	Fortifications and Military Defences	Barracks	Other	
1853–54	18,283	943	309,804	13,760	465	120,801	464,056
1854–55	10,157	524	171,923	7,987	281	70,123	260,995
1855–56	8,454	436	144,323	7,508	264	66,662	227,647
1856–57	17,610	908	299,495	21,097	743	188,261	528,114
1857–58	12,725	656	217,171	14,161	499	131,819	377,031
1858–59	2,427	5,360	191,511	2,111	10,661	118,996	331,066
1859–60	1,595	5,943	178,611	1,612	13,896	117,160	318,817
1860–61	3,473	7,759	150,815	5,939	15,052	112,574	295,612
1861–62	5,996	19,279	557,478	4,292	15,767	336,612	939,424
1862–63	5,572	50,778	666,898	12,485	14,502	217,270	967,505
1863–64	4,744	14,227	584,840	26,791	8,491	179,018	818,161
1864–65	6,022	14,253	578,163	21,163	7,608	190,748	817,957
1865–66	56,093	1,411	548,998	46,136	5,519	181,246	849,403
1866–67	71,929	6,587	764,165	47,774	6,473	239,681	1,146,609
1867–68	59,126	23,781	834,101	40,762	12,697	252,928	1,233,395
1868–69	59,253	22,894	682,491	24,825	20,761	719,052	1,529,276
1869–70	35,376	11,093	385,921	30,296	19,396	155,661	637,743
1870–71	8,808	2,159	201,281	9,729	8,591	137,077	367,645
1871–72	11,141	391	45,955	6,589	6,079	126,527	196,682

*Based on Army Strength Returns.
†Ontario and Quebec after July 1, 1867.

EFFECTIVE STRENGTH OF THE BRITISH ARMY IN NORTH AMERICA, 1860–1869*

Stations	Years (as of April 1)	Cavalry	Artillery	Engineers	Military Train	Infantry	Colonial Corps	Army Hospital Corps	Commissariat Staff Corps	Total
Canada†	1860	—	266	7	—	820	1,170	—	—	2,263
	1861	—	229	6	—	879	1,138	—	—	2,252
	1862	—	1,966	272	634	8,728	1,144	91	114	12,949
	1863	—	1,922	248	308	7,967	1,267	39	82	11,833
	1864	—	1,759	112	307	7,411	1,349	34	64	11,036
	1865	—	1,601	121	—	5,373	1,051	33	59	8,238
	1866	—	1,647	232	—	5,903	1,023	35	67	8,907
	1867	499	1,770	218	—	8,218	1,093	54	71	11,923
	1868	453	1,655	207	—	7,709	1,070	50	66	11,210
	1869	520	1,675	216	—	4,577	1,014	47	69	8,118
Nova Scotia (including Newfoundland and New Brunswick)	1860	—	166	92	—	1,525	254	—	—	2,037
	1861	—	227	90	—	1,488	227	—	—	2,032
	1862	—	1,067	215	—	3,126	172	30	40	4,650
	1863	—	677	121	—	2,560	252	15	10	3,635
	1864	—	660	240	—	2,387	212	12	8	3,519
	1865	—	767	373	—	2,883	225	15	21	4,284
	1866	—	563	204	—	2,202	212	13	8	3,202
	1867	—	546	108	—	2,851	198	13	10	3,726
	1868	—	568	194	—	2,683	213	12	8	3,678
	1869	—	607	59	—	3,023	186	13	8	3,896
British Columbia	1860	—	—	156	—	—	—	—	—	156
	1861	—	—	139	—	—	—	—	—	139
	1862	—	—	134	—	—	—	—	—	134
	1863	—	—	131	—	—	—	—	—	131

*Based on Army Strength Returns.
†Detachment of Royal Canadian Rifles at Fort Garry until 1861 is included in the strength of Canada.

INDEX